MAUREEN WALLER

A FAMILY
IN WARTIME

MAUREEN WALLER

A FAMILY IN WARTIME

HOW THE SECOND WORLD WAR SHAPED THE LIVES OF A GENERATION

Published in association with Imperial War Museums

First published in Great Britain in 2012 by
Conway
An imprint of Anova Books Ltd
10 Southcombe Street
London W14 0RA
www.conwaypublishing.com

Produced in association with
Imperial War Museums
Lambeth Road
London, SE1 6HZ
www.iwm.org.uk

Distributed in the U.S. and Canada by
Sterling Publishing Co. Inc.
387 Park Avenue South
New York
NY 10016-8810

A catalogue record for this book is available from the British
Library.

10 9 8 7 6 5 4 3 2 1

ISBN 9781844861514

Edited by Alison Moss and Christopher Westhorp
Picture research by Jennifer Veall
Design by Georgina Hewitt and Will Ricketts

Printed and bound by G.Canale & C. S.p.A., Italy

Frontispiece: Children step down into the Anderson shelter in
the garden of their home. The little boy carries his gas mask box
with him.

Contents

The Model House

The centerpiece of 'A Family in Wartime' exhibition is a 1940s Model House, based on the terraced house in London in which the Allpress family lived during the early years of the Second World War. Commissioned by the Imperial War Museum in the 1980s, the 'dolls' house' measures 1.3 metres tall by 0.80 metres wide by 2.9 metres deep, and was constructed and furnished to show what life was like for an ordinary family living through the war years.

At first glance the model house reveals a wealth of period detail: a downstairs lavatory but no bathroom (a tin bath hangs on the wall outside); a small scullery with a copper on the wall above the sink for heating water, and a mangle outside for wringing out the laundry. There is a 'front room' and a sitting room and four bedrooms for a large family – nine family members were living there at the outbreak of the war. But the house also shows the telltale signs of wartime: the windows are criss-crossed with tape to prevent them shattering; fire buckets and a stirrup pump are on stand-by in the hallway; and

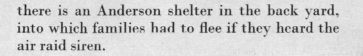

there is an Anderson shelter in the back yard, into which families had to flee if they heard the air raid siren.

The exhibit was made by model-maker Cyril McCann, who saw wartime service in the Royal Army Medical Corps until he was taken prisoner by the Germans after the invasion of Crete. He spent the rest of the war in a prisoner of war camp in Stalag VIIIb Lamsdorf in Silesia. He was a lifelong friend of Harry Allpress, and in 1946 he married Harry's sister Betty, and later used her family home as the inspiration for his model.

1
A State of War

'*We knew war was coming, really, in our hearts.*' [1]
Harry Allpress

There had been a thunderstorm in the night and Sunday 3 September 1939 dawned fresh, with bright sunshine and a clear blue sky. Like so many other British families on that memorable day, the Allpresses of 69 Priory Grove, Stockwell, in southwest London, were doing their best to carry on as normal.

The head of the family, William Allpress, was an engine driver for Southern Railway and he had gone to work, as he did every other Sunday. Although the family was poor, William had been fortunate to remain in work all through the Great Depression of the 1930s – a period of mass unemployment; indeed, on the eve of the Second World War more than one million people were still unemployed. William had been employed on the railway since he was a boy, working his way up from porter to cleaner to fireman (shovelling the coal into the firebox), before becoming an engine driver. He worked long hours to support his family.

Left: The house on Priory Grove as it stands today. It was just big enough to accommodate the large Allpress family, and was always a happy and welcoming household.
Right: The railways were so busy in wartime, carrying troops, war workers, civilians and freight, and continued during the blackout.

9

Top left: Alice (right) had been in service before she married William. She had ten children, nine of whom survived into adulthood, and worked very hard to look after them all. She is seen here with her eldest daughter Alice.

Bottom left: The two eldest daughters, Alice and Jessie, had 'lovely' weddings at their local church, All Saints in Lansdowne Road, and receptions in the church hall, around which much of the family's social life revolved. Alice is seen here on her wedding day in 1931.

The railways had been particularly busy in the last few days, with many abandoning their holiday under the threat of war and rushing home, and millions of others leaving the big cities and retreating to safer areas in country and coastal districts. It was a taste of things to come, because once war came Britain's railways would have to transport unprecedented numbers of passengers – civilians, troops and workers – as well as vast amounts of freight. Even those who owned cars would find themselves travelling by train, owing to petrol rationing. So hard pressed was the railway service in wartime that every station would display posters asking 'IS YOUR JOURNEY REALLY NECESSARY?' William and his colleagues would soon find themselves working a 14-hour day on a regular basis.

William's job would be classified as a 'reserved' occupation, because of the vital importance of the railways in wartime. The job would not be without its dangers. Priory Grove stood less than a couple of miles from Clapham Junction, where William signed in when he arrived at work. Between Battersea, where the railway station of Clapham Junction is actually located, and the mainline station at Victoria lay the railway marshalling yards at Nine Elms. These were all places of strategic importance in the transport system and therefore would be targets of enemy bombing. Railway lines would be hit and the smooth running of the trains disrupted, and this meant that on several occasions William would not manage to get home at night. This was a great worry for his wife and family, especially as there was no telephone at Priory Grove and he had no way of contacting them to assure them he was safe. Often, too, he would leave work late at night, or in the early hours, and have to walk home during an air raid, sometimes needing to throw himself flat on the ground as he crossed Clapham Common as the bombs fell and the ack-ack guns shot back in defence.

The house at Priory Grove was big enough to accommodate the large Allpress family, albeit with four of the girls sharing one large bedroom and the boys another. In the words of the second son, Harry, it was full but not overflowing. People then were used to living in crowded households, space still being something of a luxury.

Between the wars Britain had enjoyed a building-boom of relatively cheap suburban housing – for example, the neat semi-detached houses with gardens back and front, which were strung out along the great arterial roads leading out of London – and home ownership had increased among the middle class and skilled manual workers. However, like most families of the time, the Allpresses rented their Victorian terraced house from a private landlord.

At home at Priory Grove that Sunday morning were William's wife Alice, at 53 only a year younger than her husband, and four of their six grown-up daughters – Nellie, Eva, and twins Betty and Gladys, ranging in age from 28 to 18. Being unmarried, all four still lived with their parents and shared two double beds in the large bedroom at the front of the house. Having left school at 14 – the minimum school leaving age until the Education Act of 1944 raised it to 15 – they knew they were fortunate to have jobs when so many others were unemployed; unfortunately Gladys, who had a hole in her heart, was too frail to work.

The two oldest Allpress daughters, Alice and Jessie, were married and no longer living at home. The eldest, Alice, had married in 1931, and Jessie in 1936 – the year of the three kings and the Abdication Crisis, when George VI came to the throne. Tragically for the family, a seventh daughter, Vera Allpress, died that same year of a heart condition, aged only 13.

Top: Gladys was a gentle girl with a heart condition. Unlike her twin sister Betty and her unmarried sisters, she was unable to work. She died in 1940.

Above: John Allpress was the baby of the family. He was 10 years old at the outbreak of war, when he was evacuated with his school. He was so miserable that his parents decided to bring him home.

Two sons in their early 20s, William, known as 'Bill' or 'Billy', who had turned 21 in 1936, and Harry, who had earned the nickname 'Pad' because of his bad temper as a baby, had taken advantage of the fine weather to go out on an expedition with their cycling club. Neither had followed William on to the railways; Bill was an upholsterer and Harry worked as a French polisher in the same firm as his brother at King's Cross.

Only the absence of the youngest, 10-year-old John, indicated that something was badly wrong. For John, along with thousands of other children from London and the big cities throughout Britain, had been evacuated with his entire school two days earlier. If war came, civilians would be on the front line and the government had taken steps to remove the most vulnerable – 1,473,000 unaccompanied schoolchildren, mothers with toddlers, expectant mothers, the blind and those disabled people it was feasible to move – from the crowded cities of Britain before the worst happened.[2] In addition, two million individuals had made their own, private arrangements to leave the big cities and take up accommodation they had reserved months ago in the safer areas. It was reported from Southampton that 5,000 people had left within 48 hours for the United States of America (USA).

Sunday in pre-war Britain was a day of rest for most, with businesses and shops closed. However, instead of being able to enjoy the lovely weather and relax with their families on this particular Sunday, the British people were tense.

They had lived with an uneasy mixture of anticipation, relief and dread for some time, especially since the Munich Crisis of 1938 when it looked as if war was imminent. Ever since the coming to power of Adolf Hitler and the Nazis in Germany in 1933 there had been disquiet at the intentions of the German dictator. Although William was a loyal Labour Party supporter, the family was not particularly 'political', but they must have been only too aware of the dangers posed by fascism. Indeed, Nellie had had a holiday in Germany in 1937 and had been acutely aware of the sinister nature of the regime.

The 1920s and 1930s had been a time of mass unemployment and civil strife. Nellie remembers the General Strike of 1926, when her father accompanied her to and from work to protect her from angry strikers – she was only 15. Fascists and communists representing the extremes of the political Right and Left fought it out on the streets all over Europe. In England, Oswald Mosley had formed the British Union of Fascists in 1932, and in October 1936, in a scene horribly reminiscent of what was going on in Nazi Germany, Mosley's 'Blackshirts' had attempted to march on Cable Street, a district in London's East End with a large Jewish population. The ensuing street battle between the 'Blackshirts' and those determined to confront them prompted the government to pass the Public Order Act 1936, which banned political uniforms and quasi-military organizations.

The Nazi threat in Europe would be less easy to quell. After the horrors of the First World War, which had ended only 20 years before – just long enough for a new generation of potential soldiers, sailors and airmen to grow up – the British people wanted peace, but at what price?

A State of War

No one wanted war. Ordinary people feared the loss of home, of loved ones, of security; politicians feared the breakdown of national defence and the morale of the people, even mass panic. How long could Britain stand by and do nothing in the face of Nazi aggression?

Hitler believed that the Treaty of Versailles of 1919 was grossly unfair. He wanted to push back Germany's frontiers to where they had been before the First World War – and beyond. In 1936 he took the first step. The Rhineland, a buffer zone between Germany and France, had been de-militarized after the First World War. The territory belonged to Germany, but the Germans were forbidden to station troops there. Hitler decided to test the waters by sending troops to occupy the area.

Crucially, the French, preoccupied with political troubles at home, did nothing. Britain, which had always felt that the terms of the treaty were rather hard on the Germans, did nothing either. Encouraged by this complacence, Hitler reasoned that if the French could not stir themselves to act against his incursion into the Rhineland in their own backyard then they would be unlikely to object if he turned his attention eastwards.

The German people, he argued, needed *Lebensraum* ('living space') – in particular, the vast farmlands in central and eastern Europe where food would be grown to feed Germany's large population and make her self-sufficient – even if it meant seizing territory from

Below: The Munich Crisis in 1938 thrust Britain on to a war footing. Trenches were dug in public parks, where those caught out in an air raid could take shelter. Many of these became waterlogged over the following months and had to be reinforced before the outbreak of war.

other sovereign nations. Some began to suspect that Hitler would not be satisfied until he dominated the whole of Europe, perhaps the world.

In March 1938, in what was known as the *Anschluss* (the 'union' or 'link-up'), Hitler absorbed Austria into the Reich. Democratic Czechoslovakia, a new country of many different ethnic groups formed after the First World War from part of the former Austro-Hungarian Empire, was Hitler's next target. By inciting and exploiting unrest among the largely German-speaking population of the section of Czechoslovakia known as Sudetenland, mainly in the north and west, he proposed to annex that part of the country. Not only would this leave the remainder of Czechoslovakia along the German border exposed and vulnerable, but the Sudetenland contained the bulk of the fledgling republic's minerals and industrial strength. Hitler's appropriation of the Sudetenland would also prompt the further dismemberment of Czechoslovakia by its other neighbours, Poland and Hungary, in support of their respective native speakers.

In a desperate bid to avoid war, the British prime minister, Neville Chamberlain, flew to Germany on 15 September 1938 for discussions with Hitler. Hitler was far too devious and unscrupulous an operator for a gentleman of the old school like Chamberlain. The talks broke down and they seemed to have reached an impasse. On 22 September Chamberlain returned to Germany to try again, but Hitler would not modify his demands. France had promised to come to the aid of Czechoslovakia, but Hitler knew that France was far from ready for war. Nor, indeed, was Germany as ready for war as Hitler liked to pretend. At the last minute he drew back from the brink and invited Chamberlain back to Germany a third time for talks. In the early hours of 30 September 1938, at an international conference to which representatives of the Czechoslovak government were not invited, Britain was party to an agreement to cede the Sudetenland to Germany.

Top: The government feared that poison gas would be used against civilians. Decontamination squads were trained in anti-gas measures. Civilians would be alerted to a gas attack by the sound of a rattle.
Above: Special gas masks were issued for babies, as demonstrated here on Neville Mooney, the first baby to be born in London after the declaration of war.

Chamberlain returned triumphant. Emerging from the plane at Heston aerodrome, he waved a piece of paper, which bore Hitler's worthless promise to halt his territorial aggression. 'I believe it is peace for our time', he told a cheering crowd at Downing Street that evening. After the initial euphoria and relief that war had been averted, there was an underlying feeling of shame that Britain could not have done more to stand up to the bully, Hitler, and defend the freedom and independence of the little faraway country, Czechoslovakia.

The Munich Crisis had thrust Britain on to a war footing. The horror of aerial bombardment on the civilian population during the First World War, when 1,413 people had been killed and more than 3,000 injured in just over a hundred raids, was a foretaste of far worse to come in a second world war, with the ever-increasing strength of the Luftwaffe. The next war, it was believed, would open with a massive and sustained air attack on Britain, in which 600,000 people would be killed within weeks and twice that number injured. The objective would be to crush the people's morale and force them to urge the government to sue for peace.

It was expected that London, home to one-fifth of Britain's total population of 47,762,000[3], would be the primary target. The death toll would be so high that flat-pack cardboard coffins would be needed, because there would be insufficient supplies of wood to meet the unprecedented demand. The government could not rule out mass burials and the burning of bodies in lime.

Hospitals, mortuaries, ambulances, shelters, rest centres and feeding stations, all fully equipped and manned, would be needed immediately that war broke out.

Government planning placed considerable emphasis on the likelihood of poison gas attacks. Poison gas had been used during the trench warfare of the First World War – many British civilians knew someone who had suffered from gas poisoning in that conflict – and the Italians had used it in Abyssinia as recently as 1936, therefore there was every expectation that gas would be used on British civilians in this new, ferocious war and the consequences

Above: Lambeth Civil Defence post card. There was a huge recruitment drive for civil defence personnel.

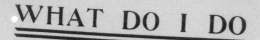

WHAT DO I DO

when I hear guns, explosions, air-raid warnings ?

I keep a cool head. I take cover.
I gather my family, with gas masks, and go quietly to my shelter or refuge room.
I do NOT try to "have a look."
I do NOT rush about alarming people.
I remember that a lot of the noise is GOOD noise—our guns firing at the enemy.
And I remember the odds are thousands to one against my being hurt.

CHEMWORTH, PRINTER, 291, KENNINGTON ROAD, S.E.11.   Issued by The Ministry of Information.

Above: Public notice, Lambeth. During an air raid it was important to keep calm. The Allpress family always did so, even though Nellie admitted that they were all 'terrified'.

---

would be absolutely hideous. For example, mustard gas left survivors blind or with damaged lungs.

It was the job of government to think the unthinkable and prepare for all these contingencies. As early as 1924 discussions on air raid precautions (ARP) had begun and in July 1935 the government issued a circular to local authorities in which it urged them to prepare plans on ARP. After the passing of the Air-Raid Precautions Act in 1937, local authorities were formally required to submit their plans for government approval. Some set about it with a will, others dithered, still not wanting to believe that war would really come. Progress was often slow and faltering, much of it piecemeal.

The London metropolitan borough of Lambeth, in which Priory Grove was situated, was one of those councils that attacked the problem head on. In April 1936 Lambeth's Air Raid Precautions Committee was set up to work in cooperation with the Home Office and devise an ARP scheme for the borough; a draft scheme was completed and submitted to the Home Office for approval by July that year.

The borough was 7 miles in length, had 142 miles of roads, a population of 600,000 and nearly 60,000 separately occupied buildings or parts of buildings.[4] For the purposes of ARP, the borough was divided into 18 areas.[5]

As soon as the committee was established it set about deciding the number of men who would be required for, say, 'decontamination' (poison gas) squads, as well as the personnel for rescue parties for the dead and injured, and demolition squads for the clearance of debris. Dispatch riders would be needed to carry urgent messages to and from individual warden's posts up to the control room in the town hall during an air raid. One hundred and eighty volunteers were to be recruited from the council's employees, although the men in the demolition squads were generally drawn from the building trade.

ARP personnel would need to be trained in anti-gas measures.[6] Fortunately a member of the borough engineer's department had undergone such training during the First World War and he would now do a refresher course at the civilian anti-gas school, established by the Home Office at Falfield in Gloucestershire, before undertaking the

training of 300 men in the borough. A long list of equipment was drawn up for ARP personnel, including hydraulic jacks, crowbars and hurricane lamps. In addition, the men were to be supplied with protective clothing, boots, gloves and respirators.

First aid posts, situated no further than two miles apart, were to be used for the decontamination of persons and their clothing from poison gas by a plentiful supply of hot water. For this reason some of these posts were initially situated in the public swimming baths and laundries. Gas-contaminated clothing was to be soaked in chloride of lime solution.

By the end of 1936 the ARP committee at Lambeth was locating suitable premises — basements and cellars — which could be made gas-proof and reinforced for use as public shelters.[7] Eventually, they would be able to shelter 100,000 people.

The Air Raid Wardens' Service (ARWS) was created early in 1937. Recruitment began tentatively, netting 200,000 citizens across Britain. There were to be ten wardens' posts to the square mile on average. Each area was divided into sectors, each covering a few streets with around 500 residents. There were to be three to six wardens for each sector. In Lambeth, ARP personnel gave a demonstration of gas masks at the Granada Cinema in Wandsworth Road.[8]

A year later, in March 1938, appeals on behalf of the City of London, the London County Council (LCC) and the metropolitan borough councils were published in the press, urgently asking volunteers over 30 years of age to join the ARP services, as air raid wardens, 'decontamination' squad and heavy and light rescue workers, first aid and ambulance personnel, stretcher-bearers, messengers and clerical assistants. Lambeth itself was asking for 3,000 wardens for its 600,000 inhabitants.[9]

On 25 September 1938, as Chamberlain's talks with Hitler showed no sign of progress, the ARP services were mobilized and now, with war a real possibility, thousands of new volunteers came forward to enlist.

That same month the need to find suitable premises for public shelters or to build them was given renewed impetus and thousands of sandbags were ordered to protect public buildings, giving the Scottish jute industry a boost. In parks and playing fields in cities and towns across Britain, long zigzag trenches were dug, in which members of the public caught out in an air raid could take cover. In Lambeth there were six such trenches,[10] designed to provide for 40,000 people, and over the coming months, as these became increasingly waterlogged, work was done to make them more permanent.

During the Munich Crisis, plans were hurriedly drawn up for the evacuation of two million people from the capital, with parents of schoolchildren being invited to register them for evacuation. In London there was an 83 percent take-up of this offer.[11] Many people were also making their own, private, arrangements to leave. Some rushed to get married – although not as many as in August and September of 1939 when the number of marriages taking place hit an all-time record; others to write their wills. Remembering the shortages of supplies that occurred during the First World War, food hoarding began. There was a feeling of barely suppressed panic.

In spite of his 'appeasement' of Hitler, Chamberlain had not entirely neglected to prepare for war during his time in office. Far from relaxing them after the Munich Agreement, Britain now stepped up its preparations for war. Men flocked to join the Territorial Army, while aircraft production was increased, outstripping Germany's by 1940. Expenditure on ARP tripled. A further campaign to recruit civil defence personnel involved public meetings, advertisements on buses, in places of business and shop windows, loudspeaker vans trawling the streets, appeals at the cinema, National Service stands at local bazaars, door-to-door canvassing, and an invitation to company bosses to join in order to set a good example to their staff.

In March 1939 Hitler reneged on the Munich Agreement and swallowed up what was left of Czechoslovakia. He was already making further territorial demands over Danzig and the Polish Corridor, claiming that the port on the Baltic rightfully belonged to Germany. Clearly, it was time for Britain to take a stand. Chamberlain's government promised to support Poland in the event of a German attack.

War was surely coming. In July 1939 the passing of the Civil Defence Act was the signal for greater progress to be made in the practical implementation of plans, many of which had so far existed only on paper.

On 9–10 August London and southeast England were plunged into the blackout, in a trial run. It was a bit of a fiasco, as thousands of 'sightseers' converged on London's West End.

On 23 August the sense of impending disaster was reinforced by the news that Nazi Germany and the Soviet Union were close to concluding a non-aggression pact – an unexpected and unlikely alliance between the fascist Hitler and the communist Stalin. In return for a slice of Poland and other territories fringing the Soviet Union, Stalin agreed to stand by, leaving Germany free to wage war. Knowing that once war was declared, Germany would be blockaded by Britain's Royal Navy, the Soviet Union also agreed to supply Germany with food and other vital materials.

Poland was now exposed on both sides to powerful enemies and it was only a matter of time before they would carve her up. On 25 August Britain signed a treaty of alliance with beleaguered Poland. Military conscription was already under way, the first time ever in peacetime.

Thirty-eight million gas masks had been produced. In Lambeth, the council had kept them in storage, ready for distribution.[12] The Allpresses went to collect theirs at the local library,[13] queuing for hours before trying them on for size and making sure that they fitted tightly. Inhaling the sickly odour of rubber and disinfectant for the first time must have made the reality of war – and the terrible fate that might await them – seem chillingly imminent.

Top: Residents of Muswell Hill, London, take their delivery of Anderson shelters in February 1939.
Above: The shelter had to be buried in a pit 4 feet deep and covered top, back and sides with a thick layer of earth. Flowers or vegetables could be grown on top.

Ration books for everyone in Britain had already been printed and by the end of August the machinery of food control was ready, although no decisions had been taken by the Cabinet as to what foods were to be rationed or how soon rationing would be enforced after the outbreak of war.

The government had already issued a million death certificates to local authorities[14] and in Lambeth the council ordered 2,000 canvas shrouds.[15]

In the year after the Munich Crisis one and a half million Anderson shelters – named after Sir John Anderson, the Lord Privy Seal, in charge of air raid precautions, subsequently Secretary of State for the Home Department and Minister of Home Security – were distributed to households in the areas thought to be most vulnerable to attack. Lambeth had its first delivery of them on 27 March 1939. The shelters were free of charge for any householder who earned £250 or less a year – Mr Allpress earned £3 10s[16] a week; a householder who earned more than £250 a year had to pay £7 for the shelter. Fortunately, the Allpresses' home in Priory Grove possessed a small garden rather than just a backyard, so that it was able to accommodate an Anderson. Small as this steel shelter was, measuring only 6½ feet long, 4 feet wide and 6 feet high, it would enable the family to seek protection at home in their own garden, rather than having to run to a local public shelter in an air raid – the nearest ones of which were at Lansdowne Gardens,[17] Stockwell Underground Station and Stockwell Memorial Gardens.

Council workmen delivered the sheets of corrugated iron and householders were[18] warned not to erect them, for fear of damaging gas mains, electric cables and

Top: Entrances to buildings were protected from bomb blast and flying debris by sandbags.

Above: Wooden battens or shutters served as blackout, but also provided protection against the effects of blast in a raid, when the windows were likely to be blown out, injuring the occupants. This family have also reinforced their windows on the inside, using sticky tape.

drains, until the council's officers had had time to visit each house and mark out the most suitable site for the shelter. Lambeth Council had erected Anderson shelters in various localities throughout the borough, to provide examples of the finished object. The nearest one to Priory Grove was to be seen at Stockwell Memorial Gardens,[19] at the junction of Clapham Road and Stockwell Road.

Fifteen thousand homes in Lambeth were judged suitable to receive an Anderson shelter,[20] but not all householders wanted to have one. For those households who did take one, the onus seemed to be on the householders themselves to erect them, although the council's minutes reported that its workmen had erected 5,555 of the 8,729 shelters in the borough.[21]

At Priory Grove the corrugated metal sheets lay in the garden for months before anyone bothered to erect the shelter.[22] Suddenly, on the brink of war, everyone was frantically digging. Harry's friend Cyril McCann, who was later to marry Betty Allpress, came round to help and the Allpress brothers in turn helped Cyril, who was an only child and lived with his mother in Stockwell, to put up his own shelter.[23]

Once the shelter was dug into a pit 4 feet deep, it was important to cover its roof, back and sides with earth. The earth had to be 15 inches deep on the top, 30 inches thick at the sides and 30 inches deep at the back. It was this layer of earth rather than the steel which would protect the occupants from shrapnel and flying glass and debris in an air raid, although of course the shelter would not protect them if it received a direct hit – as was to be the case in November 1940 when one fireman was killed and three others injured while sheltering in the Anderson at nearby Priory Grove School.[24] The entrance to the shelter would also have to be protected by some sort of barricade, and householders were advised to place padding at the top of the entrance so that the occupants would not injure themselves when entering the shelter in a hurry. It would be possible to grow vegetables on the roof as part of the Dig for Victory campaign, although the Allpresses opted for flowers.

An Anderson shelter could accommodate four adults and two children, so that even with William at work and Bill and Harry away at the war, it would be a bit of a

Above: There were innumerable accidents in the blackout, with people bumping into each other, into lampposts and falling off pavements. In this picture white lines are being painted to signpost the way to the nearest air raid shelter.

"No. 17 Verbena Road? Turn left just the other side of a blue light over a front door, then left again opposite a long yellow streak, then turn right between a bright glow above some curtains and a white gleam from a basement, and No. 17 is the third really bad light from this end."

Above: An ARP warden gives directions in a blackout, by the celebrated wartime cartoonist, Fougasse.

Opposite: Sunday 3 September 1939 began tensely. A crowd stares up at Big Ben as it strikes the eleventh hour – the time of the expiration of Britain's ultimatum to Germany to withdraw its troops from Poland.

squeeze for the large Allpress family. Many owners installed bunks, which enabled two people to lie down, but other members of the family would have to try to sleep sitting up all night. The main difficulty was keeping the floor dry. Householders were advised to dig a proper trench for drainage round the shelter. In due course, Lambeth was to find that concreting the bottom of the Anderson was a great help.[25] Although many strove to make their Anderson shelter as cosy as possible, even installing electricity, it must have been grim and uncomfortable trying to sleep there night after night, especially when the weather was cold and wet.

Meanwhile, in London the work of sand-bagging, shuttering and blacking out was being pursued energetically. There was a rush to the shops for blackout material to make night-time coverings for the windows. Mrs Allpress was busy making the blackout curtains herself from thick black material. To add to her many other household chores, she would now have to ensure that all the windows in her house were completely covered half an hour after sunset every night; the blackout curtains could not be opened again until half an hour before sunrise. With the introduction – on 4 May 1941 – of British Double Summer Time (BDST) during the war to help the farmers, 'doing the blackout' could be very late on summer evenings when it was still light at ten o'clock.

The occupants would have to get into the habit of never entering a room and switching on a light before ensuring the blackout was up and never opening outside doors without first switching off the light. Some people seemed to think only the windows at the front of the house needed be covered – somehow imagining that the German bombers couldn't see the back. Even the merest sliver of light would earn a stern reprimand from the local warden on patrol – 'Put that light out!' – and possibly a fine.

Priory Grove lay in a densely built-up urban area, which was highly vulnerable to bombing. The neighbourhood consisted of terraced houses, as well as shops, a Thermafelt factory, a builder's yard, three public houses, and at the end of the road the looming edifice of the Victorian school that John Allpress would eventually attend. Also in the vicinity lay a tyre yard, giving the family some disquiet, because if that was hit in an air raid it would send out choking, toxic smoke. Because any bomb falling within half a mile would shatter the windows, every household and business was well advised to criss-cross their windows with sticky tape to prevent shards of flying glass injuring the occupants.

On 24 August parliament was recalled and passed the Emergency Powers (Defence) Act 1939, empowering the King – that is, his government – to make such Defence

Regulations as appeared to be necessary or expedient for securing the public safety, the defence of the realm, the maintenance of public order, the efficient prosecution of the war, and for maintaining supplies and services essential to the life of the community. A whole spate of new wartime regulations – covering such matters as compensation for air raid injuries and the repair of war damage – followed within days.

Military reservists were called up: all over Britain men were leaving their wives and children, some still on holiday, or quitting the tennis club and cricket pitch, the office desk and the factory workbench, and donning uniform. The ARP was placed on full alert. Hospitals were ordered to get ready to receive air raid casualties. Thousands of patients were either sent home or removed by rail or ambulance to hospitals in safer areas; new admissions were restricted to acute cases. Additional beds were set up. On 31 August the government gave the order for the long-planned machinery of evacuation to roll: transport authorities signalled that they were ready.

In the small hours of 1 September, appropriately under cover of darkness, German troops moved into Poland and by the early hours of the morning its capital, Warsaw, was being bombed.

War was inevitable and since it was expected that it would open with a massive aerial attack on British cities, the evacuation of the most vulnerable began promptly that same morning. Clutching his little case and gas mask, a snack for the journey and an identification label on his lapel, 10-year-old John Allpress was taken, with the entire intake of St. John Bowyers school in Clapham on board a series of red double-decker buses, to the country, destination unknown. He was given a blank postcard to send to his mother to let her know his whereabouts once he was billeted. Until then, she was consumed with worry.

That evening, the blackout was applied for real for the first time and there were to be innumerable accidents, with pedestrians being run over by slow-moving vehicles without headlights, or bumping into each other, into lampposts and trees, and falling off pavements. It was so dark outside, and therefore dangerous, that families turned inward, preferring to spend their evenings at home and in the process drawing strength from each other.

Even if they had wanted to venture out, places of entertainment, including cinemas, theatres, clubs and concert halls, were temporarily closed. Much of the Allpresses' social life had anyway revolved around functions at their local church, All Saints, where three of the girls were Sunday School teachers. Indeed, it was thanks to a Bible class teacher at the church that Nellie had got her first job at a bakery. The sisters attended regular dances, sometimes two or three a week, at the church hall – where Alice and Jessie had held their wedding receptions – and many of their friends or the young men they met came through this association.[26]

The Allpress household at Priory Grove was a lively one. Although as children they had never been allowed to play in the street, the brothers and sisters had lots of friends, all of whom were welcomed into the family circle. The boys would come in from their cycling club and bring their friends; Nellie recalls that two or three loaves would be cut up to feed them all and the two dozen jam tarts she had made would be eagerly consumed.

After the First World War, family sizes had diminished; the middle classes, in particular, had limited the number of children they had, and members of the extended family were more likely to be living further away.[27] The family unit was therefore smaller and more isolated, so that in times of trouble – particularly in wartime – there would be fewer persons to come to the rescue or lend their support.

However, this could hardly be said to apply to the Allpress family. Mrs Allpress had given birth to ten children, nine of whom survived into adulthood. Holding their hard-working parents in huge respect, they were a close and supportive family, loyal and good company for each other. 'We were a family that was really happy together,' Eva recalls.[28] Now, in wartime, they would rely on and draw support from each other more than ever.

Above: The first air raid sounded shortly after war was declared. Here Londoners descend into an air raid shelter. It was a false alarm.

By and large they would have to provide their own entertainment. A family of the respectable working class like the Allpresses couldn't hope to own a television; television was a luxury and only 20,000 people owned one at the outbreak of war, all of them in London. The signal was switched off abruptly in the middle of a programme on 1 September 1939, not to be resumed until 1946. Like the majority of families in Britain, the Allpresses relied heavily on the wireless for news and entertainment and that weekend particularly, as they waited for the announcement that the war had officially started.

By the evening of 2 September, the prime minister, under pressure from the Cabinet, had to concede that 'all my long struggle to win peace has failed', but still he hesitated, hoping despite all the evidence of Hitler's bad faith that he would heed the British ultimatum and withdraw German troops from Poland.

It was now two days since Germany had invaded Poland and tension grew as the British nation waited to hear the official declaration of war. No doubt many, particularly the women, were still hoping that it would not come to war. For the Allpresses and thousands of other families, war would mean that their sons and brothers would be called up and possibly killed. At ten that Sunday morning, it was announced on the wireless that the prime minister would speak to the nation at 11.15am. It was then that families, neighbours, friends and workmates, huddled round to listen to the broadcast, heard the words that they had dreaded for so long:

'I am speaking to you from the Cabinet Room at 10 Downing Street,' Chamberlain began portentously. 'This morning, the British ambassador in Berlin handed the German government a final note, stating that unless we heard from them by 11 o'clock that they were prepared at once to withdraw their troops from Poland, a state of war would exist between us. I have to tell you now that no such undertaking has been received, and that consequently this country is at war with Germany. ... May God bless you all. May He defend the right, for it is evil things we shall be fighting against – brute force, bad faith, injustice, oppression and persecution; and against them I am certain that the right will prevail.'[29]

Chamberlain, a man of 70, sounded old, weary, querulous and disappointed. As soon as he had finished speaking, the national anthem was played, with many even in private homes standing up for it.

Dead on cue, at 11.27am the air raid siren – to be nicknamed 'Moaning Minnie' for its long drawn-out eerie moan – sounded for the first time over London, as well as parts of the Midlands and East Anglia: according to the wartime diary of an air raid warden in nearby Clapham, it was to be heard 1,231 times in southwest London before the war was over.[30]

In Priory Grove a man on a bicycle, possibly a wartime policeman, rode along ringing a handbell and shouting that there was a raid on and to take cover. Everyone ran to their doors to see what was going on. Mrs Allpress and her daughters then turned tail and dashed to the Anderson shelter in the back garden, frantically trying to put on their gas masks.

It turned out to be a false alarm. A lone French plane, flying in unannounced, had provoked it. By the time the 'all clear' sounded, Mrs Allpress, a worrier at the best of times, was in such a state that Nellie fetched her a glass of brandy from the bottle she had brought back from a recent holiday in France. 'We had a little swig to calm our nerves,' Nellie recalls.[31] Mrs Allpress had much to be upset about. Two sons were old enough to be called up; her husband's job on the railway would bring him into constant danger; the family was living in dense urban housing in London, the bombers' prime target; and her youngest boy had been sent away, living who knows where and with whom. Of course she was upset.

At six that evening King George VI, struggling courageously to overcome his stutter, made a moving address, the first of several which made him the focus of intense loyalty and identification among his subjects during the dark days of war. He called upon his peoples at home and overseas to stand firm and united in this time of trial.

A State of War

The Second World War would be a war fought by civilians on the home front as much as by the military on land, in the air and at sea. It would disrupt family life as no previous war in British history had done, with the possible exception of the civil wars in the seventeenth century. In nearly six years of war, there would be massive social upheaval. On a far larger scale than in the First World War, women would leave the home and take up their places in the armed services, in the civil defence and voluntary services, on the land and in the factories. Families would be separated, some never to be reunited; neighbourhoods would be torn apart, many never to be re-established; and thousands of homes would be destroyed or damaged beyond repair, further hindering the resumption of family life after the war. As an indication of the uprooting and restless, harried movement of the population, there would be 34,750,000 changes of address among civilians alone in the course of the war.[32]

For the Allpresses, as for the nation as a whole, life would henceforth be divided into 'before the war' and 'after the war', so momentous and traumatic would the intervening years be.

Below: Monday 4 September 1939. Workers go to work as usual, but carrying their gas masks. It was imperative to carry these at all times.

EVACUATION

DETAILS OF FACILITIES ARRANGED FOR

(1) OFFICIAL PARTIES

(TO BILLETS PROVIDED BY THE GOVERNMENT)

Evacuation is available for

SCHOOL CHILDREN

MOTHERS with CHILDREN of School Age or under

EXPECTANT MOTHERS

(2) ASSISTED PRIVATE EVACUATION

A free travel voucher and billeting allowance are provided for

CHILDREN OF SCHOOL AGE or under

MOTHERS with CHILDREN OF SCHOOL AGE OR UNDER

EXPECTANT MOTHERS

AGED and BLIND PEOPLE

INFIRM and INVALIDS

who have made their own arrangements with relatives or friends for accommodation in a safer area

★ *FOR INFORMATION ASK AT THE NEAREST SCHOOL*

ISSUED BY THE MINISTRY OF HEALTH

M.H. 21

2
Leave the Children Where They Are

'I went to a strange house in the dark, taken into a family that didn't really want us ... It was a very unhappy time ... there were big big gaps in my education.' [1]
John Allpress

nce of the enduring images of the beginning of the Second World War is of thousands of children at Britain's railway stations, pathetically clutching their little cases or bundles of belongings, their gas masks and perhaps a toy, identification labels pinned to them, boarding trains to take them to safer areas in the country away from the bombing. Neither they nor their parents knew when – or if – they would meet again.

To separate children from their parents and entrust them to strangers for an indefinite period was a desperate but necessary move, since it was confidently expected that the war would open with a massive aerial attack on Britain's cities, the enemy's objective being to wreak such death and destruction that the people's morale would be shattered, forcing the government to sue for peace. Such an attack, it was believed, would prompt a large-scale exodus from the big cities amidst chaos and confusion. The government was determined to take control of the situation – to prevent panic and flight and to move people in an orderly way, starting with the most vulnerable.

Left: It was expected that the war would open with a massive aerial attack on British cities. Evacuation was a military expedient. The idea was to prevent panic and flight and move people in an orderly way, starting with the most vulnerable.

Evacuation was a military expedient – there was no point in keeping 'useless mouths' not engaged in the war effort on the front line, as it were. It was also the surest means of protecting the lives of the next generation – Britain's future.

After years of discussion and planning, Sir John Anderson presented his report in 1938, the basic tenets of which were that evacuation would not be compulsory – it never was, except in the case of small children certified to be suffering or likely to suffer in mind or body as a result of enemy bombing – and that those who could afford to contribute to their children's maintenance should be expected to do so. The Ministry of Health would be responsible for evacuation.

Great Britain in 1939 had a population of approximately 47,762,000. The country was to be divided into three zones – evacuation, neutral and reception – and it was estimated that in the reception areas, home to 18,000,000, accommodation would have to be found for 3,500,000 evacuees in England and Wales and for 400,000 in Scotland.[2] The priority classes were to be schoolchildren, removed as school units under the charge of their teachers and voluntary helpers; children under five, who would be accompanied by their mother or some responsible adult; expectant mothers; and the blind and disabled, where feasible.

Not only was this intervention into family life unprecedented, but the authorities would have to overcome the innate dislike of the British of billeting in private homes. The presence of evacuees in a family's home, sometimes for years, was after all an intrusion into its privacy, a curb on its freedom, and would impose an extra burden on the housewife – more meals to shop for and prepare, more laundry, cleaning and mending. The government was, in effect, presuming on a family's patriotism and Christian compassion to take strange children into its midst and look after them for an indefinite period.

On 5 January 1939 local authorities in the reception areas were asked to prepare a survey of private homes to ascertain how many billets would be available for evacuees. It was a massive undertaking, incidentally revealing that about half of homes in rural

Above: With the outbreak of war millions of people were on the move. Troops arrive at a London railway station, while teachers shepherd schoolchildren on to a train bound for the country.

areas had no indoor lavatory, but then 90 percent of homes in London's Stepney did not have one either. The investigation covered more than 5,000,000 homes,[3] and engaged 100,000 visitors. It was found that in England and Wales there was accommodation for 4,800,000 evacuees, allowing for one person per room; however, by February 1939 more than one million rooms had already been privately reserved for people not taking part in the government's official evacuation scheme. Altogether, there was confirmation of 2,250,000 billets for unaccompanied schoolchildren in the government's official evacuation scheme in England and Wales and 300,000 in Scotland, where two schoolchildren to a room was considered acceptable.

When door-to-door canvassing took place in August 1939, inviting parents to register their children for evacuation, the take-up in London was only 69 percent,[4] as opposed to 83 percent during the Munich Crisis the previous year. In Liverpool the response was 65 percent, and in Glasgow 62 percent; in Birmingham, Coventry and West Bromwich it was as low as 24 percent. Manchester returned the most positive response, with 75 percent registering for evacuation, perhaps because they had been canvassed more efficiently.

These registration rates were taken as peacetime responses, however, and the government decided not to scale down its plans regarding train schedules and the number of billets required.

During the last week of August 1939, 10-year-old John Allpress probably participated in a rehearsal at his school – St. John's Bowyer's, a Church of England school located between Clapham Junction and Clapham Common – so that on the big day everyone would know where to congregate for evacuation.[5] John's school was not far from the railway junction where his father went to work, nor, indeed from London's mainline Victoria Station; as things turned out the boys were not to be evacuated by train, but were sent on London buses to Wokingham in Berkshire, a mere 40 miles away. Other London children, marshalled by an army of teachers and voluntary helpers holding up banners, would be taken by London Underground to the various mainline stations from where they would be dispatched by train to destinations far and wide.

On 31 August the government gave the signal to the authorities in the evacuating areas for evacuation to start the next day. The public was bombarded with announcements on the wireless and assured that anyone in the priority classes could go, even if they had not registered. In the event, even fewer Londoners went than those who had registered. Family solidarity was proving strong and enduring.

Transport had been laid on by the Ministry of Transport, working with the various railway companies, for nearly 3,500,000 evacuees. This figure turned out to be wildly optimistic. From the London metropolitan area alone 393,700 schoolchildren,[6] 257,000 mothers and children under five, and 5,600 expectant mothers were transported to safer areas. From the rest of the country, including Scotland, there were 433,259 schoolchildren travelling with their teachers, 266,670 mothers with small children, and 6,700 expectant mothers. The blind and disabled made up another 7,000 or so.

If it had merely been an exercise in removing the most vulnerable people from the big cities hours before Armageddon, the evacuation project would have been judged a great success. Indeed, the whole process was accomplished within three days without a single injury or accident. However, the fact that the take-up was significantly lower than had been planned for – less than 1,500,000 rather than the expected 3,500,000 – meant that the train schedules were thrown into disarray, with the second day's schedule being brought forward to fill up the first, and so on. As each group arrived at the railway station they were shepherded on to trains to fill vacant places, irrespective of the train's destination. One of the problems was that children bound for counties far from London, such as Devon or Somerset, were placed in trains without corridors and therefore had no access to toilets. At least one such party had to disembark en route in Berkshire, since the children simply could not hold on any longer.

In the general mix-up, reception areas which had billets ready for, say, schoolchildren, found themselves instead with a party of mothers with toddlers or expectant mothers.

In other cases the reception areas were totally unprepared for the numbers involved, never having been properly briefed. For example, 17,000 mothers, children and teachers were evacuated by ship from Dagenham to Great Yarmouth, destined for villages in Norfolk and Suffolk.[7] 'Suitable accommodation was impossible,' one of the local organizers reported, 'and they had to be housed in sheds, sleeping on sacks which had previously been used for artificial manure and malt, and crowded into a space which was by no means adequate for health and cleanliness.'[8] By the time transport was found and they were dispatched to the various villages the evacuees were exhausted, dirty and frightened. No wonder town and country met each other in critical mood!

Above: Small children examining each other's identity label.

To further aggravate matters, school parties which had been carefully sorted into groups at the point of embarkation were often split up willy-nilly on the journey, or when they reached their destination, and billeted in different villages over a large area. For example, one London school had divided the boys into groups of ten.[9] Great care had been taken to ensure that brothers and friends were in the same group. Unfortunately, the journey involved a change of trains and was completed by bus. As a result of the general confusion at all these stages of the journey and the interference of the police, who insisted on marshalling the boys into crocodiles, the composition of the groups was mixed up. To top it all, the buses took the boys not to one destination, where they would have been able to re-form into the original groups, but to an array of villages over an area of 50 square miles. In many places boys were whisked away by voluntary helpers to billets before a list of names could be taken. It was over a week before the teachers could locate the whereabouts of all their pupils.

It was painful enough for a child to be uprooted from family and all he or she had ever known and taken to a strange and unfamiliar destination. It was even more distressing if, upon arrival, the child was subjected to the indignity and humiliation of being 'picked'.

Never before had so much study and planning gone into the protection of the nation's women and children in the event of war. Unfortunately, the focus had been on the logistics of evacuating the vulnerable from the cities, but far too little consideration had been given to what would happen to the evacuees when they reached the reception areas. Billeting had been a haphazard affair with predictably disastrous consequences in many cases, and the government had been mean and tardy in supplying advance funds to the local authorities for the purchase of the necessary extra equipment, such as mattresses and blankets, or the provision of larger school premises or maternity homes.

Above: 1939: Evacuee children sitting on the ground with their luggage and gas masks in cardboard boxes slung round their necks. The children, from London, are at a station in the country after being evacuated from the city and are waiting to be taken to their new homes.

If only the human element of evacuation had been as carefully worked out as the transport, all might have been well. The ideal scenario would have been for the reception areas to be informed beforehand of what evacuees to expect and to have billets allocated and prepared accordingly, each child having been allotted his billet. Parents, too, might have felt easier if they had known where and with whom their child was to be living.

Britain in 1939 was still a very class-ridden society, yet no thought had been given to the effect of billeting, say, slum children with middle-class foster parents. Where children were billeted with people of the same social class as their parents there was less of a clash of cultures. In most of the reception areas billeting was haphazard with no attempt made by the authorities to match the children with suitable foster parents. Householders offering billets were not vetted properly and were usually allowed to take their pick of the children without any assessment of their own suitability.

There are innumerable stories of children being herded into village halls to be inspected and chosen by the 'hosts': of farmers making a beeline for strong-looking boys who could lend a hand on the farm; of shrewd housewives picking girls capable of doing some housework or acting as unpaid childminders to their own offspring; of pretty, well-dressed little girls being snapped up, while the more troublesome looking, grubby, poorly clad children were left to last.

When John Allpress's school arrived at Wokingham – only 40 miles from London, but it might as well have been the far side of the planet as far as John was concerned – he remembers that they were all taken into a hall and given a drink of milk or orange squash. There was pandemonium as everyone milled about, unsure what was to happen next. Then the adults came in and started choosing children to take to their billets. 'People were coming and taking boys from this hall and they were disappearing and I didn't know where they went to,' John recalls. The hall was emptying and for no discernible reason John was still sitting there, unwanted and 'feeling terrified'. His friend was chosen, but not John, until the billeting officer persuaded the lady who had taken his friend to take John too. 'I don't think she really wanted either of us,' John says, but she reluctantly agreed.[10]

He came to suspect that she took in evacuees solely for the billeting allowances she received for them – 8s 6d (the equivalent of £10 today) a week for each child if there were two of them, or 10s 6d a week for a single child. Only too obviously she favoured her own two boys over the evacuees. Town children in the country, John and his friend were always made to feel second best.

Mothers with small children were even harder to billet. Householders would be given five shillings for the mother and three for each child for board only. They would not be provided with meals. Such women found themselves in the invidious position of having to use the kitchen in the house only when the householder permitted it. More often than not, she and her small child or children were confined to their bedroom trying to keep as quiet as possible and forced to spend most of the day trawling round the small town or village to kill time. Unlike the lively streets of home, the rural backwater she had landed in offered very little entertainment. Boredom soon set in. No wonder some of them resorted to the pub as soon as it opened, much to the disgust of the locals. Separated from husband, family, friends and neighbours and living very much on sufferance in the billet under the critical eye of the householder, it is no surprise that the majority of these women turned tail and went home.

The aerial bombardment expected in September 1939 did not materialize; after the 'phoney war', when nothing much happened, the 'Blitz' came in September 1940 instead. Had the bombing occurred immediately on the outbreak of war, householders in the reception areas would presumably have felt a higher sense of moral purpose that they were sheltering evacuees and been prepared to overlook their shortcomings. In the absence of bombing, there was a dramatic change of mood from sympathy to hostility. The lull gave people in the reception areas time to question the point of evacuation and to voice their shock, disgust and frustration at the state most of the evacuees had arrived in and their subsequent behaviour.

The newspapers were full of stories of outrage. Rural and middle-class Britain had never before encountered children from the deprived, impoverished inner cities of Britain and it was horrified. If nothing else, evacuation served to open the eyes of comfortable,

Top: Life in the countryside opened up new horizons for evacuees. For some it was a happy experience, but sadly some were exploited by farmers looking for cheap labour.

Above: These evacuees are scrambling to look at a horse. They were part of the intake at Dartington Hall, Totnes, Devon, where they were lucky enough to be encouraged to learn arts and crafts.

middle England to the conditions of life in Britain's slums – slums long overdue for demolition.

There were complaints that some of the children were unruly, disobedient, bad-mannered, ungrateful, and swore like troopers. Many were inadequately clothed, they complained; some were actually sewn into their underclothes for the winter or wrapped in an inner lining of brown paper. Used to a diet of fish and chips or bread and dripping, the evacuees refused to eat the plain, wholesome, regular meals provided and they had no idea how to use a knife and fork. They possessed no nightclothes, no underclothes and no change of clothes. Some of them were affected with scabies, impetigo and other skin diseases associated with dirt. Some were not 'house-trained' and soiled their clothes or did their business on the floor; after all, at home they might have to share a lavatory with many other tenants too far from their own flat to be practical for a small child. Perhaps the most vociferous complaints were about bed-wetting.

Above: Town children were often experiencing country life for the first time, benefiting from the fresh air and nature walks.

'Every morning every window is filled with bedding, hung outside to air in the sunshine,' a report observed.[11] Although some of the children might have been perennial bed-wetters, for the majority this was a temporary problem. Uprooted for the first time from home and family – all they knew and loved – and transported to a strange environment where they were sometimes given a cool reception, not surprisingly the loss of stability and protection caused a regression to infantile behaviour. On a more practical note, town children were unused to the darkness of the countryside at night and were often too scared to get up to use the lavatory, especially if it was an outside one.

It was unfortunate that evacuation took place at the end of the long school summer holidays, when children had not been under the supervision of the school medical service for several weeks. As for the inadequacy of their clothing, the outbreak of war followed a long period of unemployment. Not only were more than a million people still unemployed in 1939, but about four million were living in hand-to-mouth poverty. The purchase of new boots and clothing, let alone a change of clothes, for growing children was simply beyond the resources of many families, even more so after a 30 percent rise in the cost of clothing in the first eight months of the war. At home most of them managed with family hand-me-downs and second-hand clothing from markets, while if boots and shoes needed mending it was done at home rather than paying the cobbler. In the Allpress household, William was always mending the family's shoes.

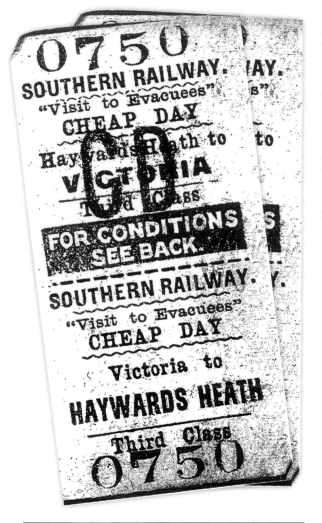

Above: The government granted parents one free travel pass a month to visit their children. Here Southern Railway, the company for which Mr Allpress worked, is offering a cheap day return fare as a bonus.

All this was impractical once the children had been evacuated – although in John's case his father continued to repair his shoes and his family would bring him fresh, clean, mended clothes every weekend, as well as his pocket money.[12] Winter in the country required warmer clothing and more of it; boots wore out quicker. Foster parents expected the children in their care to be as well turned out as their own children. Some generously put their hands in their pockets and bought the children the clothing they needed; others, ignorant of their straitened circumstances, wrote to the parents demanding they send the requisite clothing or the funds to buy it. Children were sensitive to any criticism or slur on their parents. The unemployed father of one boy was reduced to tears by his son's letter, which said that because he knew his father could not supply the ten shillings being demanded by his foster mother for clothing, he would rather come home than endure the situation any longer. It was embarrassing, both for the children and the parents – so much so that some of the parents brought the children home instead.

At the end of August 1939 the government had sent a confidential letter to the evacuating authorities authorizing the purchase locally of boots and clothing up to a limit of £1 for every 200 children, but this was hardly enough to meet the needs of so many deprived children.

Class differences worked both ways. Some parents in the cities feared that their children were living 'above their station', which would alienate them from home and family, and removed them. Others brought their children home because they were disgusted at the primitive conditions of the billet or worried at the erratic nature of the education on offer. Mothers would be torn: they would want their child to be settled and happy with a kind foster mother, yet fearful that she would steal her child's affections. There might be friction between the evacuees and the host family's own children, jealous of the attention their mother was giving the 'interlopers'. It was hard for foster mothers, too; not only must they discipline a child not their own, but they might genuinely come to love a child and have to suffer the pain of loss when he or she eventually went home.

It was not all doom and gloom. Town children were experiencing country life for the first time, broadening their horizons and improving their health. They were benefiting from the fresh air – urban, industrial Britain was then still heavily polluted with coal smoke – and a good plain diet containing plenty of fresh vegetables, as well as the early bedtimes prevalent in the country. The children were helping with the harvest and growing food, enjoying nature walks and open spaces.

Above: Separation was hard for mothers and children. Mothers were torn. They wanted their child to be settled with a kind foster mother, yet feared she might steal the child's affections.

Experiences of evacuation were as varied as the number of children involved – it was very often just down to luck, good or bad. Many were living in better home conditions, which affected their behaviour, deportment, culture and vocabulary. In some it instilled a taste for finer things, an ambition to live that life for themselves one day. Some were introduced to books for the first time, beginning a life-long love of reading that they would never otherwise have had. However, while there was a considerable amount of 'levelling up', the opposite occurred too and some children were shocked to find themselves in rural billets vastly inferior to what they had left behind at home, without electric light or running water and with an outside privy.

Whatever the material considerations, almost all evacuees missed their parents' love and many were deprived of affection during crucial childhood years. Some children were abused – emotionally, physically, or even sexually – and exploited, too fearful or unable to tell their parents or another adult and suffering in silence; others had a succession of foster homes, contributing to the disruption and uncertainty of these years. The most fortunate found a second family in their foster parents, people who were genuinely kind and loving, with whom they and their families forged life-long friendships.

Unfortunately, that was not to be the experience of young John Allpress. In spite of visits from his parents or sisters every weekend – cheap day return fares had been abolished at the outbreak of war to discourage unnecessary travel, but the government granted one free travel pass a month for parents to visit their children in the reception areas – John was desperately homesick. Alice and William could not bear to see their son so miserable and after a few months Alice decided to 'chance it' and bring him back to London. The foster mother who had so reluctantly taken him in was extremely cross – no doubt, John thinks, because she would miss the maintenance allowance she received for him. John thinks that his father, like so many parents, took the view that if they were going to die, they would all die together.

The bombs had not come and by Christmas 1939 the government was powerless to stop the drift of evacuees back to the cities. By January 1940, nearly two-thirds – 900,000 – of the official evacuees in England, Wales and Scotland had returned home.[13] Eighty percent of them were mothers and small children and nearly half were unaccompanied schoolchildren, leaving only 570,000 official evacuees in the reception areas.

Significantly, the proportion of children returning to the poor areas of East London was higher than that to the better off districts of West London. 'Economic and educational poverty, a stronger sense of family solidarity, a higher rate of rejection by householders in the reception areas may all have operated to cause this difference between east and west,' according to the official war historian, Richard Titmuss.[14] The heaviest and most rapid rate of return, inevitably, was on the part of mothers with small children from the most impoverished parts of London, Liverpool and Glasgow. They had not been made to feel at home in the reception areas and were uneasy at this separation from husbands, family and community. Being a wife and mother and keeper of the home was the whole *raison d'etre* of such women; it made no sense to them not to be there.

Those children who had been evacuated privately to stay with friends or relatives in the country – and therefore not subjected to the trauma of being billeted with strangers – were more likely to stay put for the duration of the war. More often than not, they had been enrolled in private schools, where they would stay to complete their education, perhaps coming home occasionally for the holidays if the bombing allowed. Their parents understood that although the bombing had not come yet, it would come.

234 Buckland
Rd

Dear Mummy,
Thank you for sending the bracelet, it does fit.

I am enclosing negatives. I showed the snaps to some of the mistresses and they thought they were very nice.

Miss Davies has invited me to go to a piping rally on Saturday. I am longing to go & I shall unless Mrs Waller doesn't let me,

By the way,

on the 5th of July Edna Vinall is bringing Audrey & Irene Hills up to London on a for a weekend. They wanted to know if I could come, after all Edna is in form 4. I said that you might say no; on account of air raids, though I should love to go come.

Exams soon! I am still revising, (when I'm not composing poems about mistresses or historical characters (poor old Shakespear!! how he suffers)

State education in the reception areas was haphazard, to say the least. Evacuees either shared the premises of local schools and each group – town and country – was taught in shifts, meaning that the evacuees would attend school for only half a day, or else they were taught as a separate body in oversize classes of different ages and abilities in village halls. Thrown into disarray by the evacuation, state education was no better in London and the big cities, if it existed at all.

When John returned to London his school remained officially billeted in the country so he went to Priory Grove School at the end of the road. He was fortunate to find it open, because two-thirds of London's schools had been commandeered for civil defence and other wartime purposes. It had never been envisaged that two tiers of education – one in the evacuating areas, the other in the reception areas – would be in operation concurrently. The government's official evacuation plan had assumed that all children and their teachers in the evacuating areas would leave for the reception areas and stay there for the duration of the war. Indeed, this is exactly what happened in the case of private schools, such as St. Paul's, Westminster and City of London, which were evacuated en bloc to safer areas and stayed there until the war was over.

By going to a different school, John, like so many other children, lost touch with his former teachers and therefore suffered a loss of continuity. Before the war London schools had been relatively advanced and well supplied, but now there were fewer teachers and elderly teachers were being brought out of retirement to replace younger ones who had

These pages: Few families owned a telephone, so that the best way for parents and children to keep in touch was by letter.

Above: A group of young children trying on shoes, which have been donated by the English Speaking Union in Seattle.

gone to war, class sizes were larger even though there were fewer children, and there was a shortage of textbooks. John Allpress, when he left school at 14 in 1943, felt that he was two years behind in educational terms and that his real education began when he left school – and his experience was all too common.[15]

Most of the teachers had accompanied their pupils to the reception areas, but some followed the drift of their pupils back to the evacuating areas. The more enterprising of them tackled the problem of school closure by offering private tuition or volunteering for the Home Tuition Scheme, visiting children's homes and inviting them to join impromptu classes held in private homes or in whatever premises could be commandeered for the purpose.

Education, which had been compulsory, had to all intents and purposes become voluntary, at least until such time as the government could reopen schools in the evacuating areas. During the winter of 1939–1940 many of the 200,000 children who had stayed in London or who returned home in time for Christmas were receiving no education at all.[16]

'Back home after five weeks of evacuation and filled with the elation of perhaps a never-ending holiday for schools were closed,' wrote one London boy. 'Maybe the war wouldn't be so bad.'[17] He spent the days in Hamleys in Regent Street and looking into the windows of other toy shops.

Others were not so innocently engaged. There was a marked rise in juvenile delinquency in London, Glasgow and other big cities, which was to grow worse as the war took its toll on family life. There was less parental supervision; with fathers absent and mothers sometimes engaged in war work and generally distracted by the demands of wartime (rationing, shortages and more red tape generally, not to speak of the disruption wrought by the bombing), some children were left to run wild.

The lesson of the first evacuation was that the public never behaved in the way the government wanted or expected it to. The government vowed that there would be no more official evacuation schemes en masse for mothers and children; in future it would offer assisted travel to those who requested it when the need should arise. Henceforth, the possibility of evacuation served as a safety valve for mothers and children, allowing them to escape the bombing whenever it became too intense, or giving them a much-needed break for short periods. Residential nurseries for unaccompanied children under the age of five provided a safe and stable haven for them and released their mothers for war work, while expectant mothers increasingly resorted to maternity homes in the reception areas away from the bombing.

Meanwhile, the 'phoney war' and the return of so many evacuees by January 1940 gave the government the chance to investigate the complaints emanating from the reception areas and make the necessary improvements. Strenuous efforts were made to persuade parents that it was their patriotic duty to send their children back to the reception areas, with the Ministry of Information producing posters warning mothers not to be tempted by Hitler, who was depicted urging them to take their children back home, but to keep their children safe in the reception areas. 'DON'T do it, Mother – LEAVE THE CHILDREN WHERE THEY ARE', screamed the poster.

In future, doctors would examine children the day before they were evacuated to ensure they were free from infection and 'from vermin, nits, abrasions, lesions or scratches of any nature'.[18] They were to be cleaned up and adequately clothed before their departure, while school nurses who had been consigned to hospitals to deal with the expected casualties of bombing were now reassigned to the reception areas to keep up the good work. Social services in the reception areas, which had been inferior to those in the big cities and inadequate even for peacetime, were to be spruced up. They were, after all, going to have to deal with the social casualties of war: children whose mothers were ill or expecting another baby and whose husband was in the services; children of mothers – perhaps war widows – who needed to work; children out of control; children whose parents were homeless; or children of broken homes.

There were to be hostels for mothers and children, hostels for disabled children, and hostels or camps for 'difficult' and 'problem' children; maternity and convalescent homes; residential nurseries for children under five, day nurseries and play centres; and

canteens offering cheap meals for mothers and children living in billets. All these ongoing projects improved as the war went on.

Teachers who had accompanied their pupils to the reception areas had to do a great deal more social work than their role usually entailed, not only guarding the children's moral welfare but also taking care of practical matters. The teachers had to make sure that the children had adequate clothing and their footwear was in good repair, going through the appropriate channels to recover the costs from parents where necessary. More generous clothing grants were confidentially allotted to the local authorities in the evacuation areas to distribute to the most needy cases, while the Women's Voluntary Service (WVS) was doing a valiant job setting up regional clothing depots with liberal contributions from the American Red Cross and the Canadian Red Cross.

Billeting allowances had been considered inadequate, although this was a question of relative values. A sum of, say, 8s 6d a week per child, which was considered derisory by a middle-class householder anxious to maintain standards, might have been welcomed as a lavish contribution to the household budget by an agricultural labourer on 30 shillings a week. From April 1940 there would be a billeting allowance of 8s 6d a week for children under ten; 10s 6d a week for each child aged ten to 14; 12s 6d for those aged 14 to 16; and 15s for those

Top: Invitations poured in from all parts of the English-speaking world on behalf of families willing to offer homes to British children for the duration of the war. Here a party of children arrives in New York.

Above: Children evacuated overseas – the seavacuees – were unable to see their parents for many years. However, these three are communicating with their parents in a two-way transatlantic broadcast from the USA.

aged over 16.[19] However, by June 1940 the cost of living was 17 percent higher than it had been at the outbreak of war.

The government picked up the tab for the transport costs of evacuation but it was left to the local authorities to assess incomes and collect the cost of billeting from parents. In October 1939 parents had been asked to make a weekly contribution of 6s to the billeting allowance,[20] or 9s if they had the means – this had prompted some to bring their children home – although those who could not afford to do so were means tested and did not have to pay. Forty percent of parents of evacuated children paid the full 6s or more. Sadly, there were cases where householders were sometimes pocketing the billeting allowance and helping themselves to the child's rations into the bargain. Some children were going hungry. It was up to teachers, school nurses and social workers to keep an eye open for such abuses.

In spite of all their efforts to make evacuation more palatable it was an uphill struggle to convince parents of its merits. After the first evacuation families knew what it was like to be divided and to live in unfamiliar and unsympathetic surroundings. Nor was the government having much more success in persuading householders in the reception areas to take in evacuees. Those who offered were usually the ones who had taken evacuees the first time round. It tended to be the least well off householders, rather than the comfortable, bridge-playing middle class, who were often the most generous in opening their doors to the evacuees. There was always the threat that billeting would be made compulsory, but billeting officers who wanted to keep in with the local bigwigs tended to let them off and lean on humbler householders to provide billets.

The 'phoney war' ended when Hitler invaded the Low Countries in April and then swept through France in May. The British Expeditionary Force (BEF) was evacuated from Dunkirk, with John's elder brother Harry playing a courageous role in helping to carry the wounded on board the boats. The general feeling was that Britain would be next. The fact that the Germans were now only 20 miles across the English Channel and poised to invade concentrated minds wonderfully.

The instinctive reaction of parents to the threat of invasion was to send their children as far away as possible. Those with money, and some who knew they would be on the Nazis' 'most wanted list', accepted offers of homes for their children in the USA. They were entirely self-funded. Some went

Above: Tragically, the *City of Benares*, carrying among its passengers 90 children evacuated under the auspices of the Children's Overseas Reception Board (CORB) and 20 others being evacuated privately, was torpedoed by a German U-boat in the Atlantic on 17 September 1940 with great loss of life.

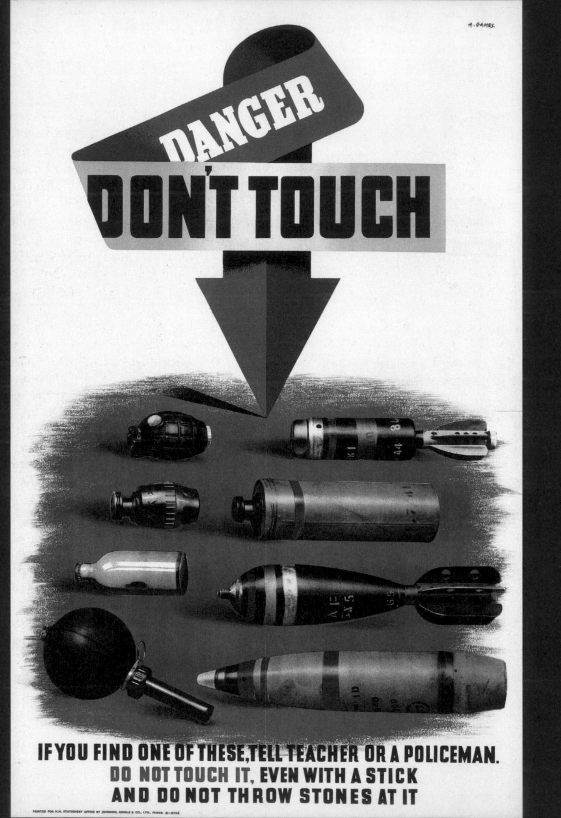

on a private basis, staying with friends or contacts; some in groups under the aegis of religious bodies, such as the Quakers, or Anglo-American companies, such as Kodak and Ford; others as part of exchanges organized by academic bodies, such as Oxford University. The children – about 13,000 of them – were enrolled in local schools in the USA and benefited hugely from the experience.

The government felt it had to sponsor a similar scheme for those unable to afford evacuation overseas, much to the disgust of the new prime minister, Winston Churchill, who saw such action as defeatist. Invitations had been pouring in from the English-speaking USA, Canada, Southern Rhodesia, South Africa, Australia and New Zealand, as well as from South American countries, on behalf of families willing to offer homes to British children. No sooner was the Children's Overseas Reception Board (CORB) established in June 1940 than it was inundated with thousands of requests from parents wanting to send their children abroad. The response can only be described as desperate, because they were entrusting their children to total strangers thousands of miles away and if the children were unhappy there was not much their parents could do about it. In all likelihood the 'seavacuees', as they were called, would have to stay put until the end of hostilities.

Families had to keep secret the fact that their children had secured a place as a 'seavacuee'. Children had to say goodbye to their parents at the railway station, because they were not allowed to accompany them as far as the port of embarkation – Liverpool or Glasgow. Medical inspections were strict and more than 300 were turned back at the port. Lessons had been learned from the earlier domestic evacuation of 1939: siblings should be kept together where possible, if not in the same house, then in the same locality; those who had become friends during the voyage should be housed close by; and children should be placed with families of the same social class as those they had come from – although this was tricky, since for the first two years the British government was not paying billeting allowances, so that in practice it was only well-to-do families who could afford to take the children.

Sixteen of the 19 ships which set sail in the late summer of 1940 arrived safely at their destination. Of the other three ships, the first was the *Volendam*, which was torpedoed, although without loss of children; the second was the *City of Benares*; and the third was the *Rangitata*, which returned to port only hours after hearing of the fate of the second.

On 17 September 1940 the *City of Benares*, en route from Liverpool to Canada and carrying among its passengers 90 children being evacuated through CORB and their escorts (one voluntary helper to each party of eight), as well as ten children being evacuated privately, was torpedoed 253 miles southwest of Rockall, sinking 40 minutes later. Thirty children were killed instantly in the explosion.

Left: There was always a danger that children playing on bomb sites would come across some dangerous object and be curious enough to pick it up or poke it. Boys, in particular, loved to collect shrapnel and other mementoes of the war.

There was chaos. One of the problems was that many of the crew were Lascars and could not understand the captain's orders given in English. The children had practised lifeboat drill over the previous days, but when it came to the real thing

some of the lifeboats tipped over as they were lowered, drowning escorts and children in the cold, stormy sea. In their haste, most of the children had left their cabins without putting on shoes and warmer clothes or taking the blanket placed for the purpose at the end of the bed, so that if they did manage to get away from the sinking ship in one of the lifeboats many died of hypothermia.

Many of the lifeboats had taken in water, so that besides hypothermia the children suffered from 'immersion foot' from being submerged in seawater for too long.

One lifeboat containing six CORB boys and two escorts, as well as other passengers and crew, survived at sea for over a week before being picked up. A couple of girls survived by clinging to a raft; they were rescued 19 hours after the attack. Altogether 77 children and 171 passengers and crew perished in the *City of Benares* incident.

Surprisingly, requests to evacuate children overseas did not diminish after the tragedy of the *City of Benares*, but it was enough to make the government close the scheme.

Meanwhile, the onslaught of the Blitz in September 1940 provoked the second great wave of domestic evacuation. More than 1,250,000[21] escaped the bombing and joined the existing evacuees in the reception areas. This time even areas which had been considered safe previously fell into the evacuation category, with over 200,000 evacuees as well as local children being moved from coastal towns in the south and east. In December 1940, three months into the Blitz, there were still 80,400 schoolchildren in London and 39,000 children under five.

Those children who, like John Allpress, remained in London and the big cities

Top: An unexploded bomb (UXB) was a real hazard and caused a great deal of inconvenience, as the area had to be cleared until the bomb disposal men could deal with it. This boy seems quite blasé about the danger.

Above: This little girl should not have been in London when she was injured in an air raid in September 1940. Evacuation was never compulsory, but children under 5 deemed to be at serious risk physically and psychologically could be compulsorily evacuated by the authorities.

under attack had to endure all the fear, danger and noise of air raids, nights of disrupted sleep in the shelters, the very real possibility of being bombed-out, as well as death, maiming and destruction all around them. Although he spent some time with his mother in Woking, where she went to be at the bedside of her dying daughter Gladys, who by then had been evacuated from St. Thomas' Hospital, John would have spent many nights with his family in London during the Blitz, trying to get some sleep in the Anderson shelter.

John was 11 years old during the Blitz, which must have been frightening enough for a boy of his age. It would be absolutely horrific for a small child, especially if the adults he or she relied on were showing signs of fear. As an ARP warden later wrote, 'Nothing, surely, could have a more serious effect on a child's stability than than [sic] to feel the earth itself heave, and the shelter rock to and fro, or, worse, to have the whole house crash down on him.'[22]

Once more the numbers of evacuees in the reception areas ebbed and flowed, according to the geographical location and intensity of the bombing. As they began to drift back to London and other cities after the Blitz it was often to find schools closed again, their premises turned into rest centres for those temporarily rendered homeless by the bombing. Teachers again went from home to home gathering the remnants of different schools and classes to offer some formal education, even if it took place in half-day shifts.

The chief inspector of education in London regretted that children's education was seriously retarded by the war. Children who should have started school at the age of five were instead starting at six or seven and, not surprisingly, a large proportion of children who should have been reading were not able to do so by the age of seven.[23]

His fears were borne out within two years of the end of the war, when boys who had spent the last two to three years of their school life in the disrupted conditions of 1939–1942 began to enter the British Army in 1946 and 1947. They were given intelligence, mechanical and educational tests and these were compared with scores achieved by men who had left school during the years 1935–1945 and joined up during the war. There was no recorded decline in native intelligence or mechanical aptitude, but there was a very definite drop in the level of scholastic attainment, and a serious increase in the numbers graded educationally backward.

Apart from scholastic retardation, there were also behavioural problems in all age groups. Teachers found that the disruption of war had dealt a serious blow to the children's powers of concentration. They were easily distracted and showed little application for hard work. They were restless and noisier than usual.

A period of stability was essential for teachers to recover lost ground, but unfortunately the unleashing of Hitler's first 'Vengeance' weapon, the V1 or 'doodlebug', directed at London and the southeast of England from June 1944, once more derailed an organization that had been approaching peacetime standards. One million people were again evacuated, with help from the government, from the areas being hit by the V1s. As before, many others also made their own private arrangements to leave. In June

Above: Children's education was seriously disrupted by the war. Here pupils are retrieving books after their school in Coventry was hit in a night raid in April 1941.

1944 there had been 237,000 schoolchildren in London, but this number rapidly dipped to 136,500, before creeping up to 173,000 in December 1944 and 192,000 in March 1945.[24]

Ironically, just as the onslaught of the V1s eased and evacuees started returning to the capital, another new weapon, the V2, was launched by Hitler on 8 September 1944. These rockets were hurled indiscriminately at London day and night; since it took all of four minutes for them to journey from their launch pads in Holland to London, there was no time to sound the air raid warning or to take shelter.

As if sitting for examinations was not bad enough, children in London often had to take them under aerial bombardment. In March 1945 a Catford boy recalls:

'The form master had just given out the English language papers when a distant rumble roared across the heavens. It did not distract us unduly, not after months of far bigger thunder crashes. The paper before us was a more immediate cause for panic, as with trembling fingers and anxious eyes we scanned it for a question we could attempt without too much head-searching.

Children who had not been evacuated or returned home despite the bombing had to endure all the fear, danger and noise of air raids, as well as nights of disrupted sleep and discomfort in the shelters. Here a mother has tied ropes from the bench to the wall, to prevent the children from falling on to the shelter's wet floor.

'The essay topics transported us to a world far removed from the reality of our own lives. The war fell away behind a halcyon mist of an eternal peace-time summer with topics like ... "A School Outing in the Countryside". We had had a few of those, only we called it evacuation. "An Evening Spent at Home". Gripping stuff. Did they mean the air raid shelter?

'Two hours later a great bang smacked the sky outside the classroom windows and subsided with a heavy thump somewhere to the north. We looked up momentarily from our ink-stained pages. The teacher, a tall, spare man in a ginger suit who never smiled in our presence, turned from the window to face us. His eyes met ours impassively. "You have one hour left," he said, without a change in his expression. To finish the paper, or to live?

'He was telling us our time was nearly up just as a mighty crack seemed to arc over the heavens and rend them apart. A giant thud shook the floor and windows. Our time will be up if they come any closer. He did not bat an eyelid ... We took our cue from him and showed no reaction ... Around us, within a radius of a mile or so, something like twenty rockets must have come down already. So close, yet so far. Had the campaign gone on for but a single day longer than it did, who knows if our luck would have held out?'[25]

On 2 May 1945 the local authorities in the reception areas at last received the signal to activate the return of all remaining evacuees to London.

Evacuees from other cities had been returning home in stages for some months now, but since London had been under attack from the 'Vengeance' weapons as late as 28 March 1945, its remaining children in the reception areas were the last to come home.

If evacuation had been fraught with problems, coming home to Britain's bombed cities and trying to resume family life again after months or years of separation had its problems, too, as we shall see in Chapter 11. Some children never got over the trauma of being separated from parents at an early age; others lived with deeply suppressed feelings about their evacuation experience for the rest of their lives. Almost all had had their education disrupted and had a lot of catching up to do.

However, on a more positive note, the evacuation scheme had been designed to save lives, and while 7,736 British children were killed as a result of enemy action during the course of the whole war, many thousands of lives were saved by evacuation.[26] An unlooked for but highly significant benefit was that evacuation had thrown the focus of attention on the welfare of children as never before. Had it not been for the war, the conditions many of these children were living in in the most deprived areas would probably not have been brought to public notice as soon and as dramatically. As it was, evacuation began to work as a kind of disguised welfare agency with the government assuming responsibility for the well-being of its people. War, of which children were the innocent victims, provided the catalyst for much-needed improvements in child welfare, health and education.

Above: Playtime: children have fun on makeshift swings that have been rigged from a lamppost amidst the rubble left by a bombing raid on London during the Blitz.

3
Go to It!

'*We did a lot of war work. We used to do ARP, you know... We were on call practically every night when the sirens went.*' [1]
Eva Allpress

O n the day war was declared, 3 September 1939, an Act of Parliament was passed introducing conscription for all men between the ages of 18 and 41. In response to the Military Training Act, the first peacetime conscripts, aged 20 to 21, had registered on 3 June 1939 and been called up on 1 July and sent away for training. Others – Harry Allpress among them – awaited the call-up. It took several months to register all the men for conscription.

Exemptions were given to those in 'reserved' occupations – jobs vital to the country or the war effort, which could not be abandoned or performed by others. Although he was too old to fight, engine driver William Allpress was in such an occupation, because railway transport was vital to the war effort. Medical practitioners, police officers and teachers also fell into this category, although in practice many of the younger men opted to join the forces, leaving older, retired personnel, or women in the case of teachers, to hold the fort in their absence. However, neither Bill nor Harry Allpress was in a 'reserved' occupation and at 24 and 21 respectively they were eligible for conscription.

Bill was in the volunteer reserves, until he was called up in 1940.[2] He had originally applied for the Army, but ended up joining the RAF. As a member of a Spitfire squadron he would serve in North Africa and Italy, not seeing his family for three whole years. As a former upholsterer, it was appropriate that Bill's

Left: The government soon realized that it would have to harness all the available 'woman power' for the war effort.

main job would be to mend the seats of damaged aircraft. This sometimes included the gruesome task of scraping off the remains of the dead pilot.

Both keen cyclists and members of a cycling club, the brothers were extremely fit, which certainly helped Harry when he came to do his Army training. Called up three weeks after war was declared in 1939, Harry joined the Rifle Brigade and did two months' initial training in Winchester, before moving on to Tidworth, where he was taught to drive trucks and motorcycles.[3] After that he was transferred to the 8th Battalion Royal Northumberland Fusiliers at Denton, outside Newcastle, where he joined a motorcycle reconnaissance unit. In March 1940 he was sent to France as part of the British Expeditionary Force (BEF), where as a lance corporal responsible for ten men he joined a party making runways for the RAF.

By the end of May 1940 the Germans had advanced so rapidly across France – the Blitzkrieg – that the British, in danger of being surrounded and captured, had been forced back to the English Channel. Crucially, the Germans halted their advance just short of the port of Dunkerque, or Dunkirk in English, giving the British just enough time, between 26 May and 4 June, to evacuate the troops trapped there, although not without the vicious attentions of the Luftwaffe.

Top: Bill Allpress, the eldest son, joined the RAF and served in the desert campaign in North Africa.

Above: Harry Allpress courageously volunteered to carry stretcher cases on to the boats at Dunkirk and was among the last to leave. He was twice mentioned in despatches during the war.

Opposite: 'Wars are not won by evacuations', Churchill warned. Nevertheless, the rescue of quarter of a million British troops from Dunkirk was seen as a triumph.

Harry and his men were machine-gunned as they approached the town but made it to the beaches, to meet a scene of barely contained chaos. Lines of men looking like long dark shadows in the sand stood waiting to embark. They were tired, hungry, thirsty and anxious – terrified that their turn would not come, that there would not be enough ships to take them off, or that they would be killed in the process. As the Luftwaffe bombed and strafed them from above, it was no wonder that Harry found 'the men around him … they'd been there so long trying to get a ship home, that they were going mad …. They almost had to fight them to stop them from really going beserk'.[4] Eventually rescue came, on one of the Royal Navy vessels or 'little ships' – fishing boats and pleasure craft commandeered from private owners in coastal towns all over England – which defied the fury of the Luftwaffe to bring the men back. Coincidentally, one of their rescuers was a neighbour, an old retired sea captain who lived opposite the Allpresses in Priory Grove.[5]

Afterwards, Winston Churchill, who had succeeded Chamberlain as prime minister on 10 May, confessed in the House of Commons that he had feared that no more than 20,000 or 30,000 men of the BEF might be rescued.[6] But thanks to the courage of the British and French seamen manning 220 warships and 650 other vessels, and to the skill of the young men flying Hurricane and Spitfire fighters combating the Luftwaffe, which outnumbered them four to one, disaster had been averted. Altogether 225,000 British, approximately 110,000 French and some 2,000 Belgian troops were taken off the beaches and to safety, to fight another day.[7] Others who had not made it to Dunkirk subsequently managed to embark from other French ports.

Being tall and strong, Harry volunteered to carry stretcher cases on to the boats — a courageous act, since it meant that he had to wait almost to the end before being persuaded to embark himself. Although Harry's ship, seriously overloaded, crossed to England at night, it was bombed all the way to Folkestone.[8] Next morning — no doubt after being offered tea and sandwiches by members of the Women's Voluntary Service (WVS) — the men were put on a train that skirted round London via Clapham Junction. Being so close to home, Harry would have liked to have jumped out there, but instead was taken to Ludlow in Shropshire to recover from his ordeal, before being given a week's leave.

At home in Priory Grove the family waited anxiously for news of Harry. Nellie describes it as a 'dreadful feeling', not knowing whether he had been killed or captured. Eventually, a little card, looking rather like a luggage label, arrived to tell them the good news — he was safe and would write to them soon.

Harry was to remain in Britain for the next four years, undergoing further training and becoming a physical education (PE) instructor of young recruits — who had to be fit enough to carry a man of their own weight for 100 yards. Promoted to sergeant, he did not return to France until several days after the D-Day landings in June 1944, when he went as part of a reconnaissance unit, whose job it was to go forward in armoured cars to discover the whereabouts of the enemy before the rest could follow. Guarding the left flank of the advance, he fought through Belgium and Holland and eventually into Germany. He was to be mentioned in dispatches twice and received the Military Medal.

Dunkirk could have been one of the greatest military disasters in British history, but the heroic rescue of the men from the beaches allowed it to be portrayed as a triumph. Churchill called it 'a miracle of deliverance, achieved by valour, by perseverance, by perfect discipline, by faultless service, by resource, by skill, by unconquerable fidelity', but deliverance must not be confused with victory. 'Wars are not won by evacuations,' he warned.[9]

On 10 June Italy entered the war on Germany's side, while on 22 June Marshal Pétain, the new French premier and former First World War hero, accepted the German terms for surrender. Hitler exacted his revenge on the French by insisting that the armistice be signed in the same railway carriage in the forest of Compiègne that Marshal Foch had used to impose his humiliating terms on the Germans in 1918.

Britain, with its Empire and Commonwealth, now stood alone, facing the very real possibility of a German invasion. Refusing to countenance pleas for a negotiated peace from Foreign Secretary Lord Halifax, with initial tepid support from Chamberlain and the War Cabinet,

Left: By the end of June 1940 one and a half million men had joined the Home Guard, relieving the Army of routine tasks.
Below: The Home Guard were at first short of equipment, although these two are training with a Vickers machine gun.

Churchill outmanoeuvred the would-be appeasers and vowed that Britain would fight on to the end. Therefore, when Hitler offered peace on 19 July, Halifax formally rejected the proposal.

If everyone did their duty, Churchill told the nation, he had no doubt that victory would eventually be achieved: '… we shall fight on the seas and oceans, we shall fight with growing confidence and growing strength in the air, we shall defend our island, whatever the cost may be, we shall fight on the beaches, we shall fight on the landing grounds, we shall fight in the fields and in the streets, we shall fight in the hills; we shall never surrender …'[10] His mood of stubborn defiance and dogged courage against almost insuperable odds exactly fitted that of the nation.

Nobody, not least soldiers like Harry Allpress who had been members of the BEF and witnessed military disaster for themselves, was under any illusion about Britain's unpreparedness for war or an invasion, but at least the successful Dunkirk evacuation meant that Britain had a considerable army on its shores, even if it had left all its equipment behind in France.

In mid-May, Anthony Eden, the new Secretary of State for War, had warned of a new form of warfare recently observed in Holland and Belgium, whereby German troops had been parachuted into those countries to weaken their defences before the arrival of the army on the ground. A similar tactic could be used against Britain. He therefore called upon all men between the ages of 17 and 65, not presently engaged in military service, to come forward to offer their services. The new force was to be called the Local Defence Volunteers, but as Churchill loathed that name, it was subsequently changed to the Home Guard. We know it more familiarly as 'Dad's Army'.

Within 24 hours, over one quarter of a million men had volunteered and by the end of June nearly one and a half million had joined the Home Guard. Although unpaid, they were promised uniforms and arms, but both were a long time coming. Meanwhile, they drilled with sporting guns, pick-axes, pitchforks, brooms or any 'weapon' which came to hand. As in so many aspects of early wartime life, improvisation was the order of the day. The Home Guard relieved the Army of routine tasks such as keeping watch on coastlines, manning roadblocks, guarding aerodromes and factories, and, later, serving on anti-aircraft gun sites.

The war would require extraordinary effort on the part of all the British people, not least in supplying the armed forces with the aircraft, naval vessels, armoured vehicles, armaments and munitions they would require to 'finish the job'. The Emergency Powers (Defence) Act, which was passed on 22 May, gave Churchill's all-party coalition government unlimited scope for coercion – complete control over persons and property – so that Ernest Bevin, the new Minister of Labour and National Service, could direct personnel to perform any service he thought fit, whether in the armed forces or the war factories, with wages, hours and conditions set by himself. He could 'freeze' people in essential jobs, and prosecute those who failed to comply. As one of the founders of the powerful Transport and General Workers' Union and its general secretary from 1922 to 1945, he was especially well equipped for the job.

Above: Lord Beaverbrook asked the British people to contribute anything made of aluminium for aircraft production.

Herbert Morrison, the new Minister of Supply, called on Britain's workers to 'Go to it!' Lord Beaverbrook, the press baron put in charge of aircraft production, was determined to cut red tape and he ruthlessly commandeered supplies – even going so far as to call on British housewives to hand over anything made of aluminium. Pots and pans poured in from all over the country. Beaverbrook's War Weapons Weeks brought in over one million pounds a month from the public. It must have been very satisfying to know that one's individual donation – say, £22 for one bomb – was making a direct contribution to destroying the enemy.

The aircraft industry was soon spilling out large numbers of Spitfires and Hurricanes and fixing damaged ones. Beaverbrook insisted that contractors work on Sundays and bank holidays, and works-weeks (when factories closed down to give the entire workforce a week's holiday) were cancelled. To save valuable production time factory workers were discouraged from taking shelter during an air raid; 'Jim Crows', employees acting as plane spotters, on the roof warned them when enemy planes were almost directly overhead, so that they could take shelter then, rather than sitting in the shelter during the entire air raid alert period.

The normal working week under the Factories Act (1937) was 48 hours, but now many workers, including women, in the Royal Ordnance factories making guns, shells and explosives, or others producing aircraft, were doing a 55-hour week, which meant a 10-hour day for five and a half days. Some employees even worked continuously for 36 or even 48 hours without a break. Studies in the First World War had already shown that long hours did not increase production – and, sure enough, this began to lag behind owing to worker fatigue. Fatigue led to accidents and absenteeism.

◆

Britain's war was fought on the home front as much as on the battlefields. Indeed, it was not until September 1941 that the death toll of civilians killed in air raids was exceeded by that of military personnel in the other theatres of war. The role of the civil defence services in protecting civilians during air raids and rescuing the dead and injured from the debris of bombed buildings was therefore vitally important.

For the purpose of civil defence the country was divided into 12 regions. In the event of invasion and the disconnection of any region from central government, the regional commissioner – London had two – would take over the autonomous control of that region.

The London civil defence region – Region 5 – was so large that it was subdivided into nine groups. Group 3, for instance, incorporated the City of London, along with the eastern boroughs of Bethnal Green, Finsbury, Hackney, Holborn, Poplar, Shoreditch and Stepney – which would be some of the most devastated by bombing. The borough of Lambeth was in Group 5. To reflect the size of their populations, some of the groups were subdivided further still. Within each group, every borough was divided into districts, which were then subdivided into wardens' posts, each covering a number of sectors composed of several streets. Ideally, there was one ARP warden for approximately every 1,000 people.

The war room network was organized hierarchically, with the wardens' posts reporting to a borough control, usually located in a bomb-proof shelter near or beneath the town hall, which reported in turn to a group control that reported to the regional headquarters. In London Region the headquarters was housed in and underneath the Geological Museum on Exhibition Road, South Kensington. At the top of the organizational pyramid, with a view of the entire picture, was the Home Security War Room.

As each incident – anywhere a bomb fell was described as an 'incident' – occurred the warden would note the location, extent of the damage and the estimated number of casualties, and run or cycle to his post to report by telephone to the borough control centre, where someone in turn would pass the message to group control and so on up the hierarchy. Each of these bodies would mark the site of the incident on its wall map, so that they were always up to date and had an instant picture of the resources currently available to be deployed at any incident. The whole exercise took minutes.

Communication was the key. Connected to group control on one hand, on the other the borough control centre was linked by banks of telephones and messengers to the wardens' posts, fire and ambulance stations, rescue depots, first aid posts and the cable and utility services. The latter – in London these were the Gas Light and Coke Company, the County of London Electric Supply Company and the Metropolitan Water

Top left: These women working for the Auxiliary Fire Service move the pegs on the wall map to show the location of appliances, giving an instant picture of resources available to be deployed at an incident.

Above left: There was one ARP warden for approximately every 1,000 people. Each warden shared his or her post with a number of others. They had to patrol the streets in their district during a raid and report details of any incident to the borough control centre.

Top right: A civil defence worker in the borough control room takes down details of an incident, which is then marked on the borough map and reported to group control and on up the hierarchy to regional headquarters. The officer in charge at the borough control centre would plan his response to the incident.

Above right: A field kitchen at the ARP wardens' post, where baked potatoes are available.

Opposite: A stirrup pump and one in action, as family members work together using the chain bucket system.

Board – all had their own control centres, working closely with the boroughs' control centres. Each borough surveyor had plans showing the exact location of pipes, wires and cables under every road, so that he was able to gauge the extent of subterranean damage not always apparent to the warden on the spot. Once the call came through to the borough control centre from the ARP warden, the officer in charge – who was supported by specialists such as the city engineer, the medical officer of health, the director of public cleansing, the chief warden and the district rescue officer, or their representatives – would immediately organize his response to the incident.

The ARP service had begun to recruit in earnest in 1938 and by the outbreak of war numbered 1,500,000 men and women, of whom 400,000 were full time and paid. They were drawn from all walks of life, from bank managers to actors and barrow boys to shop assistants. During the period of the 'phoney war' civil defence personnel attracted a great deal of criticism from civilians who resented the fact that they seemed to be pretty idle, earning money for nothing. From some of their diaries, it seems they did indeed spend a lot of time at the wardens' post playing cards and darts, but they also held mock practices in the streets, with some posing as casualties while the rest bandaged and rescued them and loaded them on to stretchers. Apathy set in during this long period of inactivity and many of the recruits began to drift away out of boredom, while some of the younger, fitter men were called up, but it did provide valuable time in which to weed out the good recruits from the bad and to get themselves organized.

Stanley Rothwell, a full-time member of a squad of the heavy rescue service in south Lambeth, recalls:

'It was the shock of Dunkirk that altered the attitude towards training; we were now really and truly at war, we were coming to terms with reality. I still do not dare to think what might have been our fate had Hitler followed his successes in France and invaded us there and then and started the bombing of London that came later.'[11]

Like Eva and Betty Allpress, Barbara Nixon started out as a voluntary part-time ARP warden; she later opted to become full time. As Nixon explains, part-time volunteers were expected to turn up for duty on two or three evenings a week, for about three hours. If a 'Yellow' warning – a 'Yellow' meant that enemy planes were 22 minutes away, whereas a 'Red' meant that they were only 12 minutes away, which was the signal for the air raid sirens to alert the public to the need to take shelter – came through on the post's telephone from 'control', a messenger would come and bang on the front door, asking the part-time warden to come and patrol their sector.[12]

In reality during the Blitz it was much more onerous than this, even for the part-timers. Eva says they were on duty nearly every night – and these extra hours came on top of a day's work.

Eva recalls that they underwent training exercises every Sunday in the park. She did first aid, but they also had to learn how to put out incendiary bombs – cannisters 18 inches long containing phosphorous, which burst into flame after landing if not dealt with quickly enough. As incendiaries were so light, weighing only 2 pounds, thousands of them could be dropped from an aeroplane over a wide area. Wardens were kept busy on the lookout for them and running to put them out before the fires burnt out of control. They could be extinguished using a device called a stirrup pump or by throwing sand or earth on them.[13]

Using a stirrup pump was a rather onerous task, as Barbara Nixon explains:

'One or two [incendiaries] fell in houses and needed stirrup pumps, and I made the great mistake of getting landed with the pumping. The first bucketful [of water] is easy, the second begins to be irritating, by the third one becomes breathless, by the fourth exasperated, and one wishes the plunger had more resistance so that one could work it more slowly, instead of jigging up and down at an exhausting speed.'[14]

Nixon thought the ARP training rather rudimentary:

'We were given several lectures on the smells and effects of the different war gases. We were told of the various standards of shelter protection, authorized by the Government. We were taught three ways of dealing with the small incendiary bomb, and we were told that the blast from high explosive travels, like sound, in all directions, and has an outward and a suction wave. That was all.'[15]

The rest was left pretty much to the initiative and common sense of the individual warden; he or she had to learn on the job. But what they lacked in knowledge and experience at the outset, they made up for with their zeal to help.

ARP wardens were recruited by the local authority and were drawn from the community they served, so that they were familiar with the neighbourhood. The Allpress sisters had lived in Priory Grove all their life, so were at an advantage in this respect. Wardens had to know their sector intimately – who the residents were, where they lived, what their shelter arrangements were, and what part of the building they were most likely to be in if a bomb struck. The warden had to keep a census of the residents and it was incumbent on the residents to inform their local warden if they were going away, or if they had been away to let them know they had come back. During an incident, the ARP incident officer would refer to the census in order to tell the rescue workers how many residents there were in a building and where they were likely to be. Sometimes, too, relatives and neighbours were admitted to the incident site if they could indicate the probable whereabouts of the casualties.

It was the warden's job to marshal the residents into the shelters when the sirens sounded, helping the old and infirm. Some of the wardens had their 'specials' whom they carried to the shelter as soon as the siren went. During the raid the wardens would regularly look in on the shelters, reporting what was going on outside and trying to offer cheer and reassurance.

If a bomb struck, the warden informed 'control', giving location, type of bomb, area of damage and number of casualties, while an incident inquiry point was set up under the direction of the incident officer in charge of the whole rescue operation. The warden's job was to help the rescue services where possible, to comfort the victims and arrange for the homeless to be sent to a rest centre. Practice was one thing, but once the Blitz started all this had to be done in darkness, amidst the noise and fury of a raid, with the bombs whistling and exploding all around them and fires raging. Often the telephones would be cut off and the warden had to cycle furiously to another post to make the necessary calls, as Nixon had to do on many occasions: 'Communications alone, in a place like London, were an enormous problem, and though there was often inevitable confusion during the night, when telephone exchanges were knocked flat, by morning a makeshift scheme was always working.'[16]

Top: The air raid siren earned the nickname 'Moaning Minnie' for its long drawn-out eerie moan.
Above: The destruction of St. Paul's Cathedral would have had a devastating effect on morale. Fortunately, the cathedral had a first-rate team of dedicated men to defend it.

The fire service was often first on the scene. Incendiaries, HE (high explosive) bombs and oil bombs were all designed to ignite fires, but only the incendiaries were within the scope of the ARP wardens.

Top: During a heavy raid water mains were often fractured. In London firemen had to drag heavy suction-pipes from fireboats in the Thames to the bank to tackle the conflagration.

Above: Incendiary bombs had to be tackled immediately before they developed into full-blown fires blazing out of control.

'The siren went on Monday at 10 minutes to eight in the evening,' noted a new ARP warden in east London. 'I reported at the post. The guns were already blazing away and planes were overhead. I walked back to the house – dodging into doorways when I heard shrapnel falling ... and then it came – a "Molotov [Bread] basket" of 50 incendiary bombs on our street, a few on the flats behind us and a number on the railway embankment ... I rushed out and blew my whistle to summon the wardens (3 of them) who were standing by. The whole street seemed ablaze with white magnesium glare. There were ten fires between our house and the post ... I tackled one which was blazing under a front window and got it out quickly. Then the woman screamed out that one had fallen on a shed full of timber in her back garden and was blazing away. I rushed through the house and tackled the bomb with sand. Then I put out the blaze in the shed with buckets of water. The other wardens were working singly on other fires down their end of the street ... The AFS [Auxiliary Fire Service] was tackling the blazing school & Jerry was using it as a landmark & letting drop salvo after salvo of high explosives and the guns were blazing furiously. It was like hell let loose.'[17]

Sometimes incendiaries fell so thick and fast over a wide area that it was impossible to smother them all and they raged out of control – a situation Barbara Nixon encountered when she was on duty one night:

> 'Fires were everywhere; the one in Cannon Street now looked nearly a mile long; to the south of that there was a vast conflagration at the Elephant. As I went along the main road, lifting my bicycle over tangles of hose-pipe, piles of debris and glass, about every third turning was blazing. We had sweated and struggled with repeated loads of incendiaries, and got them under control, all to no purpose: down came an oil bomb and the whole building would go up in flames.'[18]

Recruitment into the AFS had begun in March 1938. At the outbreak of war there were 15 auxiliaries to every one regular firefighter. Auxiliaries undertook 60 hours' training. Needless to say, the regulars resented the interlopers and there was a certain amount of friction between them. It also emerged that different districts in the country at large used different sized hydrants, so that when, say, the Manchester fire brigade came to help out in the Plymouth raids it found its equipment useless. Clearly, there had to be a national fire service, with conformity in equipment, but this did not come into being until August 1941, after the Blitz.

Apart from the almost extraordinary strength required to manoeuvre the heavy firefighting equipment in the most adverse conditions, the firemen were often hampered in their efforts by lack of water, not least during the great conflagration in the City of London on 29 December 1940. The group coordinating officer of the London civil defence region noted the plight of the firemen:

> 'The water supply of London failed, important mains being shattered by HE bombs … only by dragging heavy suction-pipes across the mud from the fireboats in mid-stream could water be brought to the bank. In the river-bed, hour by hour, firemen toiled in the eerie glare from a wall of fire, heaving, straining and coaxing slimy pipes and slippery couplings into a battery of lines for vital water supply.'[19]

Not only did the firemen need to be robust, they were often in mortal danger, as Barbara Nixon observed:

> 'Our interval was terminated abruptly by yet another oil bomb on a firm two hundred yards away and close to an existing fire; it was the only part of that street that was yet unburnt, and now it was blazing fiercely. The firemen did their best with a miserably low pressure of water, but a little later with a resounding crash the building fell in, burying two of the crew. Their bones were not found till three months later.'[20]

The heavy rescue service was responsible for digging and releasing any trapped casualties, while the light rescue service or stretcher party put the victims on stretchers and, if the injuries could not be attended to by the mobile first aid unit or the nearest fixed first aid station, sent them by ambulance to hospital. Victims emerged from the debris absolutely covered in thick mortar dust, giving them an aged appearance and making it difficult at first for even their own close relatives to identify them. The incident doctor provided immediate diagnosis and treatment and the doctor alone could verify if someone was dead and issue the death certificate.

Doctors and nurses might have to crawl through tunnels of debris after the rescue men to help the injured or amputate on the spot in the dust and grime, sometimes even with water rising or leaking gas from fractured mains threatening their own lives as they worked.

Unlike the female ARP wardens and those in the Auxiliary Ambulance service, who wore trousers – not only were trousers practical, but they were warm, which was vital for patrolling the streets during long cold winter nights – the unfortunate nurses had to do all this still wearing their uniform dress. Too bad then if they found themselves being lowered head first into a void in the debris to administer aid – usually an injection of morphia – to a trapped casualty.

Each heavy rescue service squad was supposed to have a lorry containing cutting and lifting tackle, and baulks of heavy timber for shoring up buildings, although in the early days of the war such equipment might be scarce and the rescue workers often had to use their bare hands to remove the debris to get to the victims. The men in the squad tended to come from the building or engineering industries, because they had to have the knowledge and experience to be able to foresee how brickwork, floors, steel-framed structures and reinforced concrete might behave when subjected to the eccentric strains and stresses that followed bomb damage. Combing through the debris in search of casualties – often asking for quiet so that they could listen for any tapping or crying from beneath the debris – was a delicate art, as J.H. Forshaw, the deputy to the London County Council's chief architect, describes in his unpublished history of the department in wartime:

> 'He knows that the steel joist above him would hold the collapsed roof of timber and the weight of the tiles piled upon it, but he also knew that the fractured pier upon which the joist itself was resting might at any moment give way, crushing him and the casualty he was trying to reach. He knew how to cut through the cast-iron of the bath which lay across the route he was tunnelling and how to use the mahogany frame of a wrecked piano to shore up the walls and roof of cave-like working space so that he could bring the casualty safely away. He learned to sense the value of every brick and piece of wood that lined the dark dust-filled channel. In the hours of patient working, handing out piece by piece and handful by handful the crumbled plaster and rubbish, he did not stop to think of the many places which needed only a touch to set the whole mass moving, but he knew them as he knew his own hand. He did not let bombs, flaming debris, rising water or escaping gas deter him whilst he was physically able to carry on. Nor until he had guided, carried or dragged his casualty inch by inch to safety did he open his mind to the risks he had himself undergone, and then it was only to dismiss it as a joke.'[21]

Twenty thousand Londoners, he concluded, owed their lives to this dogged, persistent work in the worst conditions imaginable.

Above: Dogs were sometimes used to sniff out casualties in the debris.

The rescue workers were responsible for many personal acts of kindness, often risking their lives to go back into an unstable building or burrow into debris to recover some object – perhaps even a beloved pet – which would mean so much to the person who had just lost their home. The Reverend George Markham, working many hours a week as an unpaid civil defence worker on top of his parish duties at St. Peter's church, Walworth, recalls one such occasion:

> 'We cut a hole through a pile carpet, so that one of my wardens could squeeze under the old lady's bed below, and find the tin box which contained her few treasures. It was hot, dusty work, after a long noisy night, but I always felt that these little salvage efforts were worthwhile … these small things made such a difference to the morale of so many people.'[22]

Inevitably, there were times when the rescue workers discovered it was their own family under the rubble, as Barbara Nixon witnessed one night in Finsbury:

> 'The other end of the borough was getting it much more heavily than we were, and a quarter of a mile away there was a shocking disaster when an HE hit a large building which contained a reinforced basement shelter. The whole structure collapsed, and a large water tank and a main burst. One hundred and thirty people, including many children, were crushed or drowned. The entire family of one of our

Rescue Service men was buried there. For days on end he watched the digging, although there was no hope at all. They tried to persuade him to go away, but he only shook his head. His wife had wanted to stay at home that night, and he had himself insisted that she and the children go to the shelter.'[23]

The rescue workers had their rewards as well, not least in being witness to the stoicism and good humour of many of those they saved. Typical was the old woman in the East End brought out from under the debris of her ruined house, where for many hours she had been protected by the solidity of the dining table. Spotting her son among the rescue crew she yelled triumphantly, 'I told you that was a good table!'[24]

The demands made on the rescue workers as the Blitz unfolded were unimaginable, as Stanley Rothwell describes:

Above: This casualty has been marked on the forehead with 'M ¼', indicating that she has received quarter of a grain of morphine before arrival at the hospital.
Opposite: A nurse works at a first aid post situated in the Savoy Hotel, in the Strand.

'The next nine or ten weeks was a continuous nightmare, the enemy visited us every night. Casualties got heavier, we were saturated with blood, dirt and stinking sweat. Our uniforms by now stiffened with clotted blood, we were impregnated with the acrid fumes of cordite and explosives and old brick dust. The only sleep I had been able to snatch was an occasional nap between raids in a chair in the depot on the alert ready for the next call out, gas mask at ready and tin helmet hanging by to be snatched up and put on.'[25]

Rescue workers needed courage and fortitude, sensitivity, and a strong stomach. Rothwell recalls an incident where a bomb scored a direct hit on an Anderson shelter, flanked by one on each side. The occupants of the two on the outside were all right, just shocked and dazed with a few minor cuts, but a large crater now occupied the space where the middle Anderson had stood:

'It had been blown out of the ground with its inhabitants. I kept this knowledge from them [those in the neighbouring shelters] as they did not know and were unaware of what had happened. Then I looked up at the wall of the house, and as I lifted my torch (which I had been shielding and keeping the light on the ground because of enemy observation from above) I could see what looked like treacle sliding down the wall. I realized what it was, and seeing that nothing could be done in the darkness, I took my squad back to the depot to report what I had seen and to prepare to come back at daybreak with shrouds and the death wagon to do the unsavoury job of picking up bits and pieces. This macabre business was to be my lot for the rest of

If **you** can't go to the factory help the neighbour who **can**

How you can help

Arrange now with a neighbour to look after her children when she goes to her war-work—or give your name to

CARING FOR WAR WORKERS' CHILDREN IS A NATIONAL SERVICE

Issued by the Ministry of Health

MH 17

Above: During the war women managed jobs traditionally done by men. One of the most iconic images is of women welders, shown here making stirrup pump handles.

Left: Married women could go to work for the war effort if they had someone – a relative, friend or neighbour – to mind the children. The government opened wartime day nurseries for war workers' children, and promptly closed them again once the emergency was over.

the war. During training I had instructed my men to treat the dead with reverence and respect but I did not expect to have to shovel them up. Now this job had to be done with a stiff yard broom, a garden rake and shovel. We had to throw buckets of water up the wall to wash it down. The only tangible things were a man's hand, with a bent ring on a finger; a woman's foot in a shoe on the window sill. In one corner of the garden was a bundle of something held together with a leather strap; as I disturbed it it fell to pieces steaming. It was part of a man's torso. The stench of it was awful and it clung to my nostrils for sometime after; in fact I never lost that smell until sometime after the war was over. We gathered up about six bags of bits and pieces; one pathetic little bundle, shapeless now tied with bits of lace and ribbon, had been a baby, as we loaded the death wagon two dogs came along sniffing into the dust and rubble. I threw a clod of earth at them to chase them off.'[26]

One man remembers his father, a rescue worker, being physically sick when he came home from a job and he was not alone, as Stanley Rothwell admits on a night when a public shelter was bombed:

'There was a vast crater with bodies of women and children all strewn in the rubble and debris round its edge, the shelter that they had occupied had gone sky high. Enemy planes were still droning overhead ... We got busy shrouding the dead and mangled bodies; people who less than half an hour before had been alive and singing. We tried to check on the number of people involved but found that there were some missing; we laid the dead behind a fence to be collected later and out of sight of the public gaze ... There were a number of people unaccounted for from this shelter; we found them the following morning lying some hundreds of yards away on some waste ground spreadeagled like tailors dummies; they had been tossed there by the blast, heads and limbs missing. After the last of them had been collected and delivered to the mortuary, I went to one side to vomit.'[27]

The public was shielded from such sights as far as possible. At least during the Blitz most of the raids occurred at night, allowing ARP personnel the chance to 'bag' body parts under cover of darkness. The dead were not to be left exposed to public gaze, but respectfully covered until they could be picked up by the mortuary crew.

The mortuary workers had perhaps the most gruesome task of all – trying to reassemble bodies, or at least to get them into a sufficiently recognizable state for identification by a relative. A young woman who had been an art student at the Slade School of Fine Art and had studied anatomy found herself engaged in this grim work:

'We had somehow to form a body for burial so that the relatives could imagine that their loved one was more or less intact for that purpose. But it was a very difficult task – there were so many pieces missing ... The stench was the worst thing about it – that and having to realize that these frightful pieces of flesh had once been living, breathing people. After the first violent revulsion, I set my mind on it as a detached systematic task. It became a grim and ghastly satisfaction when a body was fairly constructed – but if one was too lavish in making one body almost whole then another one would have some sad gaps.'[28]

Above: Nellie Allpress (left) worked in catering, which was a 'reserved' occupation, while Eva (right) had a job in a local draper's shop. During the war the sisters also did ARP duty, fire-watching, and worked for the WVS.

It was the police's responsibility to visit hospitals and mortuaries to take particulars of casualties. Lists of casualties occurring in any Metropolitan Police district would be distributed to all police stations, so that relatives who had not had the opportunity to inquire at the incident inquiry point might approach their local police station for information. The information was collated at Scotland Yard, whose Casualty Bureau kept an alphabetical list of casualties. Official reports were compiled at regular intervals and sent on to the regional headquarters.

If a casualty died in hospital his or her relatives would be informed by the hospital authorities. Otherwise, it was the duty of the police to inform the next of kin of the death as soon as possible; the local authority also had an obligation to notify next of kin and to send a message of sympathy reading, 'The Minister of Health asks me to express the deep sympathy of His Majesty's Government with you in your loss'.[29] A certificate of death due to war operations would be issued. Relatives had to attend the registrar's office to register the death and to obtain permission for the disposal of the body.

Three-quarters of all burials of war casualties were done privately, but failing this it was the duty of the local authorities to bury victims of enemy attack, the government grant being £7 10s per burial. Local authorities were reminded that the burial of a civilian who had died as a result of enemy action 'should be regarded as no less honourable than burial of a soldier by his comrades'. Members or a member of the council should attend burials, especially those of Civil Defence workers, and the use of the Union Jack as a pall at such funerals was encouraged.

Unexploded bombs (UXBs) – some were due to delayed action fuses, others simply to malfunctioning – presented another hazard, as Barbara Nixon describes:

'It was impossible to make a direct journey; at about every third street one was confronted with a yellow "Diversion" notice. Unexploded bombs – "UXBs" – were everywhere. At first the papers had referred to these "time-bombs", as they were then called, as a particularly devilish German invention, despite the fact that since they provided time to evacuate residents in the neighbourhood, they were in reality more humane than the reverse. A few people were exceptionally stupid about them, and would wheedle their way back past the police at the barrier on the excuse of a pet or indispensable treasure left behind ... They [the UXBs] caused considerable transport difficulties, which was the intention [of the enemy] ...'[30]

Whatever the inconvenience to the public, UXBs presented an even greater challenge to the Royal Engineers' bomb disposal units, who during the Blitz were working night and day to detonate these things. There were so many that a huge backlog built up. There was always the danger that the device would explode while they were working on it.

The most famous UXB was the one that lodged itself almost into the foundations of St. Paul's Cathedral. As it was being painstakingly removed by the bomb disposal team it sank further into the clay. When it was eventually removed, it was placed on a lorry and taken at breathtaking speed through the City and detonated on Hackney Marshes.

◆

In 1941 Britain became the first country to extend conscription to women. The mobilization of women – and the absence of many women for long hours from the home – would be the most radical and disruptive social factor of the war.

At the outset of war, the government was reluctant to break with tradition and intrude into family life by recruiting women. After all, the family unit was the foundation on which society was based. The place of a married woman – the two eldest Allpress daughters, Alice and Jessie, for example – was in the home, looking after her husband and children. Those women who did work – such as Nellie, Eva and Betty Allpress – tended to be unmarried. They were employed mainly in factories, shops or in domestic service, and left work once they married. The government feared that servicemen would resent their wives being conscripted and that this would have an adverse effect on morale; in fact, those in the ranks were so badly paid that their wives needed to work. It ignored the recommendation of various women MPs, a cross-party group of whom sat on the Woman Power Committee (WPC), to extend conscription to women. However, from 1941 the need to harness extra labour to carry on the war effort from such a relatively small population as that of Great Britain became imperative and the government realized that it would have to bow to the inevitable and squeeze every ounce out of the available 'woman power'.

From March 1941 successive groups of women were obliged to register at their local labour exchange – an announcement giving the registration date for a particular age group would appear in the newspapers to alert them to the fact that their time had come – and in due course the net encompassed all women between the ages of 18 and 50. All of them were obliged to attend an interview and be directed, where appropriate, into war work. Any woman up to the age of 60 with nursing experience had to register, as there was a desperate shortage of trained nurses, as did former textile workers up to the age of 55. So desperate did the need for cloth become that some textile workers who had gone into munitions were ordered back into lower-paid textile jobs.

Women like the second Allpress daughter, Jessie, who had children or stepchildren under the minimum school-leaving age of 14 living with them, or women who were shouldering a domestic burden, such as elderly, infirm parents, were exempt, as well as those – like Mrs Allpress – who were above the age limit. In practice, a high proportion of these 10 million 'immobile' women – out of a pool of 17 million women between the ages of 14 and 64 – volunteered for war work of some kind.

The wives of men serving in the armed forces – for example, Bill Allpress's wife, May – were exempt from national service that took them away from home, but single women were categorized as 'mobile' workers and could be ordered to leave home and go where labour was needed. After attending a government training centre, they were often sent to work at one of the Royal Ordnance factories, producing explosives, guns and tanks.

Fortunately, Nellie, Eva and Betty were already in jobs and doing additional work in ARP and the WVS, which satisfied the requirements. Nellie was in the catering business, which was a 'reserved' occupation; Eva was working in a draper's shop, but did ARP duty and later worked for the WVS in her spare time after the day job; and Betty, whose employer had been making lampshades but immediately switched to the production of seats for bomber aircraft at the outbreak of war (Betty had to try out the seats), was usefully employed in production for the war effort. The eldest Allpress daughter, Alice, was married but had no children. After her husband died, she had to work in order to keep herself.

On the whole, women welcomed the opportunity to work and found it a rewarding experience. When asked what they enjoyed most about work, most said it was the companionship. Work alleviated loneliness while husbands were away. Many were driven by patriotism, but it was also useful to have the money. The majority of women had never had money of their own, so this was something of a novelty. As one middle-aged woman told Mass-Observation, 'When you get up in the morning you feel you go out with something in your bag, and something coming in at the end of the week, and it's nice. It's a taste of independence and you feel a lot happier for it.'[31]

Nevertheless, they were at a disadvantageous position in the workplace. Ernest Bevin had been able to persuade the trade unions to allow women into jobs hitherto done by men. Women's trade union membership doubled during the war, rising to 2,200,000 by 1944, or just over a quarter of women workers, despite the fact that many were described as 'dilutees' because they were diluting the skilled, male, workforce for the duration only. In theory, women were to receive the same pay for the same jobs. Women's average pay rose from £1 12s 6d to £3 3s 2d a week during the war. In an exceptional week in, say, a Royal Ordnance factory, with lots of overtime and bonuses this could be bumped up to as much as £8; against this, a first-year nurse's salary was only £5 a month, although she would also receive board and lodging. However, in spite of being better off, women were paid only 52 percent of men's average earnings.

All sorts of ruses were employed to short-change women and to ensure that they did not encroach too far into the male preserve. They were considered to be doing the same job as a man if they could do the

Opposite Top: This girl is in the nose of a giant Lancaster bomber working on the autopilot.

Opposite middle: Women served in an auxiliary capacity, releasing men for combat. Here a WAAF trainee driver checks the engine of her vehicle.

Opposite bottom: A young lady is being interviewed for the Auxiliary Territorial Service. If she joins, she may operate searchlights, drive lorries or fill sandbags, or do clerical work or cooking.

Above: The Women's Land Army reached a peak of 80,000 volunteers in 1943, replacing male farm workers who had joined the forces.

job without supervision or assistance, but the foreman's usual practice was to interfere in some way, so that the woman could be deemed 'unskilled' and paid accordingly. Some men even stooped so low as to tamper with the machinery, so as to hinder the progress of the woman who succeeded him on the next shift. Many women had undergone government training for the job, but found that they were not being allowed to do that job. Lots of jobs, in skilled engineering or the higher echelons of the civil service or just plain factory work where strength was required, were considered 'men's jobs'.

The conscription of women released men for combat; women were not permitted to bear arms and served only in an auxiliary capacity. Hence, the Women's Auxiliary Air Force (WAAF) and the Auxiliary Territorial Service (ATS). The women of the ATS operated searchlights, drove lorries and filled sandbags, as well as doing clerical work and cooking. The WAAFs did cooking and clerical jobs, too, but some became electricians or flight mechanics. The women in the Air Transport Auxiliary (ATA) were pilots, but they were only allowed to fly the planes from the factories to the airfields, not to engage in combat. Women working on anti-aircraft gun sites might calculate by the use of scientific instruments where the gun was to be aimed, but only the men were allowed to fire the shell.

Above: The WVS mobile canteen provided a sterling service in bringing hot tea and sandwiches to hardworking rescue workers.

The Women's Royal Naval Service (WRNS) was a popular choice among smart upper- and middle-class girls joining the forces. Women in the First Aid Nursing Yeomanry (FANY) served overseas, driving ambulances in battle areas and nursing the wounded. Some members of FANY, WAAF and the ATS also worked for the Special Operations Executive (SOE), being dropped behind enemy lines to act as secret agents. Some of these women – Violette Szabo, for instance, who fought off numerous German soldiers until her Sten gun ran out of ammunition and she was captured – were involved in direct combat with the enemy.

The Women's Land Army (WLA) was another option. Some 'land girls' were sent to live on farms, replacing male farm workers who had joined the forces; others worked in gangs, moving from place to place as they were needed. Early rising and long hours spent out in all weathers ploughing the fields, cutting logs, digging ditches, picking potatoes, milking cows, feeding pigs and helping with the harvest was not every town girl's dream.

Flexibility was what many women with domestic commitments required and this is where the WVS was so clever and adaptable, as it allowed women to contribute what hours they could. Founded in 1938 as an adjunct to ARP under the direction of Stella, Dowager Marchioness of Reading, the primary role of the WVS – initially, the Women's Voluntary Service for Air Raid Precautions, but subsequently renamed the Women's Voluntary Service for Civil Defence – was to assist civilians in air raids. Working closely with the government and local authorities, its members organized rest centres for the bombed-out, ran feeding stations and mobile canteens for the rescue workers and those whose domestic routine had been disrupted by the bombing, and collected clothing and household items for those who had lost everything but the clothes they stood up in.

The WVS played a key role in the evacuation of children and billeting in the reception areas, and subsequently it extended this social welfare work to helping servicemen with domestic problems.

The WVS was expected to be able to turn its hand to all aspects of wartime life, whether organizing knitting and make-do-and-mend groups or running clubs to welcome the American military personnel after they began arriving in 1942.

Among its many roles, the WVS was very helpful at incident inquiry points. Using the census cards, the WVS would draw up lists of the names of casualties recovered. It was then able to inform anxious relatives as to the whereabouts of their loved ones – whether they had been taken to hospital, were still missing, or dead. In some cases, a WVS member accompanied the bereaved to the mortuary. The WVS might take charge of valuables, before they could be transferred to the local authority for safe-keeping, and it even looked after pets until they could be handed over to the care of the National Air Raid Precautions for Animals Committee (NARPAC).

With their experience in ARP it was a natural progression for the Allpress sisters to join the WVS. After a busy working week, Betty and Eva devoted their Sundays to working for the WVS in the canteen at St. Thomas' Hospital, serving the hard-working doctors and nurses. Nellie was doing fire-watching at the bakery where she worked one night a week, while for two nights each week Betty worked in the town hall for the WVS preparing sandwiches for the mobile canteens which travelled to bomb-sites to bring much-needed sustenance to the rescue workers and those in damaged houses without fuel.

Betty's only regret was that she was too tall to go out in the mobile canteen itself – 'They'd have to cut a hole in the roof to carry me!' Tired? 'I don't really think you took any notice of being tired because you still got up the next day and went to your jobs.'[32]

4
The Blitz

'War is a terrifying thing in every aspect.' [1]
John Allpress

Night after night during the Blitz, when they weren't on ARP duty, Nellie, Eva and Betty would come home from work and go straight into the Anderson shelter, not emerging until the 'all clear' sounded, often after dawn. They would eat their evening meal in the shelter and in the morning emerge cold, cramped and tired, since it was almost impossible to sleep with the heavy drone of enemy aircraft above, bombs whistling, screaming and crashing down to earth, the crack of the guns, the trembling of the ground and the ping of shrapnel as it hit the Anderson. The noise outside reverberated in the confined space of the Anderson: a loud explosion outside became ear-splitting inside the shelter. 'It was a very nasty experience,' says Nellie. [2]

If William Allpress had been on night duty he would make them all a nice cup of tea when he came home in the morning and bring it to the shelter. Otherwise they would return to the house for a wash and some breakfast – provided the gas and water mains had not been fractured – before leaving for work, walking all the way if the transport system had been disrupted by the bombing. Tired as they were, it never occurred to them or anybody else suffering from chronic sleep deprivation during the Blitz to shirk their duty or cry off work. Sleep, or lack of it, almost replaced the weather as a topic of conversation.

Left: The survival of St. Paul's amidst the fire and destruction of the City of London on 29 December 1940 was nothing short of a miracle.

'We were all so anxious to stay alive, we just carried on,' Nellie recalls. 'There was nothing else you could do.' [3] Every day they would post a card to their mother to let her know they were 'safe' and Mrs Allpress would do the same.

Mrs Allpress was at the bedside of her very sick daughter Gladys, who had been evacuated from St. Thomas' Hospital to Woking. By the time Mrs Allpress and her youngest son John came home to Priory Grove in December 1940 the Blitz had been raging for three months.

After the 'phoney' or 'bore' war, Hitler's Blitzkrieg ('lightning war'), when his armies occupied Denmark and Norway in April 1940 and then swept across the Low Countries and France in May, left the world stunned. The British Army was evacuated from Dunkirk and the French signed an armistice. Britain now stood alone and vulnerable.

On 10 May Neville Chamberlain resigned and Winston Churchill became prime minister. On 18 June he told the House of Commons that '... the battle of Britain is about to begin. ... The whole fury and might of the enemy must very soon be turned on us. Hitler knows that he will have to break us in this island or lose the war. If we can stand up to him all Europe may be free ... but if we fail, then the whole world, including the United States ... will sink into the abyss of a new dark age ... Let us therefore brace ourselves to our duty and so bear ourselves that if the British Commonwealth and Empire lasts for a thousand years men will still say, "This was their finest hour."'[4]

There could be no successful German invasion until the Luftwaffe enjoyed air supremacy. In mid-June German bombers attacked eastern England and the first bomb fell in the London area on Addington near Croydon. June and July saw intermittent random daylight raids in the London area, on coastal towns in the south and east and as far north as the Tyne. South Wales was bombed and several people lost their lives in Aberdeen. Invasion seemed likely and towns along the coasts of Kent and Sussex were evacuated, the beaches mined.

The Luftwaffe had been dive-bombing British shipping and ports along the south coast, engaging RAF fighter planes in aerial combat, but on 13 August it switched its attention to Britain's air defences, attacking airfields, radar stations and other targets, such as aircraft repair sheds. Fortunately, Hermann Goering, Reich Minister of Aviation and commander-in-chief of the Luftwaffe, was easily distracted from his purpose of wiping out Britain's air defences by refocusing on London. If the capital was attacked, he believed, it would draw the remaining RAF fighters out to defend it and the Luftwaffe could pick them off, leaving Britain open to invasion. He underestimated the strength and skill of the RAF.

On 24 August London was hit, against Hitler's express orders. It gave Churchill the opportunity to order raids on Berlin, in expectation that Hitler would retaliate with full-scale raids on London, which would draw the Luftwaffe's attention away from Britain's aerodromes, giving them a respite and time to re-equip and recover.

On 7 September, known as Black Saturday, the air raid siren sounded at 4.45pm, as wave after wave of Dornier and Heinkel bombers, escorted by Messerschmitt fighters, appeared like a swarm of black flies over the Thames. First they dropped clusters of incendiary bombs, which illuminated the scene for the other bombers which followed. At 6.30pm the first wave of planes left, but at 8.30pm they were back, to drop 625 tons of HE (high explosive) bombs – each HE weighed anything from 500 to 4,000 pounds – on the already burning warehouses and streets in a raid lasting until dawn.

First to be hit were the Ford motor works at Dagenham and the Beckton Gasworks – the largest in Europe. By now the whole area from north Woolwich to Tower Bridge was ablaze on both sides of the river. In Surrey Commercial Dock, over 200 acres of imported timber – vital for the war effort – went up in flames. Burning spirits and paint poured out of the warehouses, while the toxic black smoke from burning rubber mixed with the fumes escaping from the gasworks prompted a rumour that the Germans were using the dreaded poison gas. Even the telegraph posts spontaneously combusted in the heat.

For many of the auxiliary firemen this was their baptism of flames, but nothing would have prepared even a seasoned fireman for the mayhem unleashed by the Luftwaffe on this night. The noise of the exploding bombs and crashing buildings and the heat of roaring flames dulled the senses, while amidst the dense smoke the firemen had to fight to stay upright, holding up their heavy hoses, while the suction and compression from high-explosive bombs pushed and pulled them in all directions. Soaking, filthy, exhausted, in danger of asphyxiation, they worked 40 hours without stopping, taking turns to hold the hoses, occasionally stooping to inhale the cool air around the nozzle; surrounded and cut off by the blaze or caught under collapsing buildings, some perished.

The sister of one fireman who lost his life on 8 September describes it poignantly:

'He was with the auxiliary fire service. They were stationed at Kings College Fire Station and there was a fire at the

Top: Leonard Rosoman (centre figure) and friends in the AFS share a moment of calm after their exertions. Rosoman became an official war artist.
Above: Firemen were at risk of being surrounded and cut off by the flames or trapped under a collapsing building.

top of Chancery Lane. He had received his call-up papers for the Army and was told that he did not have to go that night, but he wanted to be there to help his mates … The last person he spoke to was a neighbour of ours. He remembered my brother disappearing round a corner, followed by an explosion. He woke up in hospital, but my brother had been killed on the spot.'[5]

The bombers ranged as far west as Chelsea and Victoria that night, putting Battersea Power Station out of action, but the Isle of Dogs, Silvertown and Rotherhithe took the brunt of it, with Bermondsey, Canning Town, Woolwich, Deptford, West Ham, Plaistow, Bow, Whitechapel, Stepney and Poplar also widely hit – as they would be over and over again in the next few months. Nestling close to the docks and warehouses where they worked, many of the flimsy back-to-back houses of working-class Londoners were demolished or damaged irreparably. Those who did find their homes still standing were without water, gas and electricity, perhaps for days, as mains and pipes were fractured.

Four hundred and thirty-six Londoners were killed on that first night of the Blitz, including seven firemen, and 1,600 seriously injured.

Among those made homeless a group of 600 men, women and children were hurriedly put up at South Hallsville School in Agate Street, Canning Town. They were assured that coaches would be coming to take them to safety. The coaches never turned up. They were still there three days later, when just before three in the morning a high-explosive bomb scored a direct hit on the school. The official death toll was 200, but locals suspected it was far higher. There were so many bodies or bits of bodies entombed in the debris that the site was concreted over.

The Luftwaffe came back the next night and the next, killing another 800 people, and every day or night after that throughout September and October. The docks were targeted again, but so too was the transport system. On Sunday 8 September, in a raid lasting

from 8pm to 5.40am the next morning, every railway line running out of London to the south was put out of action. As the Allpresses, 'terrified', kept each other's spirits up in the Anderson shelter, HE bombs fell perilously close, in Stockwell Gardens, where a gas main was fractured, and in South Lambeth Road, where a house was demolished and five killed.[6] The house at Priory Grove would have been badly shaken and the Allpresses must have felt the reverberations in the shelter. There were many casualties in the area and by 10 September 1,000 people in Lambeth had been made homeless and the gas supply was interrupted over a large area.[7]

On 13 September Buckingham Palace was hit – a public relations disaster for the Germans, since it dispelled any suspicion that the poor of the East End and other working-class districts were being unfairly targeted and quelled any potential social unrest.

Just across the river from the Houses of Parliament, St. Thomas' was hit many times by enemy bombs (for example, on 9, 10, 13 and 15 September), but some part of it always managed to carry on. This continuous bombardment must have been a horrendous experience for Mrs Allpress, who was nervous at the best of times and determined to stay with her sick daughter who needed her. Just over a week after the onset of the Blitz, in the early evening of 16 September 1940, the hospital was so badly damaged that 131 patients were evacuated to the country.[8] Gladys Allpress was almost certainly among them. A gentle, frail girl, Gladys died in early December 1940. Harry was given compassionate leave from the Army to attend her funeral.

A young woman working in the hospital's canteen for the WVS arrived shortly after the nurses' home had been hit:

> '... five nurses were still in it and emergency crews were trying to get them out ... I always remember the one nurse left, and the doctor went in through the debris to give her an injection. The cheers when she was carried out, followed by a gasp and how we fell silent when we realized she had died, as they laid her down. It was such a disappointment.'[9]

There were even close encounters with the enemy. Three crew members of a Dornier bomber that crashed outside Victoria Station managed to parachute to safety and land 'among a hostile population' on Kennington Oval, where they were arrested.[10] Later in the month a Clapham couple sleeping in their basement were woken up by a German pilot who had landed on the roof and wanted to give himself up.[11]

Opposite: Once Buckingham Palace was hit Queen Elizabeth declared that she could look the heavily bombed East End in the face.
Top: Located just across the Thames from the Houses of Parliament, St. Thomas' Hospital was hit by enemy bombs several times.
Above: On 16 September 1940 St. Thomas' Hospital was so badly damaged that patients had to be evacuated. Among them was Gladys Allpress.

Above: Letters addressed to wrecked homes were marked accordingly and returned.

In spite of almost constant night-time bombardment, morale in Lambeth was reported to be good.[12] There were even moments of light relief and miraculous delivery – such as the lady who was rescued from the ruins of her block of flats, having ridden down three floors of the collapsing building, sitting upright upon the loo, with a cup of cocoa in one hand and a sandwich in the other.[13]

Certainly in the Allpress household everyone kept calm, even though the sisters admitted they were 'dreadfully frightened'. William Allpress was a steadying influence on his family. They, too, had their moments of mirth, such as the night later on in the Blitz when William was caught in a raid near a flour factory and came home covered in white flour, to find his wife and John – sheltering in the coal cellar under the stairs – emerging covered in coal dust and absolutely black.

By the end of September 1940, 5,730 people had been killed in London Region and 9,003 seriously injured – the names of the deceased made public on notices posted outside the town halls and available at police stations.

In the air, however, the battle had already turned in Britain's favour. The RAF's Bomber Command had been targeting the barges Hitler had assembled on the French coast for Operation 'Sealion' – the invasion of England. On the morning of 15 September, subsequently hailed as Battle of Britain Day, the horde of German bombers heading for London in a daylight raid received a rude shock when RAF Spitfires and Hurricanes rose up to challenge them. In the skies over Kent and London the German planes were

Above: No matter how bad the damage, people kept calm and carried on.

attacked, shot down and dispersed. The survivors turned tail for France, but in the afternoon another force was back. Again, they encountered RAF fighters. That day the RAF shot down 57 German planes for the loss of 26. On 27 September another full-scale daylight raid on London was launched, but again met fierce resistance from the RAF, so that only 20 out of 300 raiders reached London and the Germans lost 55 planes to the RAF's 28. It was clear now even to Goering that the RAF was not vanquished; indeed, it had the edge on the Luftwaffe. With winter approaching, on 17 September Hitler decided to postpone Operation 'Sealion' indefinitely.

In London, meanwhile, it was business as usual. People got to work, whatever the difficulties, sometimes finding their place of business a smoking ruin, as Betty did one morning in Holborn. Milk and post were delivered as usual. Many of the shops in the West End were damaged. John Lewis was burnt out, but put up a defiant notice: 'Reopening on October 5th.' Others continued to function even though their plate glass windows had been shattered: 'More open than usual' was the pithy message. Locally, the draper's shop where Eva worked was destroyed, but reopened in premises round the corner.

Just after eight o'clock on the evening of 13 October an HE bomb demolished a public house in the vicinity of 69 Priory Grove, burying a number of people. Twenty-three were killed. A neighbouring house was burnt out and once again water and gas mains were damaged, adding to the overall misery, since it was impossible to wash or cook until they were repaired.[14]

Two nights later, guided by a bomber's moon along the shining Thames, there were 410 raiders over London, dropping 538 tons of HE bombs. Four hundred civilians were killed and nearly 900 seriously injured. Nearly all rail travel in and out of the capital was temporarily suspended, although the worst day for Southern Region was 17 October when all the automatic signalling within two and a half miles of Waterloo was knocked out. A particularly bad experience for Mr Allpress was the time he found himself stalled at a red light on Holborn Viaduct at the height of a raid with a train full of passengers. They all had to get off and make a dash for the shelters.

Fog and low cloud brought a welcome respite on 3 November, the first night of quiet in London since the Blitz began nearly two months previously, but on 4 November the raiders were back. At Priory Grove School, a few hundred yards from the Allpress house, an Anderson shelter where four members of the AFS had taken cover suffered a direct hit. One fireman was killed, while the other three were seriously injured and taken to hospital.[15]

Above: Trench shelters were always liable to flooding, but in spite of the damp conditions these shelterers sleep soundly on the narrow benches.

Opposite: At the beginning of the Blitz families clutching their bedding started queuing early in the day for a place to sleep on an Underground platform that night.

The natural instinct of people under constant aerial bombardment is to seek shelter as far underground as possible. It soon became apparent to Londoners that the street, or surface, shelters constructed prior to the war and during the 'phoney war' were not just inadequate but positively dangerous. At least 5,000 of them were deficient, thrown up by cowboy builders. Inside, they were dark, cold, damp, poorly ventilated and uncomfortable. The pre-war planners had not envisaged raids lasting all night, so that the facilities in these shelters had been rudimentary. Consequently, shelterers had to spend long hours on hard benches or bunks and the toilets behind sack curtains were soon overflowing, the stink adding to the smell of sweat of the frightened people who cowered there as the bombs fell. Built deeper than the Anderson shelters, the street, or surface, shelters protected those inside from shrapnel and flying debris, but shook alarmingly from the effects of blast and very often collapsed on the hapless occupants. They offered no protection in the event of a direct hit.

Nor were reinforced basement shelters much safer. On 13 October 1940 the residents of a block of flats in Stoke Newington dutifully filed down to the basement shelter when the siren sounded. An HE bomb hit the building and penetrated all five floors to explode in the basement. Those who were not killed outright subsequently died a horrible, lingering death, drowned in water and sewage that poured into the basement from broken mains, or poisoned by seeping gas. It took rescue workers a week to extract the bodies of all 154 victims.

The trench shelters hastily dug during the Munich Crisis and reinforced and improved in the succeeding months proved equally hazardous. On 15 October a bomb landed in the middle of Kennington Park on trench shelters packed with over 200 local people, blowing part of the shelter into the air and burying many in the falling debris.[16] The rescue work went on for days and the final death toll was 104 people – the largest single loss of life from a bomb incident in Lambeth.

There was a tendency to seek safety in numbers, to draw comfort from being in the company of others when under attack. This herd-like instinct to follow the crowd often lacked rationale. At the notorious Tilbury in Whitechapel – part of Liverpool Street Station's goods yard – 6,000 to 10,000 people poured in nightly, although only the vault beneath, which held up to 3,000, was an authorized shelter. On the surface, the rest of

NOTICE

SHELTER
IN UNDERGROUND STATIONS

London Transport asks those who seek shelter in Underground stations to help in maintaining the essential transport facilities which are used by roundly one million passengers daily.

Passengers must be afforded free and uninterrupted use of the platforms and stations and the space used for shelter must therefore be limited. Only the space within the white lines may be used for this purpose. The police have been instructed to enforce this arrangement and those seeking shelter are asked to help them in carrying it out.

Stations and platforms must be vacated in the early morning and before the heavy passenger traffic begins.

Only a limited amount of personal baggage, etc., will be allowed on the premises.

Stations and platforms must be kept free from litter which should be carried away or placed in receptacles provided for that purpose.

LONDON ⬤ TRANSPORT

CONDITIONS OF ISSUE

1. This Ticket is issued subject to the London Regional Commissioners' Shelter Rules, copies of which are exhibited at the stations.

2. This Ticket does not permit the holder to travel on any portion of the London Passenger Transport Board's system. Where, however, the entrance to the station where the holder is entitled to shelter is closed, he will be entitled to travel free between the nearest open station and his shelter station.

3. The holder enters or remains on the premises of the Board for the purpose of air raid shelter at his own risk in all respects and neither the Board nor their servants or agents shall be responsible to him or his dependants for personal injury (whether fatal or otherwise), loss of or damage to property, or any other loss, damage, costs or expenses, however caused or incurred.

4. This ticket may be withdrawn or cease to be valid without any reason being given and, in particular, in ANY of the following circumstances :—
   a. If the station ceases to be available.
   b. If the holder ...

LONDON CIVIL DEFENCE REGION No. *B4A*

METROPOLITAN BOROUGH OF LAMBETH

Admit person named below for shelter at

WATERLOO STATION

Name .... Age ....

Full Postal Address ....

Nature of Employment ....

Date of issue .... National Registration No. ....

Signature of Holder ....

O. L. ROBERTS, Town Clerk.

Signature of Issuing Officer ....
NOT TRANSFERABLE.   FOR CONDITIONS OF ISSUE SEE BACK.

This ticket expires on 3 1 AUG 1941

Above: A ticketing system was introduced guaranteeing shelterers a place in the Underground so that they did not have to spend valuable working time in a queue.
Left: Shelterers were urged not to interrupt the normal flow of passengers on the Underground platforms.

---

this makeshift shelter was highly vulnerable. Lacking basic facilities, the conditions were appalling. Others sheltered under railway arches, believing them safe – until the Stainer Street incident near London Bridge, when 60 were killed.

Fifteen thousand Londoners sheltered nightly at Chislehurst Caves in Kent; special trains took them there before the raids started in the evening, returning them to London in time for work in the morning. East Enders took to 'trekking' out to Epping Forest; others drifted as far west as Reading and to Oxford, where hundreds occupied the Majestic Cinema.

Some took refuge in the crypts of churches. At Lambeth Palace the Archbishop of Canterbury hosted at least 250 shelterers nightly, while at Christ Church Spitalfields the living occupied the tombs of the dead. In the West End, where the buildings generally fared better than those in the East End owing to their reinforced concrete structures, hotels such as the Savoy and the Dorchester offered sleeping accommodation for their well-to-do clients in their basement shelters. One night in September a group from Stepney boldly invaded the Savoy. West End stores had basement shelters – the one at Dickins & Jones, which accommodated 700, was clean and offered refreshments, being particularly popular.

For the frightened people of London's poorer, heavily bombed districts another option beckoned. They began to occupy the London Underground, or Tube. Queues of people clutching their pathetic bundles of precious belongings and night-time necessities would begin to form early in the day; some would send a child to secure a place for the family. The London Passenger Transport Board was powerless to stop the shelterers, since they simply bought a ticket and made their way down to the safety of the platforms. It did not take long for organized gangs to exploit the situation by bagging places on the platforms and selling them to the public for 2s 6d.

The government's first instinct was to ban the Underground as a public shelter. It did not want to encourage a shelter mentality – a population of troglodytes living a parallel existence down in the Tube and not contributing to the war effort. On the other hand, to have police barring the way, preventing these desperate people from seeking safety, might provoke a collapse of public morale. It seemed that the only course of action was to give way to the inevitable. Admiral Sir Edward Evans, one of London's two regional commissioners, immediately introduced a ticketing system for Underground shelterers, ending the tyranny of the racketeers.

Eighty tube stations, including disused stations at British Museum, South Kentish Town and City Road, and non-traffic tube tunnels at Aldwych, Bethnal Green and Liverpool Street were to be used as shelters. Southwark's 70-foot deep shelter in the old City and South London railway tunnel was the largest with space for 10,000 people, although the disused tunnel to the east of Liverpool Street had a similar capacity. Bethnal Green's tunnel could hold 7,000. Two stations that were interchange points – Piccadilly Circus and Leicester Square – were not to be used for dormitory purposes, while eight other interchange stations – Bank, Paddington, Euston, Leicester Square, Tottenham Court Road, King's Cross, Oxford Circus and Strand – would offer limited dormitory space.

In October Herbert Morrison succeeded Sir John Anderson as Home Secretary and Minister of Home Security, responsible for all aspects of civil defence and for coordinating the efforts of ministries affected by air raids – Food, Transport, Health. Morrison appointed the Labour MP Ellen Wilkinson as his parliamentary secretary, giving her special responsibility for shelters.

Improvements were swiftly implemented. The official entry time was to be 4pm. Two white lines were drawn along the platforms: the first was eight feet from the edge of the platform, and might not be crossed until 7.30pm, to allow commuters sufficient space to get on and off the trains; the second was drawn four feet from the edge and shelterers might advance this far after 7.30pm.

Even so, travellers alighting from the trains would be greeted by the smell of hundreds of bodies in close confinement and have to step past their recumbent forms. One night Nellie Allpress almost stepped on to someone's plate of salad.

At 10.30pm the trains stopped for the night and the current was switched off, allowing shelterers to move forward to the edge of the platform, to the escalators or even on to

Above: Once the power was switched off for the night shelterers could move on to the track and sleep between the rails. Note the shelter warden keeping order on the platform.

the lines themselves to snatch a few hours' sleep. The lights would be dimmed on the platforms, although not in the corridors.

Anyone breaking shelter rules would be summarily arrested by the police, who might also be called on by the paid shelter warden or voluntary marshal to eject those exhibiting drunken, disorderly or quarrelsome behaviour. Even so, the noise of excited children and the snores of fellow shelterers could prove an irritation.

By mid-October most shelters had chemical lavatories and there was the prospect of sleeping on a bunk rather than on the dirty platform. Six people would be able to occupy six feet of platform length – allowing three to sleep in a three-tier bunk and three to stretch out on the platform in front of it. The first three-tier metal bunks – wood was ruled out, since it harboured bed bugs and other nasties – were installed at Lambeth North Station on 25 November and by early March 1941 7,600 had been erected at 76 stations. A standard reservation ticket corresponding to a specific bunk or platform position was issued by the local authority to each shelterer, assuring the holder of a place – so that they did not have to waste valuable working hours during the day queuing. The onus was on the ticket holders to keep their area clean. In addition 10 percent of the total accommodation at each station was kept free for casual shelterers. No charge was made to shelterers to enter the station.

One of the biggest fears of the authorities was that epidemics of diphtheria, measles or whooping cough would break out among the densely packed shelterers, but this never happened. Tuberculosis was still a prevalent disease and any family with a known sufferer was forbidden to use a public shelter – special arrangements were made for them – and in the Underground the medical officer in attendance was to keep an eye out for anyone showing signs of tuberculosis and isolate the case. For less contagious health problems, there were first aid posts and a nurse on duty.

Frequent routine visits were made by local authority public health inspectors to eliminate rodents, bed bugs, fleas and mosquitoes. There was always a danger that bugs would be introduced into the Underground on people's clothing and bedding. Shelterers were urged not to shake out their bedding on to the platforms and tracks, but to take it home and shake it. Gradually, laundries were opened at or in the vicinity of certain Underground stations so that bedding could be washed

Above: Many people emerged unscathed from a Morrison shelter, even when the whole house collapsed around them.

and aired the same day, ready for the evening. Adequate numbers of public toilets were introduced and mobile showers began to tour the shelters offering people a chance to wash before work.

The WVS and the Salvation Army ran platform canteens, while trains offering 'Tube Refreshments' toured the system. Shelterers could soon enjoy some of the entertainment laid on for them – borrowing books from the lending libraries serving the Tube shelters, listening to programmes of gramophone music or taking night classes. There were Christmas parties for the children, concerts, and in some cases their very own shelter magazine.

At the height of the Blitz a shelter census in September 1940 showed that 177,000 – 4 percent of London's population – was sheltering in the Underground, as opposed to 27 percent using Anderson shelters (such as the Allpresses) and 9 percent using other kinds of public shelters.[17]

Sixty percent, however, still preferred the comfort of their own homes, chancing fate. The introduction of the Morrison shelter – a steel structure deemed sufficiently robust to survive a house collapsing on it – in March 1941 would at least offer them some protection. At just 6½ feet long, 4 feet wide and 2½ feet high, it could shelter two or three people. The Allpresses acquired a Morrison for their new home in Wimbledon, but Betty hated it: 'It was like being in a cage – horrible!'[18] Nevertheless, many people did manage to walk, or crawl, free from their collapsed homes, having sheltered in the Morrison.

Before the war steps had been taken to safeguard the Underground system from flooding in the event of a direct hit to the Victoria Embankment or the under-river tunnels. For example, a single bomb dropped in the proximity of the Charing Cross–Waterloo tunnel could have flooded half London's Underground system. Floodgates and diaphragms to act as a second line of defence had been installed at every vulnerable point. The old Strand–Charing Cross loop tunnel, which had been out of use for years, had been sealed at either end. In 1940 it received a direct hit – the only one suffered by any of the Underground's Thames tunnels – and a section over 200 yards long was flooded by the river and would have swamped the Underground in all directions had not these safety measures been installed.

Large sums of money had also been spent on constructing various protective devices in the neighbourhood of important water mains and sewers. Hydrophones had been installed on the Thames riverbed so that the impact of a delayed-action bomb or mine falling near any of the under-river tunnels could be promptly detected. The sound was recorded in the control room at the South Kensington regional office's headquarters of the chief engineer. The floodgates were manned round the clock, controlled collectively from a small room in the passage between the Piccadilly and Northern lines at Leicester Square Station. The time required to close them was 30 seconds.

Top: A bus plunges into a 60-foot crater in Balham High Street. In the Underground below, 68 people were killed, drowning in water and sewage.

Above: An HE bomb penetrated Bank Underground station and exploded, opening up a crater in the street above – so wide a bridge had to be built across it.

However, these precautionary measures did not mean that the Underground was exempt from accidents. In October 1940 a bomb in Balham High Street burst the water main, opening up a 60-foot crater.

A bus fell into the crater. Six hundred people sheltering in the Underground below were buried in sludge, as gas seeped from a broken main. Sixty-eight were killed, many drowning in water and sewage.

In November a 2,000-pound HE bomb scored a direct hit on Sloane Square Station, just as a train had disgorged its passengers and was pulling out of the station. Most of them were killed by the blast, which stripped off their clothing. Others were hideously mutilated. The heavy rescue service had to work for days under the naked bodies of two young women who had been hurled up and impaled on the steel girders above. The carnage was so horrendous that there could be no accurate tally of the dead.

In January 1941 an HE bomb fell into the booking hall at Bank Station in the City. The explosion opened up a massive crater in the road above – so huge that a bridge subsequently had to be built across it. Blast shot down the escalator, which collapsed, killing the people on it. Others were blown off the platform into the path of an approaching train. One hundred and eleven people were killed, including 54 shelterers and four members of staff.

At Bethnal Green Station in 1943 people were filing into the Underground after an alert when there was a sudden deafening noise, possibly an anti-aircraft ('ack-ack') battery trying out a new anti-aircraft rocket in Victoria Park. Whether this made the crowd press forward too quickly or not, a woman carrying a baby tripped down the final steps. People tumbled down on top of her, leaving 173 dead, mainly from suffocation. A Home Office inquiry into the disaster attributed it to loss of self-control, although it was pointed out that the number of steps before a landing contravened safety requirements.

In spite of these tragedies, the London Underground acted as an essential safety valve, offering shelter to thousands of people who might otherwise have been killed in the raids or whose loss of nerve might have contributed to a breakdown of morale and public order.

Knowing that Hitler's war machine was planning even heavier bombs and more lethal weapons, as early as October 1940 the government approved plans for the building of a series of deep shelters 130 feet underground, although the first of these – coincidentally, at Stockwell, just round the corner from Priory Grove – would not open to the public until July 1944.

◆

London was Hitler's primary target, but to win the war he would also have to beat the heart out of industrial Britain and destroy the ports where vital supplies were being brought in.

On the night of 14–15 November the Luftwaffe turned its attention to Coventry. With major companies such as Armstrong Whitworth, Dunlop, Rolls-Royce, Daimler and Courtaulds all given over to the war effort, Coventry was an obvious target and had suffered intermittent raids since August 1940. Over 400 of its people had already been killed or seriously injured.

Operation 'Moonlight Sonata' took place on the night of the full moon. Five hundred German bombers dropped 500 tons of HE bombs, including 50 parachute mines, of which 20 were incendiary petroleum mines, as well as 881 incendiary canisters, each containing 75 incendiary bombs. The point about parachute mines – missiles the size of a pillar box and weighing up to 4,400 pounds, which floated down on green silk parachutes – was that they exploded on the surface, so that the blast from the explosion went sideways, affecting entire streets. Bombs containing oil or petroleum were designed to spread and intensify the fire risk; certainly at Coventry the aim was to cause fire and destruction.

Wave after wave of Luftwaffe planes came over, dropped their load, then went back to France to replenish and return. As fires raged all over the city, the fire brigade's headquarters were hit, disrupting its control of the situation. Added to which, there was a fatal shortage of water, because the utilities had been deliberately knocked out at the beginning of the raid. Large craters in the roads further hampered the firefighters trying to get through to tackle the blazes.

One hundred acres of the city's historic centre, including the 600-year-old cathedral, were destroyed or seriously damaged. Four thousand homes and one-third of its shops were destroyed. Three-quarters of Coventry's factories, many making vital components for aircraft and ammunition, were destroyed or temporarily put out of action. Railway lines were blocked and roads rendered impassable by debris and UXBs. Bodies and bits of bodies were strewn widely around.

London could absorb the strain of continuous bombing without danger of collapse; it was so big that if one area, such as the East End, was knocked out, it was business as usual in the rest of the capital. But when a compact city the size of Coventry, with a population in the region of 230,000, suffered a raid of this force the impact was absolutely devastating. Nearly everyone lost a friend or a relative or knew someone who had been killed, seriously threatening morale. Historic and cultural landmarks – symbols of the city's proud identity – were obliterated. Such was the level of destruction that a new word was coined in Nazi Germany by Joseph Goebbels, the Reich Minister of Propaganda – *Coventrieren*, to Coventrate.

The people of Coventry were in a state of shock. On the day after the raid Mass Observation noted that there were 'signs of hysteria, terror, neurosis … Women were seen to cry, to scream, to tremble all over, to faint in the street, to attack a fireman, and so on … There were several signs of suppressed panic as darkness approached.'[19]

Above: Southampton, like other provincial cities, suffered devastating raids. Thousands of its people sought to flee, 'trekking' into the open countryside.
Opposite: Much of Coventry's historic centre, including the 600-year-old cathedral, was destroyed in an epic raid on the night of 14–15 November 1940.

Those who had not left the still smoking ruins during the day hastened to do so before dusk, but the Germans did not return that night to complete the final destruction.

The known death toll was 568, but might have been much higher. It is impossible to be exact, since so many of the victims were literally burned, blasted or crushed beyond recognition. A highly industrialized city such as Coventry would have attracted many war workers to its factories from other parts of the country with no relatives on hand to report them missing.

Normally after a raid, the dead were taken to a temporary mortuary, numbered consecutively in the order in which they arrived. There were special procedures to observe. A body must be labelled, ideally with details of name, address, sex, age, place of death, and the time and date the body was recovered – such labels to be attached to the body by the rescue workers, stretcher-bearers or mortuary vehicle attendants.

Unfortunately, at Coventry the temporary mortuary had lost its roof and it rained, washing these vital identifying details off the labels. It was hard enough at the best of times to identify the badly mutilated or dismembered remains of a loved one; parents in particular would find it hard to make that extra leap of the imagination to identify their child in the broken, mangled remains they saw before them. In Coventry, in lieu

Above: On the night of 29 December 1940 the City of London suffered the greatest firestorm since the Great Fire of 1666. After this, fire-watching became compulsory.

of labels, they resorted to confirmation of the presence of the deceased through personal effects – perhaps a watch or a piece of jewellery, an item of clothing or some distinctive feature described to the relative. There was to be a mass funeral in two stages, taking place a few days apart as more bodies were dug out of the ruins, all of them placed in a communal grave. The line of mourners seemed to stretch into infinity, with each person placing a flower on a coffin – any coffin, since there was no means of telling whether or not it held the remains of their loved one.

In spite of the destruction, Coventry's factories were partially operating again within days – often with the roof blown off and the rain and sleet pouring in – and were fully functioning again by Christmas. The night after Coventry it was Birmingham's turn. Home to Austin, Rover and GEC – all now involved in aircraft production – and the Metropolitan-Cammell Carriage and Wagon Company, making tanks and radar vehicles, the city was very much an engine of war. Formerly a centre of the jewellery industry, requiring precision workmanship, Birmingham had brought these skills to the manufacture of radar equipment, rifles and aeroplane instruments. The Birmingham Small Arms (BSA) company factory was making Browning machine guns and cannons for aircraft, Lee-Enfield rifles, as well as bicycles and motorbikes for dispatch riders.

After several subsequent raids, including a 13-hour raid on 11–12 December, Birmingham became Britain's third most bombed city, after London and Liverpool. The city's death toll in these raids was 2,241, while 302 factories and 12,391 houses were destroyed.

On 23 November large areas of Southampton were destroyed. Following a typical pattern, the Luftwaffe returned on the nights of 30 November and 1 December to finish the job. Mass Observation recorded that public morale was seriously low; that there was a feeling that 'Southampton is finished'. The government attributed this feeling

Fire-watchers at their post on the roof of the Houses of Parliament. This photograph, taken by Bill Brandt, was originally published in *Picture Post*.

to poor leadership, especially in the case of the mayor, who was 'a weak creature' – but then Southampton and other provincial cities had far less resources than London and its citizens did not have the Underground to resort to. A London civil defence worker felt genuinely sorry for these other cities, knowing how harrowing must be their experience:

> 'In those cities, shelter accommodation was less extensive; the CD Services were less well organized; the defences were not so strong, and the target area could not be compared with our vast space. In London, if one borough was getting more than it could cope with, there was always another fairly close, and fully prepared, to help it out.'[20]

Thousands of Southampton's inhabitants were fleeing the town, 'trekking' into the open countryside. The Bishop of Winchester found,

> '… the people broken in spirit after the sleepless and awful nights. Everyone who can do so is leaving the town … Everywhere I saw men and women carrying suitcases or bundles, the children clutching some precious doll or toy, struggling to get anywhere out of Southampton. For the time being, morale has collapsed. I went from parish to parish and everywhere there was fear.'[21]

On 24 November the city of Bristol, ringed by aircraft manufacturing plants, including the Bristol Aeroplane Company at Filton, and its port at Avonmouth were attacked by 134 Heinkels, Dorniers and Junkers. By 11pm the Luftwaffe had dropped 160 tons of HE bombs, 333 incendiary canisters, each containing 75 incendiary bombs, and 4.7 tons of oil bombs; 207 people had been killed and 187 seriously injured, while 175 UXBs blocked the roads, making the job of clearing up and resuming life that bit more difficult. Much of the city's architectural heritage had been destroyed. Again, Mass Observation noted an air of defeatism with such remarks as 'We can't possibly win this war' and 'We are only one little country'.[22]

On the nights of 12 and 15 December Sheffield, the home of the British steel industry, currently turning out crankshafts for the Rolls-Royce Merlin engines in Spitfires and Hurricanes, was targeted, leaving 750 dead and 500 seriously injured. The steelworks escaped serious damage, but many smaller factories and business premises were put out of action, as well as thousands of houses and shops.

Just as Christmas was approaching, Merseyside was attacked on three consecutive nights, from 20 to 23 December. Obviously the port of Liverpool, importing vast quantities of food and matériel for the war effort from North America, was a prime target, to be hit over and over again. The destruction spread out from Liverpool to Bootle, Birkenhead and Wallasey. Eight thousand of Bootle's 17,000 houses were destroyed or damaged in this pre-Christmas raid.

It was Manchester's turn on 22–23 and 23–24 December. The Free Trade Hall, the Corn Exchange, Smithfield Market, the Gaiety Theatre, Cheetham's Hospital and St. Ann's Church were all destroyed, as well as 8,000 homes – forcing many of the city's unfortunate inhabitants to spend Christmas in the rest centres.

There was a brief lull for Christmas with neither the Luftwaffe nor the RAF engaging in operations. In London, which since November had suffered six more major raids and a handful of minor ones, a Streatham woman noted: 'Jerry has obviously thought kindly about Christmas so we spent the night in our own bed and took off all our clothes, the first time since early August.'[23]

The respite was short and bombing was resumed on the night of 27–28 December. Railway lines were hit and 141 killed, including 50 in a public shelter in Southwark, and 455 seriously injured.

On 29 December, the first Sunday after Christmas, there was a bomber's moon and the Thames was at a particularly low ebb. The offices, warehouses and churches of the City of London were locked, shuttered and deserted – a soft target for a raid that would cause the greatest firestorm since the Great Fire of 1666. The siren sounded just after six o'clock in the evening. Within three hours 613 incendiary canisters, each containing 75 incendiary bombs, landed in the vicinity of St. Paul's Cathedral, and 127 tons of HE bombs followed. Nearly 1,500 fires, which roared like furnaces in the high wind, soon merged into two great conflagrations, the worst of which ravaged the area between Moorgate, Aldersgate, Cannon Street and Old Street.

Twenty-eight incendiaries landed on the cathedral itself. One of them lodged halfway through the outer shell of the dome and began to melt the lead. It was beyond the range of stirrup pumps and the dome seemed doomed; then the incendiary somehow fell outwards on to the parapet and guttered out. The cathedral was by no means out of danger – flames from buildings all around, eating up the stocks of London's book trade in Paternoster Row, were practically licking the stonework. This was the moment when a photographer on the roof of the *Daily Mail* building in Fleet Street took the iconic photograph of the dome of St. Paul's rising above the smoke as the City was engulfed in the inferno. A telegram was actually dispatched to New York with the news that the great edifice was no more. The firemen's hoses were running dry, but by foresight and good fortune the guardians of St. Paul's, inspired by the indomitable dean, had installed some of their own water supplies and the cathedral was saved.

Wren's other masterpieces were less fortunate. That night eight of his City churches were destroyed. The medieval Guildhall was burnt out, the ancient statues of Gog and Magog crashing to the ground.

By midnight the raid was over. Had the Luftwaffe followed its usual pattern and returned a couple of hours later the destruction would have been complete. Fortunately, bad weather on the continent prevented that.

As few people lived in the City the cost in terms of human life was smaller than a raid of this magnitude would have been in other parts of the capital. Nevertheless 163 people lost their lives, including 16 of the heroic firemen, 250 of whom were also seriously injured.

The conflagration prompted the government to make fire-watching compulsory. Every factory or business was required to provide for its own protection, arranging a roster of lookouts from among the staff to stand on the roof during raids to spot incendiaries, put them out or call the fire brigade if the fire looked as if it was getting out of control. Training for this Fire Guard was given by the Civil Defence Service. Although fire-watching did not become compulsory for women until 1942, Nellie Allpress did her bit, taking her turn with two other women fire-watching once a week at the catering company where she worked. She hated it, especially the night she bumped into a policeman looking for a burglar in the building.[24]

The new year, 1941, began relatively quietly in London, but then on 11 January there was a major raid. Liverpool Street Station was hit, killing 43 people, including 18 on passing buses, one of which was blown into the wall of Bishopsgate Police Station. This was the evening that the major incident at Bank Station occurred. In Lambeth the area around Priory Grove was being pounded and at 8.30 that evening the Thermafelt factory at 34 Priory Grove went up in flames and was completely gutted.[25] It was the first of four major raids on London that week.

Nor did the Luftwaffe neglect Cardiff, Bristol, Avonmouth, Swansea, Southampton, Portsmouth or Birmingham – all of which suffered repeated raids. On 12 March Plymouth had its thirty-first raid and the worst was by no means over. There were to be seven more major raids in March and April. In March both Clydebank and Hull were attacked, before the Luftwaffe extended its reach to distant Belfast in April, wreaking destruction and a high death toll on the thinly defended city. So great was the conflagration that firefighters came up from neutral Eire to help the local men. Liverpool was targeted on seven successive nights in May, killing nearly 2,000 people and rendering 51,000 homeless.

Meanwhile, in London on Saturday 8 March the Café de Paris, 20 feet underground, was hit by two HE bombs, one of which crashed through the building in Piccadilly above and exploded on the crowded dance floor, where 'Snakehips' Johnson's band was playing 'Oh Johnny … '. The club was full of sophisticated revellers – officers on leave and their glamorous girlfriends – 34 of whom were killed. 'It was a gory incident,' noted one commentator, 'but the same week another dance hall a mile to the east of us was hit and there were nearly 200 casualties. This time there were only 10/6d frocks and few lines in the paper followed by, "It is feared there were several casualties." Local people were rather bitter.'[26]

Then on 16 April, when Londoners were already exhausted after months of bombardment, came 'The Wednesday'. The raid began late afternoon and was marked by the use of Junkers Ju 88 multi-role aircraft being used as dive-bombers, 'screaming' as they descended to drop their deadly load. Four hundred and fifty enemy planes were involved, many of which made a double or triple journey. In the area around Priory Grove alone there were more than 140 HE incidents. The noise and the shaking of the ground must have been horrendous for the Allpress family clinging together in their shelter. Then, at 3.45 in the morning, the cottages opposite, numbers 44–46 Priory Grove, received a direct hit.[27] It was so close, it missed the Allpresses by yards. As it was, they must have felt the effects of blast, along with the smell of cordite in the dust-filled atmosphere.

Above: Plymouth with its naval base suffered repeated raids.

The incident report mentioned five casualties, four of them trapped. As the rescue men worked to extract the victims there was confirmation of a UXB at the Priory Grove rest centre.[28] Together with the other residents of the stricken street, the Allpresses would have had to leave their home and been escorted to a safe distance from the danger of the unexploded bomb until it was dealt with by the bomb disposal men.

The family had endured months of bombardment, with all the terror, strain and sleepless nights associated with it. With this latest incident they had come within a whisper of death itself. It was almost certainly now that Nellie prevailed upon her mother to leave Priory Grove: 'We've got to get out of here, Mum,' she urged.[29] The house itself was probably bearing scars from previous incidents during the Blitz – Harry recalls that the front door had already been blown in when he came home on leave for Gladys' funeral back in December 1940 – but it would have suffered a great deal more damage when the houses opposite were demolished by the bomb. It would have been rocked by the explosion.

It is estimated that one Londoner in six was homeless at some point in the Blitz of 1940 and 1941. In Lambeth alone, 1,000 people lost their homes on the night of 16–17 April.[30]

'It was nearly 4.30 a.m.' and the 'planes were becoming less frequent,' recalled an ARP warden of that fateful night. 'I started timing the intervals; five minutes in which there were no aircraft to be heard. We dared to hope that, perhaps, soon it would be over. The glare and smoke of the fires had almost hidden the moon for hours. All night we could have read small newsprint easily by the firelight. But now the sky grew paler and the dawn came up pink. At first it was indistinguishable from the glow of fires. To the north of us, to the south, to east and to west the horizon was red.'[31]

The raiders had offloaded 890 tons of HE bombs and more than 4,200 incendiary canisters over a wide area, including Lambeth and Camberwell.[32] On the night of 19–20 April the Luftwaffe dropped 1,026 tons of HE bombs and 4,252 incendiary canisters, concentrating on the London docks and eastern boroughs. So fierce were these April raids that the number of houses damaged was 148,000, as opposed to an average of 40,000 a week in September and October 1940.[33]

However, the worst was not yet over. May 10 was one of those nights with a full moon and a low tide in the Thames – conditions particularly favourable for the Luftwaffe. The trail of devastation it unleashed that night reads like a tourist's guide to the sights of London. Damaged or destroyed were the Tower of London and the Royal Mint; Westminster Hall, a building that dated back to William the Conqueror's son, William Rufus; the House of Commons; the roof of Westminster Abbey; the British Museum, which lost more than a quarter of a million rare books; the War Office; Gray's Inn and the Law Courts; the Public Record Office in Chancery Lane; the Mansion House; several of the City's livery company halls and Wren churches; Barber-Surgeons' Hall; the Royal Naval College at Greenwich; the Temple Church damaged and St. Clement Danes in the Strand gutted – to name but a few. Every railway station except Marylebone was put out of action, and every bridge across the Thames rendered impassable. Fires raged around Elephant and Castle. Indeed, so great was the conflagration in London generally that the evidence of their night's work was still visible to the Luftwaffe pilots as they were over Rouen, 160 miles away.

Symbolically, perhaps, Big Ben still struck two o'clock correctly, minutes after a bomb had passed right through its tower.

A little before that, at 1.29 in the morning, All Saints Church Hall in Landsdowne Way, Stockwell, was hit.[34] The hall had been at the heart of the Allpress family's social life: here the two eldest daughters had had 'lovely' wedding receptions; the sisters had taught at the church's Sunday School; they had gone to the dances they loved, met their friends and made new ones. With the hall gone, it seemed a good time to leave.

Londoners were left stunned by the intensity of the raid on 10 May and braced themselves for further death and destruction, but they did not come – not then, anyway. For Londoners, there was still the 'Little Blitz' to come in 1944 and then the V1s and V2s, but for now anyway, the Blitz was over. It had claimed the lives of over 40,000 people, approximately half of them in London, left 71,000 seriously injured and 88,136 with minor injuries.[35] One million homes in London alone were destroyed or damaged. For all that devastation, the Blitz had failed in its objectives of demoralizing the British into surrender and of significantly damaging their war economy, which in spite of the bombing continued to operate and expand. By May 1941 the invasion of England had been indefinitely postponed, as Hitler prepared to make his cardinal mistake – turning east, to Russia.

Opposite: The heavy rescue squads face a challenge finding any survivors under this mountain of debris.

5
After the Raid

'I told Mum – we've got to get out of here!' [1]
Nellie Allpress

It was just at the tail end of the London Blitz in April 1941 that the Allpresses were 'blasted out' of Priory Grove. On the night of 16–17 April 1941, numbers 44–46 on the other side of the street received a direct hit, killing two people, and some of the shops over there were damaged. Fortunately, Mrs Allpress and her family were in the Anderson shelter in the back garden, so that no one was injured, but the force of the explosion would have rocked the house on its foundations and shattered the windows. The roof remained pretty much intact, but fixtures and fittings would have been badly shaken and dislodged and the contents thrown into disarray, possibly damaged. Everything would have been covered in soot forced out of the chimney by the blast and the thick dust that swirled around a wide area after an incident.

The house was not destroyed and could be made habitable again; nor did they lose their belongings. But after living through the terror of the bombing for so many months, and all the sleepless nights and frayed nerves that entailed, it is understandable that they would want to move to a safer area.

Nellie was already working in Wimbledon, a leafy district a few miles southwest of Clapham, and had noticed that an estate agent was advertising lots of empty properties to rent. 'We could have had half a dozen houses in Queen's Road. People had just upped and left,' she says.[2] It was fortunate timing, because towards the end of the war accommodation would be almost

Left: Those who had been bombed-out retrieved whatever possessions they could from the wreckage.

impossible to come by and private landlords would be charging exorbitant rents. She and her mother went to view them and chose a house in Queen's Road, Wimbledon. They were to live there for the next 41 years. By happy coincidence, William was now driving electric rather than steam trains and his point of departure switched from Clapham to Wimbledon.

The loss of the home where she had brought up her large family and lived happily for so many years must have been a wrench for Mrs Allpress. As one observer noted, 'For many wives, their home had been their life's work. All their energy, all their attention, for 30 years had gone into polishing, patching and scrubbing; they went without luxuries to get the furniture …'.[3] Mrs Allpress at least had her happy memories of the house at Priory Grove and a new home to look forward to.

As the Allpresses had rented the house at Priory Grove they would have followed the procedure laid out in the booklet *After the Raid* to serve a 'Notice of Disclaimer' under the Landlord and Tenant (War Damage) Act, 1939, to advise their landlord that they would not be paying rent on the damaged house, which they were no longer continuing to occupy.

Their neighbours opposite were less fortunate, having lost their homes. For them, a long process of rehabilitation lay ahead.

After the dead and injured had been located and removed from a damaged or destroyed property, great care was taken to comb through the wreckage to retrieve possessions, so that they could be returned to the owner. Valuables, as well as any documents that survived, had to be handed to the incident officer or leader of the working party and from him to the police. They were then passed to the borough treasurer at the town hall to be logged and for safekeeping. The owners could claim them upon showing proof of identity. If the owner had died, the next of kin might claim them, but only on production of a valid will.

Top: It was comforting for families to rescue any memento of their former lives.
Above: People would be reluctant to leave salvaged possessions in the street at the mercy of looters. They would wait until the council's removal men turned up to take the items into storage.

If the occupants had survived the incident, they might be reluctant to leave, preferring to stay to guard their possessions from looters. Survivors would often be seen as soon as it was daylight combing through the rubble for whatever they could salvage – perhaps a handbag containing cash, marriage and insurance certificates, ration books and clothing coupons, jewellery, or a treasured photograph. It was comforting to rescue any memento of their former lives, no matter how small or insignificant. If furniture or other household goods could be salvaged they would want to wait until the council's removal men showed up to take them away to a storage depot, rather than leave them sitting in the street, at the mercy of looters. Looting was a constant threat; although it was one of the tasks of the Home Guard and the police to guard damaged, vacated homes, they could not be expected to be everywhere at once.

For the bombed-out the local rest centre was often the first port of call. At an incident the newly homeless were counted and the information conveyed to the local authority report centre, so that the billeting officer could organize their transfer to the rest centre. These centres were open only to people made homeless as a result of enemy action and who had no alternative accommodation. Board and lodging were free of charge, and, after the usual wrangling between local authorities – responsible for providing for their own people, but not for 'refugees' who, unwittingly, might have entered a shelter a few streets away in a neighbouring borough – and a Treasury reluctant to advance sufficient funds, costs were met ultimately by the government.

Pre-war planning had assumed that aerial attack would leave thousands dead; it had not envisaged thousands made homeless. Nevertheless, by May 1941 two and a quarter million people had lost their homes, almost two-thirds of them in London and very little thought had been given to what was to happen to these homeless people or preparations made to receive them.

At first the rest centres, commonly situated in schools and church halls, were overcrowded and ill-equipped. People generally arrived dirty and dishevelled, caked in dust and grime, even blood-soaked, but washing facilities were minimal. No provision had been made to supply hot meals; instead, there were endless cups of tea and sandwiches. Worse, since responsibility for administering financial relief rested with the Poor Law authorities, the bombed-out – shocked, dejected, confused – were treated like 'public assistance' cases asking for charity rather than the innocent victims of war.

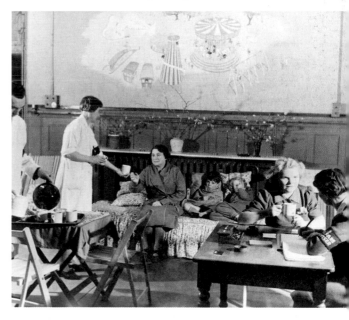

Above: A bombed-out family is given refuge in a rest centre. The grandmother and two children sit on the sofa and are served cups of tea, while the welfare officer gives the mother advice.

As with evacuation, however, improvements were quickly implemented after the initial dismay and barrage of complaints. More rest centres were opened to relieve overcrowding and more realistic funds allocated to them. The old Poor Law attitude was ditched. Every effort was made by the rest centre staff to ensure that the bombed-out were welcomed with the kindness, sympathy and compassion they deserved. Rest centres competed with each other to provide the best facilities and most attractive surroundings. ENSA (Entertainments National Service Association) was invited to entertain the residents.

Social workers, working for the Ministry of Health, who had responsibility for the welfare of the homeless through local authorities, were brought in to help. They liaised with the borough's billeting officer in finding the most suitable housing for individuals, ensuring that the rest centre did not become 'dammed up' and that there was a fast, efficient flow of homeless people in and out of its doors.

Although the wartime leaflet *ARP at Home: Hints for Housewives* advised people to pack a suitcase containing spare clothing and leave it at a friend's house in another part of town for this sort of emergency, this advice was often ignored and the homeless arrived at rest centres having lost everything they possessed. Lending their support to the initially scarce and harassed staff at the rest centres, the invaluable WVS was on hand to provide some essential clothing, very often from generous donations made by Canada and the USA in their 'Bundles for Britain' drives, but also financed by the Lord Mayor's Air Raid Distress Fund. Grants were obtainable to replace clothes, spectacles, false teeth, furniture and tools essential to the person's work. A sum in cash was offered for immediate needs, to be deducted from the subsequent war damage claim.

It was quite likely in an incident that the bombed-out would have lost vital papers, such as National Registration identity cards, ration books and, after their introduction

---

Below: Every billboard was covered with posters. The local Citizens' Advice Bureau was a good place to go for information.

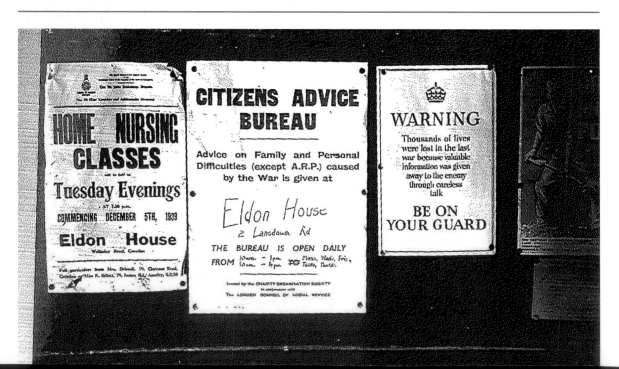

in 1941, clothing coupons. The National Registration card had to be carried at all times and had to be produced for police inspection on demand. Initially, the homeless would have to go from office to office, queuing for replacement documents, as well as to make applications for war damage compensation and to arrange for the removal and storage of furniture by the local authority and the reconnection of utilities, where appropriate. By the end of the Blitz, however, all this could be done in the rest centre when the relevant officers came to visit.

Top: Families whose home had been destroyed or damaged would have to apply for compensation from the War Damage Commission.
Middle: An air raid warden indicates where people can go for information in the aftermath of a raid.
Right: Furniture in damaged houses had to be kept safe from the weather and thieves. If a house was totally destroyed, any furniture that could be salvaged was taken into storage depots, at the government's expense.

Top: Water services were often disrupted after a raid. Here children queue up in the street to use a mobile bath unit.
Above: A bombed-out family gets some rest in a neighbour's living room.

Those who were bombed-out and did not go to a rest centre still had the same problems to tackle. They could get help and advice from the newly established Citizens' Advice Bureaux or the local offices of information established after the Blitz by every borough or district council. Both bodies offered advice on how to claim compensation, what to do about hire purchase agreements on furniture that had been destroyed, how to obtain grants for lost clothing and other goods, how to apply at the local branch of the Ministry of Pensions for an injury allowance or for a pension for the dependents of men who had been killed. These two bodies speeded up the process of resettlement by directing people to sources of assistance and by helping them to help themselves. The sooner displaced people were settled, the sooner they could return to essential work.

Those who had had their house damaged had to claim compensation by completing Form C1 – obtainable from the district valuer's office at the town hall – while for contents they should complete forms PCS3 if they were insured or form PCS4 if they were not insured.

The insurance companies would not pay for property that had been destroyed or damaged as a result of war. The War Damage Commission was set up in 1941, with responsibility for making payments for property damaged as a result of enemy action. The Inland Revenue collected war damage contributions from property owners, as a sort of tax. These payments continued for some time after the war.

The War Damage Commission would pay for the repair of a property if it was feasible; if the building was destroyed the owner would receive compensation based on its assumed value on 31 March 1939. This payment would be made at some unspecified date in the future. If the owner needed to replace his damaged home or business premises immediately, an advance sum of £800 maximum would be forthcoming. If he had a mortgage, it had to be paid off from this sum. However, the building societies had agreed that in these circumstances mortgages could be carried over to the new property, bought to replace the previous one.

The sum of compensation would be reduced if the owner failed to take reasonable steps to preserve his property from deterioration following war damage. Damaged properties left unoccupied or unprotected were often prey to looters, who removed lead, floors, doors, mantelpieces – destruction that was not categorized as war damage.

The War Damage Commission paid out to repair the property to the condition it had been in at the time it was damaged; it was not the Commission's job to fund improvements by rectifying what should have been done properly when the house was first built or in the course of time. Many disputes were to come to court after the war as to what was attributable to war damage and what was owing to original shoddy workmanship.

If a house was damaged and rendered uninhabitable, it was the responsibility of the owner to ensure that the surviving contents were protected from the elements, until such time as the local council could remove them to storage. If the house was damaged but habitable, furniture would not be removed, but had to be stored in such a way as to safeguard it from thieves and the weather. Compensation would not be paid for furniture and other items that had incurred damage after the incident as a result of negligence. If the owner could not be found, the local authority took responsibility.

Costs of furniture being stored as a result of enemy action, and its subsequent removal from store to a new home, were borne by the government.

◆

On the morning of 13 June 1944 the first V1 exploded in Bethnal Green, East London. In the ensuing weeks under attack from the V1s that summer, 1,104,000 homes were damaged in London. It was a race against time to repair them before the onset of winter. Only 700,000 of them had received an immediate stop-gap remedy known as 'first aid repairs' before Hitler unleashed his second Vengeance weapon, the V2 rocket, on the evening of 8 September 1944. The rocket continued to wreak havoc until the end of March 1945, exacerbating the housing problem, just when people were starting to return to the capital.

No one with experience of the building trade was conscripted by this time. Labour exchanges throughout the country were instructed to send all suitable men to London to work for local authorities on damaged houses. They were housed in emergency camps, rest centres and private homes.

Those just returning to London would have been shocked at the scale of devastation. Mile upon mile of houses in the inner and outer suburbs were covered in tarpaulin, applied as an immediate stop-gap remedy where roofs had been damaged or entirely blown away by blast. Workmen were busy tapping away, renewing roofs, while others restored windows. Needless to say, they were soon running short of tarpaulin, while the demand for glass was so great that it had to be eked out sparingly. Usually only the living room would be given a new glass window, while two-ply roofing felt was applied to the rest. This was subsequently replaced by 'R' glass – coarse, unpolished and almost opaque – so that damaged houses were dark as well as draughty.

In the Allpresses' old neighbourhood of southwest London, where 127,000 houses still awaited repair at the end of January 1945, it was estimated that the amount of glass required to replace windows in Battersea, Wandsworth and Lambeth alone amounted to 9,000,000 square feet, or nearly enough to cover the whole of Clapham Common.[4]

House damage fell into four categories. Class A signified that it was completely destroyed; Class B that it was unsafe and due for demolition; Class C that it was presently uninhabitable, but capable of repair; Class D that it was habitable and capable of repair.

Many houses had been damaged and repaired several times in the course of the war. In Stepney, 45,000 houses had been repaired, some of them as many as five times; and in Camberwell, not far from Priory Grove, some houses had been damaged and repaired six or seven times.

It was up to each local authority to decide the programme of work. The idea was to do essential works – 'first aid repairs' – making the property 'wind and weather tight', as quickly as possible, so that people could return to their homes, as they preferred to do, no matter how rudimentary the repairs.

That at least was the theory. In practice householders trying to get the council to carry out such repairs was a long and frustrating business, as one family whose roof had been severely damaged by blast discovered:

> 'The council men called as they promised, and told mother they hadn't any slates. She asked them to go up and first aid it – they are the first aid squad anyway. They went up, swore at it, and then went away without touching it, or knocking at

the door again. When last seen they were mending one of the easy roofs with two or three holes over the road. We have heard of two cases where they have actually removed the lino that owners had laboriously put over their holes, and taken away loose tiles, making the holes bigger.'[5]

Apart from the house itself, local authorities had to ensure that broken drains were given immediate attention, to prevent drinking water from becoming contaminated by sewage and to keep the rat population under control.

The local authority would re-house people who had been bombed-out only if their home had been destroyed or if repairs would take more than six weeks. They had the power to requisition empty houses, where the homeless could live rent-free for the first fortnight, then for a rent within their means. Alternatively, they might be re-housed in flats owned by the council or billeted with private families. There was always the chance that they might be re-housed in another part of town, but this was never popular.

For those who were successfully re-housed, there was the problem of equipping the home again, at a time when household goods were extremely hard to obtain. Mrs Allpress must have been extremely grateful that she had not given up her saucepans for Spitfires during the great salvage drive of 1940 – when council workmen came to take away the iron railings at the front of the Priory Grove house – because household items of all kinds became increasingly scarce. Indeed, the family soon learned that they must be careful to preserve everything, because it was almost impossible to replace an item – an alarm clock, for instance – or even to have it repaired. Boys like John Allpress would collect waste metal and bottles and take them to scrapyards for the war effort.

In 1942 the Utility Furniture Scheme (UFS) was introduced, with the emphasis on good design and economical use of cloth and timber, which were in very short supply. There were only three different designs for each article of furniture and two qualities. The government gave factories licences to produce furniture only if they were prepared to make it to UFS, or Utility, standards. This requirement also applied to items such as saucepans, pencils, umbrellas, cigarette lighters and pottery. Plates, cups and saucers were still on sale, but they were kept as simple as possible to save on materials – for example, cups were plain white and often without handles. So scarce were these objects that people would take their own glass to the pub, while in cafés everyone would use the same spoon – so precious it was tied to the counter – to stir the sugar in their tea.

Utility furniture was available only to newly wed couples setting up home for the first time and to those who had been bombed-out and had lost all their possessions. They had to obtain a permit, each one of which carried 60 units and was valid for three months. A piece of furniture was given a price in units as well as money.

Second-hand goods were also available. London received many gifts of such items from the provinces – the most generous donors being those cities, like Plymouth and Bristol, who had been badly bombed themselves – for distribution through WVS depots to the most needy on a points basis.

The local authority would provide the WVS with a classified list of eligible people. Each household was entitled to goods up to a value of 50 points and each member of the household was given an additional 30 points. The points did not go very far. A double bed cost 50 points, an armchair or dining table 40, a kettle or saucepan 10, a lamp 5 and a knife and fork 3. Sheets and towels were hard to come by, although blankets might be supplied by the WVS, thanks to generous donations from of the American and the Canadian Red Cross.

Understandably, after being bombed-out some people decided to leave London and the big cities, at least for a time. They were entitled to free travel vouchers if they did not have the means to pay for their journey and had to obtain a certificate so that the person they were staying with could receive a billeting allowance for them.

Those relocating were advised to send their new address to the Secretary, London Council of Social Services in Bedford Square. In this way, anyone might be found through the town hall, the local council offices and the Citizens' Advice Bureaux, all of which kept the information on record.

◆

The sight of bomb damage was considered bad for morale, so that as soon as the valuer had done his appraisal, the demolition men moved in to do their job and the debris men cleared and levelled the site. German prisoners of war (POWs) were brought in as extra labour to clear bomb-sites, on the principle that since they had made the mess they could clear it up. They were paid according to the terms laid out in the Geneva Convention, with a proportion of their pay being deducted for their keep. They were kept separate from British workmen.

At a time of severe shortages, it was vitally important to salvage building materials for future reconstruction. Bricks, slates and tiles were carefully removed, cleaned and stored; iron and steel were sorted and sent to foundries. Large quantities of

Above: Utility furniture was available only to the bombed-out or newlyweds, who had to obtain a buying permit issued by the Board of Trade. Each permit carried 60 units – not much to replenish a home, when a dining table cost 40 units, plus the cash.

timber were taken out of London for safekeeping, although there were dumps of firewood from bombed houses, to which the public were welcome to help themselves for domestic fires. Cast iron baths, taps, sinks, fireplaces, radiators, counters and safes were all rescued and put in storage. Rubble proved useful in constructing runways for new airfields.

By VE (Victory in Europe) Day, the WDDS in London had managed the salvage and removal of 331,865 tons of steel, 298,810 tons of timber and firewood, 132,659,000 bricks, 2,578,000 slates and tiles, 6,726,246 tons of hardcore and 3,897,000 tons of debris.[6] In addition, anything that could be salvaged from a historic building or church was carefully removed and preserved for its restoration.

Once the site was levelled it was ready to be built upon. Under intense pressure to provide housing urgently, the temptation for some local authorities was to erect quick, temporary housing in the form of 'prefabs'. At £1,000 apiece for the 655 square feet of space they provided, they were not cheap and there was some debate as to whether this was the best use of resources. Surely labour, time and money would be better spent on constructing permanent homes which would have a long life?

Among those desperate people who yearned for a roof over their heads and a home of their own, however, the prefabs proved popular. They were compact, but well designed, and had modern kitchens and bathrooms – luxuries that many of their occupants were not used to. The fact that some people continued to live in them for years and would not be parted from them is a testament to their qualities.

One man, who like so many others was living with his wife and two children in

Top: Utility goods had to be kept as simple as possible to save on labour and materials. Note that these cups do not have a handle.
Middle: It would cost around £100 for a newly married couple to furnish a bedroom, living room and kitchen with Utility furniture, but their points allocation would not stretch far. A double bed alone took 50 points.
Bottom: Utility furniture aimed to combine economy with artistic effect.

Top: Local authorities had the power to requisition bomb-sites for the erection of temporary housing.
Above: A Nissen hut was better than having no home at all.

a single room at the home of his mother-in-law, describes his relief and joy at obtaining a prefab:

'After we looked round Mary was worried – would it be our luck to get one? There were nine families lined up and only eight prefabs. Well, someone was going to be unlucky and as number two went, then number three, number four, so the tension was getting worse, but when it came to number eight he called my name to the table, I said "Yes, I'll have it". And of course we took it and we moved in a week after but I did feel sorry for the person who was left out and she even cried. But it's the happiest day that ever happened.'[7]

The government had given local authorities the right to requisition empty bomb-sites for the erection of temporary housing. They had to give the freeholder a fortnight's notice of their intention by posting a notice on the site. The chances of the owner actually seeing this notice when so many had left London or were engaged in the forces or war work elsewhere were slim. Some local authorities were quick to exploit their powers to grab as much land as possible. Since the requisitioning of bomb-sites was usually absolute and permanent – unlike the 'borrowing' of empty houses to provide temporary accommodation for the homeless – it was condemned as sharp practice. By the end of the war local authorities had in their possession enough land to provide 600,000 new homes, but they would be slow in coming.

◆

In 1945 housing was to be the first big problem of the peace. The new Labour government was under intense, immediate pressure to relieve the housing shortage. After all, in the run-up to the General Election in July 1945 they had promised five million houses in quick time, which certainly sounded more attractive to the voters than the Tories' more realistic pledge of half a million new homes within two years. The onus was now on Labour to deliver, especially as demobilization was soon under way.

Two million British couples had married during the war. Many of these young wives, including Bill Allpress's wife May, had been content to live with their parents or in-laws while their husband was in the forces, but now these couples would want a place of their own. Poor housing or lack of a home was not the best start to married life and it placed a strain on the marriages of returning servicemen – couples who after years of separation had to learn to live together again. In addition, a rise in the marriage and birth rate in the aftermath of war would add to the demand for housing.

Not only were millions of new homes required to replace those lost or damaged during the war, but none had been built during the conflict, so that there was a lot of catching up to do to meet future demand. A massive slum clearance programme was also long overdue. In spite of Goering's best efforts, there were still some appalling Victorian slums in Britain's major cities and large pockets of inadequate housing everywhere. Six million British homes lacked an inside toilet and five million – including the Allpresses' former home at Priory Grove – a fixed bath. Property everywhere had been neglected for five years at least; lacking new paint, houses were drab and dingy and in urgent need of maintenance repair work.

While the houses fit for heroes were slow to materialize, exhibitions to promote the goods that would be available in the post-war world drew the crowds. Some of them displayed new kitchens with all the latest labour-saving gadgets. How much easier Mrs Allpress's life would be if she didn't have to spend all day Monday, and many other mornings besides, doing the washing – which involved collecting wood to fire under the copper to warm the water, lifting the heavy wet washing from the copper and laboriously passing it through the mangle outside in the yard and hanging it up to dry – when an electric washer-dryer would do it all for her. Ironing all those sheets and clothes would be so much quicker with an electric iron, rather than having to pause and reheat the iron every few minutes. How much easier it would be for her to keep the house free of soot and dust with an electric Hoover, instead of the carpet sweeper. How nice it would be for her if she had a refrigerator, rather than having to queue at the shops every day, or every other day, for perishable foodstuffs. However, it would be many years before she and housewives like her would be able to enjoy such luxuries.

Housewives flocked to the exhibitions in their thousands, but most could only dream of this bright new world sometime in the future. As the war came to a close, the height of ambition for many of them was just to have a roof over their head.

6
What Are We Fighting For?

'Everyone rallied round in wartime.' [1]

Nellie Allpress

At the outset of war one of the government's greatest fears was that ordinary people like the Allpresses would break under the strain of a long war: of course, it was proved wrong. Nevertheless, one of the key tasks of the wartime government was to monitor morale and to offer morale-boosting incentives. After the First World War it was felt that the majority had made all the sacrifices for the privileged few, only to be let down themselves. There had been no homes fit for heroes and few jobs. There was no way this could happen again. The people had to be assured of a better world, if only they employed all their efforts into defeating the enemy.

Propaganda was vital in wartime. However, it was nonsense to say that Britain was fighting for freedom, yet limit the freedoms of the press and wireless. In a totalitarian state like Nazi Germany a Ministry of Propaganda spewing out all sorts of lies was possible. It was unacceptable in a democracy such as Britain. Her people were far too discerning to accept a diet of lies. Nor could the British sense of humour be discounted. Far from being in awe of the state's propaganda machine, as many Germans were, the British regarded it as a national joke.

Left: Dancing was one of the most popular social activities in wartime.

A free press was judged best for morale. There had to be a certain amount of negotiation between the government, the BBC and the press as to what news was permissible and how and when it was to be

Top: The Ministry of Information liaised closely with representatives of the press.

Above: The BBC acted as a beacon of freedom with its bulletins to occupied Europe starting, 'This is London calling Europe'.

Opposite: J.B. Priestley's 'Postscripts' were very popular. It was a welcome change for the BBC to use a broadcaster with a regional accent.

presented, but there could be no question of deceiving the public. On the whole, the government could rely on the patriotism of newspaper editors – and the people – to co-operate.

After a disastrous start, the wartime Ministry of Information – based in the University of London's Senate House, the skyscraper in Malet Street, Bloomsbury – quickly earned the titles Ministry of Muddle, Ministry of Malformation and the Mystery of Information. It was only when Winston Churchill's confidant, the assertive Brendan Bracken, took over as Minister in July 1941 that the whole ethos of the Ministry changed for the better. It fell more in tune with the popular mind and came to appreciate that it could rely on the common sense of the British people, who responded best to plain speaking and sound information, but understood that certain constraints had sometimes to be applied, owing to the exigencies of war.

As a press proprietor himself and on good terms with Lord Beaverbrook and other proprietors, Bracken was determined to allow the press as much scope as possible. There was constant liaison between the Ministry of Information and representatives of the press, who attended daily briefings at Senate House and submitted material for censorship.

Both BBC News and the press were to have complete freedom to keep the public – and, indeed, the rest of the world – informed as to how the war was progressing, as long as what they broadcast or wrote did not assist the enemy. Broadcasting to occupied Europe, the BBC's European Service was an instrument of war, acting as a beacon of freedom with its bulletins starting, 'This is London Calling Europe'.

At home the BBC Home Service and Forces Programme – the only two British stations that were on air until the advent of the independent, popular American Forces Network – pervaded nearly every home, factory, and many air raid shelters and had an equally vital role in disseminating information and in keeping up spirits through entertainment.

The Forces Programme, providing light music, was particularly good for morale in maintaining the link between servicemen and their families.

The novelty of listening to William Joyce (Lord Haw-Haw's) propaganda broadcasts from Germany, heralded by his trademark 'Jairmany calling, Jairmany calling ...', soon wore off. At first they caused some disquiet, such as when it was said to have claimed that the town clock in such and such a town had stopped at a certain time or that a particular city or town would be bombed that night. Far from being seen as a danger to Britain, however, the average English person regarded him as a bit of a joke.

In wartime, listening to the BBC News – broadcast at 7am, 8am, 1pm, 6pm, 9pm and midnight – was important. Families like the Allpresses, with sons fighting overseas, were keen to glean any news of the progress of the war. Naturally, they preferred to get their news straight, no matter how bad. To offer them inadequate or false news would only have fostered anxiety and rumour.

Newsreaders, the most prominent of whom included Alvar Lidell, Stuart Hibberd and John Snagge, announced themselves by name, to foil any fifth column attempts to spread disinformation over the airwaves, and weather reports were suspended, since they were considered helpful to the enemy.

There were some omissions from the media in the interests of national security. For instance, it was never revealed that after the bombing of the Houses of Parliament in 1940 and 1941 the Members had assigned Church House as an alternative to the House of Lords for their sittings. Nor were the location or movements of the Royal Family ever revealed in wartime, although the press and newsreels would record a royal visit after the event. Equally, the press co-operated with the government when disclosure would have had a detrimental effect on the war on the home front. If the press got wind that an item was about to be rationed, for example, it would not reveal this before the official announcement, so as not to provoke a run on that particular item in the shops.

The Ministry of Information would send 'private and confidential' letters to newspaper editors for their eyes and those of their top editorial staff only. Before the Vengeance weapons began to arrive in 1944, Herbert Morrison, the Minister of Home Security responsible for Civil Defence, gave newspaper editors a secret briefing about what to expect and urged them not to give too much prominence to them in the press, so as not to spread alarm.

When the Vengeance weapons started to arrive the public were well aware that some strange new weapon was being used against them, but there was a tacit understanding

on their part that if details of the new secret weapons were not being published it was for a good reason. After all, why let Hitler know if and where they were landing and what havoc they were causing? A typical bulletin might say, 'There was intermittent enemy air activity recently directed against Southern England. Damage and casualties were caused.' Press reports concentrated only on major incidents, were sparing of the facts, and appeared days or weeks after the event.

It would obviously be harmful if a particular incident could be related to a particular time for the enemy to correct the direction or range of the V-weapons. Nor did the press want to give any hint as to the effect on morale of the V-weapons, which would assist 'the enemy in deciding whether his expenditure is worthwhile.'

The main goal of 'propaganda' in a democracy had to be to promote action to win the war on all fronts. Good civilian morale was vital for full-scale war production and thus Britain's ability to prosecute the war at a time when victory was far from assured.

Posters were an obvious means of getting a message across to the people and, indeed, every billboard was in due course filled with government posters. The public was bombarded with appeals and instructions on subjects ranging from immunization against diphtheria and preventing the spread of the common cold to digging for victory and women factory workers covering their hair for safety, but it took the Ministry some time to refine the process.

There was a tendency among the largely Oxbridge-educated personnel at the Ministry to patronize, to treat the people as if they were slightly stupid, when actually they responded well to reason and clear explanation. It is notable that Churchill, from an aristocratic family, never talked down to the people. His speeches came from the heart and were great morale boosters. At the Ministry of Food, Lord Woolton, too, had the popular touch. He understood that the best results were obtained when the government took the people into its confidence.

An early poster displaying the slogan, 'Your Courage, Your Cheerfulness, Your Resolution WILL BRING US VICTORY' generated cynicism. With the disappointment following the First World War still fresh in some memories, the public read into this poster the implication that once again sacrifices would be made by the many for the few.

Well-meaning campaigns could go badly wrong. For example, one to discourage loose talk and rumour-mongers – rumour itself could be bad for morale – using such imaginary characters as 'Mr Secrecy Hush Hush', 'Mr Knowall', 'Miss Leaky Mouth', 'Miss Teacup Whisper', 'Mr Pride in Prophecy' and 'Mr Glumpot' and the instruction, 'TELL THESE PEOPLE TO JOIN BRITAIN'S SILENT COLUMN', went down badly with the public, who interpreted it as a campaign against free speech, especially as it coincided with a spate of prosecutions against individuals for spreading 'alarm and despondency'.

Above: The popular cartoonist Fougasse struck the right note – using humour to apply a gentle corrective.

In contrast, an anti-gossip campaign using striking posters by the popular cartoonist Fougasse in the 'Careless Talk Costs Lives' series and the 'Keep it under your hat!' series achieved exactly the right balance: they didn't browbeat the public, but acted as a light corrective by applying a touch of humour. They simply reminded the public that spies and fifth columnists might be anywhere, whereas the 'Silent Column' campaign had seemed to imply that any derogatory talk of the war was unpatriotic and dangerous.

Above: A fast, efficient postal service was important for the morale of the fighting forces and their families at home. Here a serviceman receives a telegram with the happy news that he has become a father.

Under Bracken the Ministry came to accept that exhortation did not work and that short, clear messages such as 'Be like Dad, Keep Mum' – if rather sexist – worked wonders.

Feedback was essential, if the Ministry was going to understand the popular mind – rather like political focus groups today. It would receive this feedback from a number of organizations. There were regular reports from its own Home Intelligence Division on the state of morale, the effectiveness of the material it was publishing, and all aspects of wartime life. The intelligence came from its own regional officers, but also from questionnaires the Home Intelligence Division issued to such bodies as the Citizens' Advice Bureaux, the WVS, W.H. Smith and Sons, the managers in the Granada cinema chains and officials of the London Passenger Transport Board. The BBC's Listener Research unit was another source of information, as were police duty room reports.

It was good for morale that a fast, efficient and cheap postal service had long been established for the forces, so that servicemen could keep in touch with family and friends at home. Like millions of others who had sons, brothers or husbands serving overseas, the Allpresses wrote regularly to Harry and Bill and waited anxiously for their letters. Sometimes they would not hear from them for weeks at a time, which was very 'distressing'. Mrs Allpress would often be on the doorstep an hour before the postman was due, so desperate was she to know that her sons were safe and well. The postal service even facilitated romance: when Betty started corresponding with her brother's friend Cyril, in a POW camp in Germany after being captured in Crete in 1941, and sending him food parcels, little did she realize that it would lead to marriage.

People did not want to worry their loved ones by telling them how bad the bombing was at home, or how frightened or miserable they were at the fighting front, so that they often wrote letters which made things sound better than they were. Nevertheless, Betty admits that she found official censorship of their letters off-putting. Postal and Telegraph Censorship, whose staff exceeded 10,000, gleaned vast amounts of information about the state of public morale and opinions from its scrutiny of mail leaving Britain.

Tom Harrisson's independent organization, Mass Observation, which supplied the Ministry with regular reports on a wide range of subjects by observing, interviewing and eavesdropping on the public, or having ordinary people such as Nella Last in the North East submit regular reports in diary form, was a very fruitful source of information.

This material was bolstered by the work of the London School of Economics, which presided over the statistical reports of the Wartime Social Survey.

It became a two-way process. The Ministry of Information acted as a filter, passing on feedback to the appropriate ministry, as well as carrying out specific surveys on behalf of those ministries, so that they might adapt their policies accordingly. Ministries were expected to do their homework, before submitting their proposals for a campaign for the Ministry of Information's approval. Public morale was more likely to be maintained if these campaigns married up with practical reality. For instance, there was no point in running a campaign urging the public to spend holidays at home, if the railways were running special holiday excursion trains.

Apart from posters on billboards, the BBC, penetrating nearly every home and workplace in the land, was the most effective medium for getting the message across. The BBC's *Kitchen Front* campaign, made in co-operation with the Ministry of Food and timed after the eight o'clock morning news just before the housewife did her shopping, achieved exactly the right balance between information and entertainment.

Such a campaign could only work if the public was in sympathy with it. Lord Woolton's light touch reconciled the public to the inevitable – rationing – and encouraged them to make the best of it. In contrast, the Ministry of Fuel and Power's

Top: The radio comedy show *ITMA* was a popular favourite – its in-jokes as familiar to people at home as to the forces overseas.
Above: Workers' Playtime was a big hit way beyond the factory audiences.

Fuel Economy campaign failed to win the public over, since they remained unconvinced that an island literally sitting on coal could be short of it. The poor in particular were unlikely to respond to a campaign which was so ignorant of the basic facts of their existence: they could hardly cut fuel consumption since they were already down to the barest minimum; they could not buy coal in the summer when it was cheap because they did not have the ready cash and often lacked a place to store it; and they could not save on bath water, since they possessed no bath.

Entertainment was good for the public mood. Although Nellie Allpress says she did not listen to much comedy on the wireless, comedy was a great morale booster, not least because it brought a sense of relief and restored a sense of proportion. Starring the popular Tommy Handley, *ITMA – It's that Man Again* – was the most successful radio comedy show of the war. It picked up on the topical news of the day, satirizing wartime institutions, such as the Ministry of Information, as well as poking fun at bureaucracy, rationing and other aspects of wartime life. A German spy, Funf, was thrown in for good measure. *ITMA*'s in-jokes acted as a unifying force, so that the likes of Bill Allpress and the thousands of others serving overseas would have become as familiar with such catchphrases as 'Can I do you now, sir', 'I'm going down now, sir', 'I don't mind if I do' and 'After you, Claude – No, after you Cecil' as family and friends at home.

Comedy was not the only BBC success. *The Brains Trust*, a serious programme in which a distinguished panel discussed science, politics, philosophy and the arts, won a widespread audience.

The BBC's *Music While You Work* and the lunchtime variety show *Workers' Playtime* were also hugely popular. Blasting out of loudspeakers in the factories, they were far more stimulating to wartime production than any amount of 'Factory Front' propaganda. These programmes also provided another link between the Home Front and those fighting overseas.

Top: 'The Forces' Sweetheart' Vera Lynn sang the romantic and sentimental songs so popular in wartime.
Above: The Joe Loss Orchestra was one of the most successful in the big band era of the 1940s, with hits such as 'In the Mood'.

Dance music by orchestras led by such household names as Jack Payne, Harry Roy, Geraldo and Joe Loss were popular. The Allpresses had always enjoyed singing and dancing as their chief forms of

Above: Cinemas drew the crowds. *Gone with the Wind* played at the Empire Leicester Square from April 1941 to Easter 1944.

entertainment. Before the war Mr Allpress had performed in a minstrel troupe with other railway colleagues, and according to Harry was 'always singing'. The whole family would go to watch him perform at Nine Elms swimming baths, although the troupe did not perform during the war. Bill, too, had been in a band before the conflict. The family also had a gramophone in the sitting room and would often have singsongs at home in the evening.

Singing was popular among women in all walks of life. They knew all the words to the popular songs and when they sang they could forget the horrors of war. The most popular wartime songs were the romantic and sentimental ones, such as those sung by Vera Lynn, the plumber's daughter from East Ham who had become 'The Forces' Sweetheart'. Her 'We'll Meet Again' and 'The White Cliffs of Dover' had a wistful appeal.

Most of the family's social life revolved around church 'socials'. The Allpress sisters loved to dance. They went out to dances frequently, although during the bombing Mrs Allpress preferred them to come home if there was a raid on. Fortunately, when they moved to Wimbledon the Civil Defence centre was right across the road and a dance was held there every Saturday night. If the siren sounded, there was time to dash home and take cover in the Morrison shelter.

Above: Filming is underway on an inspiring MOI film recalling the courage of the 'little boats' who risked all to evacuate troops from Dunkirk.

Nellie Allpress remembers going to the cinema in the West End occasionally, on the 77A bus, although there were also plenty of picture houses in the local area. A Shirley Temple fan, Nellie enjoyed films with plenty of song and dance routines – the popular ingredients of Hollywood musicals.

As ever, the cinema provided sheer escapism. It was no surprise that the most popular wartime film was *Gone with the Wind*, a four-hour epic filmed in glorious technicolor and set against the dramatic backdrop of the American Civil War. Starring the British beauty Vivien Leigh and the handsome Clark Gable, it played continuously at the Empire, Leicester Square from April 1941 to Easter 1944. The air raid sirens might be sounding outside, but the audience remained rooted in the cinema, so transfixed were they by the burning passions and fires of Atlanta up on the screen. Patriotic films such as *Lady Hamilton*, with Vivien Leigh and Laurence Olivier as the hero Lord Nelson saving his country from invasion at Trafalgar, and Olivier's *Henry V*, were suitably inspiring, reminding the audience of a past heroic age, when England won all her battles.

Apart from the main feature film, there was a B movie and at least one short film provided by the Ministry, which rightly saw the cinema with its captive audience as an ideal forum through which to deliver its message. *Food Flashes* promoting the virtues of potatoes were as common at the cinema as 'Food Facts' were in the press, but an official short film might cover anything from salvage to mending clothes.

The wartime public was always hungry for news, straining for a sight of their loved ones on the battle fronts, and the cinema programme provided a newsreel, too. Shots of enemy defeats and British triumphs provoked enthusiastic applause; they were definitely morale-boosters. Similarly, there was an appetite for realism. Documentaries such as *Western Approaches*, depicting the hazards of the merchant seamen on Atlantic convoys, were well received.

Family life was captured in *Mrs Miniver* – middle-class – and *This Happy Breed*, with its between-the-wars background – lower middle class. The threat to marital stability in wartime was exposed in *Waterloo Road*, starring John Mills. It was such a convincing cameo: the lonely wife of an absent soldier being seduced by a small-time racketeer in a flashy suit and armed with a phoney medical certificate. Love and loyalty triumph in

Above: ENSA did a splendid job touring the country and entertaining factory workers. Here they are performing for shelterers in the London Underground.

the end – a good omen for Betty Allpress, since she hired the wedding dress used in the film for her 1946 wedding to Cyril McCann.

There was a great revival of the arts, actively encouraged by the government and CEMA (the Council for the Encouragement of the Arts, which after the war evolved into the Arts Council of Great Britain), which took opera, concerts, ballet, drama and art exhibitions to the people to sustain morale, in the process winning many lifetime converts. The original intention of Basil Dean's ENSA (Entertainments National Service Association) was to entertain the forces, but then it extended its audience to embrace factory workers. Its first dinner hour show took place at Woolwich Arsenal in July 1940.

It was imperative to place the nation's historic and artistic treasures in a place of safety – the National Gallery's collection was despatched to Wales, while some of the treasures of the British Museum were hidden in a tunnel in the Underground – but contemporary art flourished. Artists such as Graham Sutherland, Stanley Spencer and Paul Nash were commissioned by the Ministry of Information to paint the destructiveness of the bombing and other aspects of the war, while Henry Moore painted his figures sheltering in the Underground quite spontaneously, before he was taken on officially. It was forbidden

for anyone without authorization to paint outdoors, and all work had to be submitted for censorship. Some wartime artists were on salary, but Leonard Rosoman's 'House Collapsing on Two Fireman, Shoe Lane', a tragedy he witnessed as a wartime fireman during the City conflagration of 29 December 1940, was bought by the War Artists' Advisory Committee acting on behalf of the Ministry of Information for £30.

Ironically, just as publishers were faced with a paper shortage and their output rationed, there was a reading boom. A big, absorbing read, such as Margaret Mitchell's *Gone with the Wind*, was just the thing to while away the long evenings spent in the shelters or on some endless wartime train journey. The classics, in which readers were transported back to the more genteel world of Jane Austen or the solid Victorian stability of Anthony Trollope, were popular. It was a good opportunity to work through a series, such as John Galsworthy's *Forsyte Saga* or the entire works of an author, such as Dickens. Tolstoy's *War and Peace*, coinciding with a fascination for all things Russian after their entry into the war on the Allied side, was *the* big read of the war.

Readers were hungry for detective fiction, *No Orchids for Miss Blandish* by James Handley Chase being one of the most popular. Escapism was also provided by historical fiction, although the salacious Restoration romp, *Forever Amber*, by the American Kathleen Winsor was considered so risqué that its critics did not think it warranted the 800 precious pages it was printed on. The public evidently disagreed.

The London theatre was expensive – too much so for the Allpresses. Harry says that he was lucky if he could afford one trip to the cinema while on leave, never mind the theatre. The West End theatre was obviously restricted in its appeal to those who could afford it and who could get there in time for the 6.30pm start demanded in wartime (5pm during the worst of the V-weapons period), since transport closed down so early. The wartime theatre enjoyed more success in provincial runs and, of course, CEMA introduced it to new audiences in the forces and factories.

◆

Regardless of the Ministry's efforts, public morale rose and fell according to how the war was progressing. From September 1939 to May 1940, during the long period of inactivity – called the 'bore war' at the time and subsequently referred to as the 'phoney war' – morale was low. Ironically, just as France capitulated and the Germans swept towards the Channel ports, it received a boost. It came as a relief to many, from the King downwards, that now there were no allies to please. Britain would go it alone – with the aid of the Empire and Dominions, of course.

The evacuation from Dunkirk in May–June 1940 had been treated as a triumph of sorts. The following year, 1941, was definitely a low point, when there was hardly any news of victory on any front to cheer people up and when food stocks were perilously low,

---

Left: Auxiliary fireman Leonard Rosoman's 'A House Collapsing on Two Firemen, Shoe Lane' is all the more moving since he witnessed this scene for himself and could have been one of the victims.

---

as a result of the U-boat campaign in the Atlantic. The news in the Atlantic continued depressing in 1942, but the entry of the USA into the war in December 1941 at least meant that eventual victory was assured.

The victory of Montgomery's army at El Alamein in November 1942 saw morale reach a high point, with the church bells ringing out all over England after nearly three years of silence. The defeat of the Germans at Stalingrad in February 1943 was also a boost to British spirits. After that morale dipped again. Turnaround at the docks and output in the war factories slowed down. Then came the successful landing in Italy, when it picked up again, although progress through Italy was slow, tough, and brought many casualties.

The euphoria felt after the success of D-Day in June 1944 and the advance of the Allies across France led many to hope that the war would be over by Christmas 1944. Instead, the Allies had come up against a strong German offensive in the Ardennes. By the end of December 1944 the final Home Intelligence weekly report recorded a marked lowering of morale – 'shock and surprise' at this turn of events, as the Allies engaged in the Battle of the Bulge. The Allpresses worried about Harry, whose reconnaissance unit was covering the left flank of the advance and penetrating deep into enemy territory, especially when they did not hear from him for weeks at a time.

After the Allied crossing of the Rhine, spirits picked up again. The last months and weeks saw daily newspaper headlines such as 'Only 200 miles to Berlin' and 'Russians in the suburbs of Berlin', while private diaries also record the increasing excitement of this countdown to victory.

Morale was less seriously affected by what was happening in the war in the Far East, with the exception of the fall of Singapore in February 1942, arguably the biggest, most shameful capitulation in British history. In vain did the Ministry of Information try to arouse any interest in that theatre of the war after VE Day in May 1945. The apathy was not entirely surprising, since the fighting was taking place in such a distant part of the world, whereas for four years the Germans had been only 20 miles across the Channel and often directly overhead.

Morale was equally affected by what was going on at the Home Front. Most people understood that sacrifices had to be made in order to win the war and were willing to put up with inconveniences and shortages, although not without a certain amount of grumbling. 'Don't you know there's a war on?' was a typical response to a complaint.

If Hitler believed he could bomb the British into submission, he was seriously mistaken. The effect of the Blitz was if anything to stiffen resolve. American reporters in London, such as Ed Murrow, did much to foster the image of a stoical people – something the people themselves came to believe, and acted accordingly.

'Britain can take it' was a popular slogan, but spirits received no better boost than when people could see for themselves that the British were giving the Germans a taste of their own medicine. Nellie Allpress remembers the satisfaction they felt when they

Above: The Ministry of Information commissioned leading artists to paint aspects of the war. This is Paul Nash's striking interpretation of the Battle of Britain.

saw RAF planes going over to bomb Germany. 'The sky was black with aircraft,' she recalls. 'We knew the Germans were going to have it that night. We were getting our own back.'[2]

With the arrival of the V-weapons it was feared that morale might break. After nearly five years of war the people were less capable of standing the strain of attack than they had been in the winter of 1940–1941. They were tired and suffering badly from lack of sleep. Under constant bombardment from the V-weapons day and night, there was no relaxation from the strain and often no opportunity to take cover. Of course, it might have been a different story had the Germans had the rockets in 1940 and now at least the end of the war was in sight.

The last few weeks of the war saw a crack in the communal spirit that had been such a marked feature of the Blitz. With the end of the fighting people did not see why they should make sacrifices any more and they were making their disenchantment felt. A Me First attitude began to reassert itself. 'The mood of the people was changing,' one Londoner noted, 'they were no longer polite, but snappy, irritable, some downright rude.'[3]

Critical for morale were the questions of post-war housing and employment. The housing shortage was even more severe this time around than after the previous war, thanks to the destruction of so many homes by enemy bombing. Now, a country which was left virtually bankrupt by the war would somehow have to provide homes urgently for a growing population, as the men came home from the war and the marriage and birth rates rose again. As for jobs, a Home Intelligence report stated, 'Workers continue anxious about redundancy in the war factories.'[4] Redundancy was recognized as a new name for unemployment and they dreaded it, as wartime industry was dismantled and peacetime industry was slow to re-establish itself.

There was evidently a great deal of cynicism about the post-war world, despite the fact that for some time the government had been holding out the prospect of an improvement in social conditions as an incentive.

One of the reasons that morale had been so low during the first months of the war was that Chamberlain's government steadfastly refused to state what Britain's war aims were supposed to be. His successor Winston Churchill was always more interested in the grand strategy of the war than he was in the home front, or in setting an agenda of Britain's war aims. Churchill's declared aim that Britain was fighting for 'Victory, victory at all costs' was apparently not enough. It was felt that a firm pledge of post-war social reform was imperative if the people were to be persuaded to give all their energies to the war effort. It was only with the German attack on Russia, diminishing the prospect of an invasion of Britain, that Churchill's government was free to pay some attention to the question, 'What are we fighting for?' although Churchill himself seems to have been reluctant to offer any hostages to fortune, at least until it was clear that the proposed welfare state could be afforded and until Britain's post-war defence needs were met.

In September 1942 the Army Bureau of Current Affairs launched a new propaganda campaign: 'Your Britain – Fight for it Now'. The war had shown that conditions could be improved if the state was willing: it seemed there was an enormous amount that the state could do when it was in its interests to do it.

It had been dubbed the people's war and so it must be the people's peace. The people were to be rewarded for their participation in the war. Plans for post-war reconstruction, growing out of the need to declare what Britain was fighting for, had come to be treated as an integral part of the war effort. The Beveridge Report, published in December 1942, promised the elimination of the five giant evils of want, squalor, ignorance, idleness and disease. It proposed a comprehensive system of compulsory social insurance to provide for all classes a minimum standard of living 'from the cradle to the grave'. For the scheme to be viable there would have to be family allowances, a National Health Service, unemployment benefit and state pensions for all.

For a family like the Allpresses, who rarely went to the doctor because they couldn't afford the fees and were so poor they never had a proper holiday – instead, the family took two or three day trips a year to a resort on the south coast, courtesy of Southern Railway – and, according to John Allpress, 'had to make every penny count', it looked as if it would be a fight worth winning.

Above: News of the war was followed avidly and public morale rose or fell according to how the war was progressing.

Needless to say, the Beveridge Report became an instant bestseller, giving the armed forces, war workers, and those doing their bit on the home front the incentive to bring about this better post-war world.

When it came to the General Election of July 1945 the Labour Party swept to power in a landslide victory. The electorate felt, not altogether justifiably, that it could not trust Winston Churchill and the Conservative Party to give their wholehearted support to the post-war welfare state with the same confidence it could Clement Attlee and the Labour Party. Labour had eagerly grasped the Beveridge proposals from the outset. Although Mr Allpress was a Labour supporter, the family appreciated Mr Churchill 'had seen us through the war' and 'we all admired him'.[5] Indeed, the rest of the world was amazed and incredulous at the apparent lack of gratitude of the British people to their wartime leader.

In the face of his election defeat, Churchill remained stoical – faintly amused that fate could play so dramatic a trick on him, and admiring of the electorate's show of independence. 'They are perfectly entitled to vote as they please,' he told an associate. 'This is a democracy. This is what we've been fighting for.'[6]

THIS PLAN WILL GIVE YOU YOUR OWN VEGETABLES ALL THE YEAR ROUND

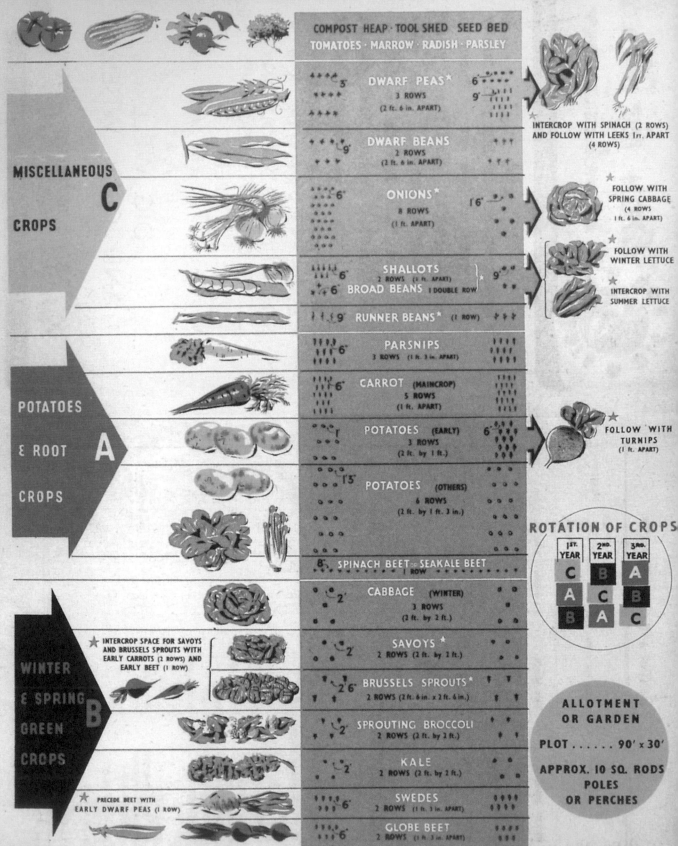

COMPOST HEAP · TOOL SHED · SEED BED
TOMATOES · MARROW · RADISH · PARSLEY

MISCELLANEOUS C CROPS

DWARF PEAS*
3 ROWS
(2 ft. 6 in. APART)

DWARF BEANS
2 ROWS
(2 ft. 6 in. APART)

ONIONS*
8 ROWS
(1 ft. APART)

SHALLOTS
2 ROWS (1 ft. APART)
BROAD BEANS 1 DOUBLE ROW

RUNNER BEANS* (1 ROW)

INTERCROP WITH SPINACH (2 ROWS)
AND FOLLOW WITH LEEKS 1 ft. APART
(4 ROWS)

FOLLOW WITH
SPRING CABBAGE
(4 ROWS
1 ft. 6 in. APART)

FOLLOW WITH
WINTER LETTUCE

INTERCROP WITH
SUMMER LETTUCE

POTATOES & ROOT A CROPS

PARSNIPS
3 ROWS (1 ft. 3 in. APART)

CARROT (MAINCROP)
5 ROWS
(1 ft. APART)

POTATOES (EARLY)
3 ROWS
(2 ft. by 1 ft.)

POTATOES (OTHERS)
6 ROWS
(2 ft. by 1 ft. 3 in.)

SPINACH BEET - SEAKALE BEET
1 ROW

FOLLOW WITH
TURNIPS
(1 ft. APART)

ROTATION OF CROPS

	1st. YEAR	2nd. YEAR	3rd. YEAR
	C	B	A
	A	C	B
	B	A	C

WINTER & SPRING GREEN B CROPS

★ INTERCROP SPACE FOR SAVOYS
AND BRUSSELS SPROUTS WITH
EARLY CARROTS (2 ROWS) AND
EARLY BEET (1 ROW)

CABBAGE (WINTER)
3 ROWS
(2 ft. by 2 ft.)

SAVOYS*
2 ROWS (2 ft. by 1 ft.)

BRUSSELS SPROUTS*
2 ROWS (2 ft. 6 in. x 2 ft. 6 in.)

SPROUTING BROCCOLI
2 ROWS (2 ft. by 2 ft.)

KALE
2 ROWS (2 ft. by 2 ft.)

★ PRECEDE BEET WITH
EARLY DWARF PEAS (1 ROW)

SWEDES
2 ROWS (1 ft. 3 in. APART)

GLOBE BEET
2 ROWS (1 ft. 3 in. APART)

ALLOTMENT
OR GARDEN

PLOT ...... 90' x 30'

APPROX. 10 SQ. RODS
POLES
OR PERCHES

7
Food, a Munition of War

'You got bored of having the same old thing but you never really went hungry.'[1]

Betty Allpress

The Allpresses were fortunate in that Alice Allpress was a good manager and worked very hard looking after them all. She was used to stretching her tight household budget to feed a large family, providing them with good, plain, sensible meals. No one ever left the Allpress household without a cooked breakfast in the morning – apart from the morning there was a raid on and the cat ate Nellie's breakfast kipper – and when they came home they could be sure that a nice hot meal would be waiting for them. Such good management would be an asset in wartime when housewives had to become adept at eeking out the rations and juggling the points to provide appetising and nutritious meals for the family from limited supplies.

Feeding a beleaguered island of approximately 47,762,000 people in wartime was one of the government's greatest achievements. The wartime diet might have been monotonous, but it was sufficient and no one went hungry. Indeed, those who had been malnourished in the poorer sections of society were now well fed. Not only were the British people in wartime consuming the correct number of calories for the energy expended, but thanks to the advice of the nutritionists, whom the government was forced to take seriously for the first time, they were including the right 'protective' foods – milk, fruit and vegetables – which provided vital vitamins and minerals to boost the body's immune

Left: People were advised to eat more vegetables – which were not rationed – and encouraged to grow their own.

139

Above: Housewives had to spend time planning nutritious meals for the family from the limited rations. A mother and daughter check a portion size against a chart supplied for a Wartime Social Survey.

system, leaving the nation healthier and fitter than it has ever been.

After mismanagement during the First World War, when food shortages led to hoarding and roaring inflation took the cost of food beyond the reach of many ordinary people, the government was determined to get a grip on the situation this time. Ministers were only too aware that in this war unprecedented sacrifices would be asked of the entire nation, not just the military, and that they must therefore take responsibility for safeguarding the food supply, providing an adequate diet for everyone at affordable prices. Above all, they recognized that the efficient supply and distribution of food to provide fair shares for all was good for morale and social harmony.

The government became the owner or virtual owner of all food imported into the country and of all home-produced food. The Ministry of Food became a bulk buyer of food with agencies established all over the world to procure supplies at the best prices, and at home it became the sole buyer of produce, with responsibility for its distribution into legitimate rather than black market channels. The slaughter of animals was controlled by the Ministry at selected slaughter houses; it also decided such matters as how much milk should be used for dairy products, how much for liquid consumption. Eggs were sent to packing stations under the Ministry's control. Strict price controls were imposed at all stages of production to the point of sale to the public and any trader infringing them would incur a heavy fine or imprisonment.

Waste was to be eliminated as far as possible. In the food industry an agreed volume of production would be concentrated into a smaller number of factories economical of manpower. All non-essential transportation was discouraged in wartime, because of a shortage of fuel and rubber for tyres, which meant that the transport of food had to be restricted and rationalized. For instance, before the war milk had been distributed by a large number of companies to hundreds of small retailers. One street might be served by six or more milk delivery carts. In wartime, however, one delivery man was to serve a compact number of streets.

Food manufacturers had to reduce the variety of products on offer. The maximum number of types of biscuits any one company could produce was reduced from 350 to 20, while the manufacturers of soft drinks agreed to eliminate all brand names for the duration of the war and sell standardized products under such designations as 'Orange Squash S.W.153'.

The use of packaging was strictly limited. Paper and board could be used to package food only as far as bare necessity required to convey the goods to the public in a proper condition. From 1943 paper bags were not provided in shops and customers had to carry goods away unwrapped, using their own carefully preserved paper or baskets or the ubiquitous string bag.

◆

Before the war Britain relied on importing two-thirds of her food. Carried on the 3,000 ships of the Merchant Navy, 22,000,000 tons of food arrived in Britain's ports annually, the key suppliers being Argentina, Canada, Australia, New Zealand, India, Burma and the USA, with the remaining small proportion coming from what would soon become enemy or enemy-occupied countries in Europe.

This vital trade was thrown into jeopardy by the war at sea. On 20 August 1940 Winston Churchill announced a total blockade of Germany and its allies and all occupied countries, but the war in the Atlantic waged by the U-boats against British shipping raged on. By February 1941 Britain was losing ships three times as fast as her shipyards could build them. The shipbuilding industry had not recovered from the Depression of the 1930s; the shipyards were rundown, there was a shortage of skilled workers, and relations between employers and dock workers were poor. All this meant that Britain was unable to repair ships or replace those which had sunk fast enough. In addition, unloading and loading of cargo and turnaround at the ports was desperately slow, reducing imports by about 10 percent. Aerial bombardment of the ports, warehouses and vital rail links further hindered the slick and efficient distribution of food.

The situation was so desperate that in March 1941 Churchill released men from the Armed Forces to lend their muscle to repairing the backlog of 600,000 tons of damaged ships.

An evocative poster showing a sailor adrift in the Atlantic, who had lost his life in the attempt to bring supplies to Britain, had a powerful impact. 'Remember the little economies are multiplied by every home in the land,' the Ministry of Food advised. 'In this way British housewives can lighten the heavy load of our Merchant Navy.' Indeed, every housewife soon understood that sacrifices had to be made to save valuable shipping space and to conserve the lives of seamen. They did their bit in making the most of the available food and not wasting a scrap.

Nazi occupation in Europe and Scandinavia denied Britain valuable imports of Danish and Dutch bacon, butter and cheese. Onions, imported from Spain, France and the Channel Islands, became so rare that one might be offered as a coveted prize in a raffle. Nor could Britain afford to give valuable shipping space to bulky fruits, such as oranges and lemons from Cyprus or bananas from the Caribbean. These fruits became almost as precious as antiques, while by the end of the war most British children could not recall ever having seen a banana.

The entry of Japan into the war in December 1941 would entail the loss of all sources of sago, tapioca, pepper, copra and coconut oil. The occupation of Malaya would leave Britain without her rubber, tin and palm oil, while the occupation of Thailand, Burma and Indo-China meant that 80 percent of Britain's supplies of rice would be lost. The Dutch East Indies would no longer supply sugar, tea and vegetable oils. The presence of the Japanese in the Indian Ocean jeopardized food supplies from Australia, New Zealand, Ceylon and India – a source of wheat as well as tea.

Clearly, Britain would have to rely less on imports of food and grow more of her own. At the outset of war, British agriculture was in poor shape, but now the race was on for the Ministry of Agriculture to stimulate British farmers into producing some of the food that had hitherto been imported or replacing it in the diet with other foodstuffs.

Before the war, large quantities of animal feed had been imported with which to maintain the domestic output of meat, bacon, poultry, eggs, milk and dairy products; several tons of animal feed were required to produce one ton of meat or eggs. This was neither practical nor economical in wartime. The priority now was to reduce the loss of energy inherent in converting edible crops into meat, by growing crops and feeding them directly to humans. The redirection of crops from beast to man meant that the number of livestock was reduced, although it was important to maintain and, indeed, increase the supply of milk for liquid consumption.

With the reduction in livestock, pastureland, hitherto used for grazing, could now be ploughed up to expand the area under crops. Ten acres of pastureland for stock raising had fed only 12 people, whereas the same area under wheat could feed 200 and under potatoes 400 people.[2] Huge reliance was placed on energy-giving potatoes in the wartime diet – so much so that one woman quipped that she was consuming so much starch that she crackled when she moved.

None of this was easy or could be achieved overnight. Many farm workers had gone into the forces and British agriculture was in competition with the better-paid war industries for manpower. It was short-handed, even with the invaluable addition of the Women's Land Army, which reached peak strength with 80,000 women in 1943, to replace some of the men.

With the virtual elimination of animal feed from imports valuable shipping space could be utilized for the import of condensed high-energy foods, which filled the protein, calcium and fat gaps in the national diet and added taste and variety. To save shipping space, meat was de-boned, telescoped or tinned, while British scientists devised a technique for spray-drying eggs to create a powder which took up only 20 percent of the shipping space required for shell eggs.

Left: The Ministry of Food's recommended emergency food store for one person included flour, porridge oats, evaporated milk, sugar, rice, baked beans, lentils, biscuits and jam. The scales were essential for carefully weighing a recipe's prescribed amount.

Above: The Minister of Food, Lord Woolton, had the popular touch and managed to make food rationing palatable to the British public.

For Britain to win the war her people needed to be fighting fit and the government was uncomfortably aware that many of them were not. This was primarily due to poverty, but also ignorance. The bottom third of society was unhealthy and malnourished, scraping along on a diet of white bread, margarine, jam or dripping, a little bacon and copious amounts of tea. Even if they ate sufficient calories, the diet of about half the population was generally deficient in calcium, Vitamin A, Vitamin B1 and Vitamin C; it was also short of animal protein and iron. Fortunately, Lord Woolton, appointed Minister of Food in April 1940, was not just a successful businessman but a philanthropist who had helped the poor in the deprived areas of Liverpool before the war. He was eager to seize the opportunity to improve the nation's health and well-being through their diet.

Enormous energy would be required for the war effort. Levels of physical activity would increase, requiring a greater calorie intake. Day after day, often after sleepless nights interrupted by the bombing, civilians like the Allpresses would have to get up and make the difficult journey to work, sometimes on broken transport systems. Not only would war workers be spending 10-hour days at the factories or on the land, but others, including the Allpress sisters, would come home from a day's work to put in more hours doing ARP duty or voluntary work. Even a housewife like Mrs Allpress would expend more energy, her chores – bad enough at the best of times without modern electrical appliances to clean the house and do the washing and with such a large family – made more onerous by the constant cleaning of dust and dirt which settled all round the house and in clothing after the house was shaken by bombing anywhere in the vicinity. Since the family did not own a car and could not afford unnecessary bus fares, Mrs Allpress had always walked to the shops, but now she had to spend long hours queuing as well.

When war broke out, a national register was set up, and everyone was given an identity card. Subsequently, everyone had to register at their local food office to obtain a ration book. Food rationing began on 8 January 1940. To succeed, rationing had to be simple and essentially democratic – guaranteeing fair shares for all.

Ration books were colour-coded according to category. Adults had a buff-coloured book, while the green ration books of pregnant women, nursing mothers and children under

5 earned them extra privileges. Children between the ages of 5 and 16, such as John Allpress, were given blue ration books. Where the rations allocated to the 5 to 16 year olds might have been generous for a child of, say, 6, they were stretched to the limit for a growing boy in his teens like John. Ration books had to be handed in at hotels and billets, but were not needed in restaurants or cafés. If a precious ration book was lost, it could be replaced on payment of one shilling and on signature of a declaration witnessed by a responsible person.

Unlike the rationing system in Germany, where some received more coupons than others, in Britain everyone received the same amounts. A slight exception was made in the case of children, pregnant and nursing mothers, and invalids, who were to receive extra supplies of milk. Before the war milk had been expensive at threepence a pint, so that pregnant and nursing mothers in the poorer sections of society had not been drinking enough of it, to the detriment of their health and that of the baby. Now, with government subsidies on food, it became more affordable. Whereas adults would be rationed to 2 pints of milk a week in winter and 3 to 4 pints a week in summer, to be used for drinking or in cooking, pregnant women and nursing mothers were given priority access to 1 pint of milk a day costing 2d if they could afford it, or free if the joint income of husband and wife did not exceed 40s a week; children under one year of age, 2 pints a day, and children over the age of one, 1 pint a day. After the launch of the Vitamin Welfare Scheme in December 1941 all children under five – Jessie's son Colin, for instance – would also be receiving blackcurrant or orange juice containing Vitamin C and cod liver oil containing Vitamins A and D.

The public had to register with the shops of their choice – a butcher, a grocer, a dairy. Housewives had to work very hard to keep in with the shopkeepers with whom they were registered, although as new ration

Top: Everyone had to have a ration book as well as a National Registration Identity Card. The housewife usually kept all the family's ration books, as she did the food shopping.
Above: Cargo space for bulky fruits was limited, so this rare consignment of oranges, with their essential Vitamin C, is marked for children only.

books were issued annually there was a chance to move to another retailer if the original one proved unsatisfactory. They had to queue almost on a daily basis – very few owned a refrigerator, and certainly not Mrs Allpress – to pick up fresh food. For someone like Mrs Allpress, who was shopping for herself and her husband, three daughters at work, and a schoolboy son, it was particularly time-consuming.

Queuing for food and other commodities became the bane of housewives' lives. A queue could be a sign that a shopkeeper's quota of un-rationed goods – perhaps including some all-too-scarce item such as torch batteries – had arrived at the shop. News would spread that a particular shop had some nice fresh fish or a rare consignment of cooking apples and housewives would have to dash off to secure them. They had to be prepared to walk a long way, going into another district or from shop to shop, in order to hunt down un-rationed goods – perhaps something as mundane as lavatory paper – the ready supply of which would be taken for granted in peacetime, and then queue. They felt bullied and slighted by shopkeepers, who sometimes took a malign pleasure in not opening until a sufficiently long queue had formed, or else pronouncing, 'Sorry, ladies, that's your lot!' before slamming the door in their faces.

Top: Housewives had to keep in with the shopkeepers with whom they were registered. The shopkeeper would tear out coupons from the ration book in exchange for rationed items.
Above: Women had to resign themselves to waiting in line. Word would go round that a particular shop had just received supplies of some rare un-rationed item and a queue would form.
Opposite: Rabbit, which was not rationed, was a treat in wartime, supplementing the meagre meat ration.

Shopkeepers would be allocated the exact amount of food to fulfill the ration quota of their customer base. When Mrs Allpress bought rationed food, she would have to hand her family's ration books to the retailer, who would cut out the coupons. The retailer would put the coupons in a large envelope, certify how many were in it, and send it to the food office, where staff did spot checks to ensure they were all present and correct. On the basis of the number of coupons returned, the food office would issue the retailer with a buying permit so that he could replenish his stock from the wholesalers.

The initial rations reflected the maximum guaranteed amount of the food available for every person with a ration book. It consisted of 4 ounces of bacon or ham per person per week, 12 ounces of sugar and 4 ounces of butter. From 11 March 1940 meat was rationed to just over 1 pound, or 1s 10d worth, per person per week. From July 1940 tea – the national panacea – was rationed at 2 ounces per person per week. In the same month margarine, butter, cooking fats (lard) and suet were limited to 2 ounces. Margarine, made from whale oil and nuts with Vitamins A and D added by the Ministry of Food, was promoted as an alternative to butter. Nellie says she absolutely hated margarine, but 'was glad to get it'. From March 1941 jam, marmalade, syrup, honey and lemon curd were rationed, varying from between 8 ounces and 2 pounds a month according to supplies. In May 1941 the cheese ration was introduced at 1 ounce a week, although miners and farm workers who relied on packed lunches, as well as vegetarians, were allowed extra. Sweets were rationed from July 1942.

The sweet-toothed British missed their sugar. In the Allpress household everyone took sugar in their tea. Mrs Allpress didn't want to waste the ration on sweetening tea, however; she resolved to pour so much sugar into everyone's cup that they quickly grew sick of it and gave it up. To overcome the fact that the family hated margarine, she mixed it with the butter ration, so that it did not taste so bad and everyone had a share of each.

In the course of the war the quantities of rationed food would vary slightly. Basic staples such as bread, potatoes and vegetables were never rationed. Fruit was seasonal and often in scarce supply. The sugar ration would be increased during the soft fruit season, so that as much of it as possible could be made into jam and bottled by assiduous housewives and members of the Women's Institute (WI) and the WVS.

Offal was off the ration, as were sausages and, if you could find it, rabbit. People became rather reliant on sausages of dubious content. Alternatively, they could consult the new austerity cookery books for recipes of stuffed ear, pig's feet in jelly, mock goose, hash of calves head, and melt and skirt pudding.

Fish was never rationed, but the few men and boats available for commercial fishing had to work in enemy-infested waters or under threat of enemy fire from the air. Icelandic fishermen did a good trade, sweeping into British ports to unload their catch and making a quick getaway. Needless to say, fish was expensive. Britain's favourite dish of fish and chips was in jeopardy. 'If it isn't a shortage of fish ... it's a shortage of frying fat,' one Londoner complained.[3]

It was difficult to ration eggs, since the supply could not be guaranteed, but from June 1941 they were rationed to about one per person per week, subsequently to about 29 per person a year in 1942 and 30 per person a year in 1943. A young woman returning to London from Canada towards the end of the war recalled:

> 'The first surprise was when I asked for half-a-dozen eggs! The elderly man behind the counter looked at me more in sorrow than in anger. He took off his glasses, wiped them, and put them on again – as if to visualize better what had drifted into his shop. Then he scribbled something upon my ration book, handed me one egg, minus a paper bag, and retired.'[4]

The ration also allowed for two packets of dried eggs a month – later reduced to one packet for two months – which could be used to make scrambled egg, omelettes, or in cakes. One packet of dried egg powder was equivalent to 12 eggs. One level tablespoonful of dried egg powder had to be mixed with two tablespoonsful of water; if two much powder was used, the mixture tasted of sulphur. Betty Allpress, who missed fresh eggs most of all, recalls that dried eggs weren't very nice, but they did go a lot further.

◆

Above: It was impractical to import shell eggs, which took up too much shipping space, so British scientists invented powdered eggs. With water added, the mixture could be used to make omelettes, scrambled eggs, and cakes.
Opposite: People banded together to run their own pig clubs. Here men of the National Fire Service tend their pigs amidst the ruins of London.

The autumn and winter of 1940–1941 was the worst period of the war for food. By January 1941 there was only two weeks' worth of reserve stocks of frozen meat in Britain's warehouses, mainly owing to the bombing. For the first and only time in the entire conflict, the ration could not be honoured and the meat ration had to be cut down to 1s worth per person per week.

By this time, too, Britain's gold reserves – the money it needed to pay for imports – were running low. With its whole economy geared to the war effort, its overseas exports were dramatically reduced, leaving a yawning gap in the balance of payments. Partly because it was importing only essentials, Britain had cut its expenditure on American food imports from £62 million in 1939 to £38 million in 1941.[5] Faced with a sudden surplus of foodstuffs, the US Department of Agriculture urged its government to find some way of selling more food to Britain. In March 1941 President Franklin D. Roosevelt introduced Lend-Lease as a means by which the neutral USA could aid Britain's war effort – and preserve its level of exports. Lend-Lease solved the problem of the British balance of payments by 'loaning' Britain raw materials and food for the duration of the war. It also provided for the repair of British ships in American ports, alleviating the pressure on British shipyards.

The Japanese bombing of the US naval base at Pearl Harbor on 7 December 1941 and Hitler's declaration of war against the United States on 11 December 1941 finally brought the Americans into the war. At the Arcadia Conference held in Washington later that month, Churchill and Roosevelt discussed their future strategy. The Combined Food Board and the Combined Shipping Board were established to co-ordinate the production and distribution of food throughout the Allied territories, including the USA, Great Britain and its Empire and Commonwealth, the Belgian and French colonies, Latin America, the Caribbean, the Middle East and the Soviet Union.

Everything, of course, depended on the available shipping. The British representatives at the Combined Food Board in Washington had to lobby hard to have shipping allocated for food imports to Britain. Competition for shipping was fierce, especially now that vital supplies, including 500,000 tons of food a month, had to be transported to Britain's new ally, the Soviet Union, on the dreaded route to Murmansk.

The U-boat war in the Atlantic was particularly savage in the autumn and winter of 1942–1943, exacerbating the shipping crisis. One of the consequences was that the government was forced to ban white bread. The soft white bread the British favoured at that time was made according to a method devised by the Americans, whose flour was highly refined but lacking in nutritional value. The loathed greyish-brown National Loaf, made from wholemeal flour with additional calcium, became the only bread available, saving one million tons of shipping space a year. People complained that it tasted disgusting and made them sick. It was high in iron and Vitamin B content, however, so that, like it or not, the working-class diet, which relied so heavily on bread, was greatly improved.

The advent of Lend-Lease meant that Britain was able to import more supplies of American frozen and tinned meat, notably Spam – Supply Pressed American Meat – tinned fish, dried egg, tinned and dried milk, tinned and dried fruits and beans, cereals, pulses, fats and oils. In practice, small consignments of these foods were often squeezed into the odd cabin or small space when a ship was being loaded. There was never a sufficiently large or consistent quantity of these goods to honour a blanket ration for the whole population, however. 'It is only possible to ration if there are sufficient supplies for everybody to have some,' Lord Woolton declared, 'and this multitude of different articles that indeed made life tolerable for people, were all in such short supply that it would have been impossible for everybody to get even the smallest quantity.'⁶ So the Ministry devised a new, ingenious scheme.

Points rationing was introduced in December 1941, just in time for Christmas. Every holder of a ration book received 16 points a month, later raised to 20 and then 24, before dropping to 20 again, to spend as he or she wished, at any shop that had the items. Multiplied by six – the members of the Allpress family living at home – this would give Mrs Allpress 96, 120 or 144 points a month to spend on items of her choice, injecting some variation into the family diet. The items that were in the shortest supply cost the largest number of points and vice versa.

One of the most popular items proved to be a tin of American sausage meat. It cost 16 points, plus the cash, but it provided several meals and in addition contained a thick layer of nearly half a pound of fat.

For months before the introduction of the points system the Ministry had stockpiled the food, so that there would be enough in the shops to launch the system with confidence. Points rationing was a morale booster, in that it offered an incentive to break the routine of the dreary wartime diet. Housewives scanned the 'Changes in Points Value' that appeared in the newspapers. It also offered the Ministry the means of controlling the market. If the demand for any one article became excessive the points value of it was increased until consumption had been checked.

Above: Nothing must be wasted. Every neighbourhood had its pig bin for leftover kitchen scraps.

Opposite: Everyone could do their bit digging for victory, whether it was looking after an allotment, or growing vegetables in the garden, or even in a window box.

In addition, there was 'personal points' rationing for chocolate and sugar confectionary. Betty Allpress saved up her chocolate ration to send to her friend – and future husband – Cyril in the POW camp in Germany. She made do with carrots instead – much healthier.

◆

'Food is a munition of war. Don't waste it,' urged one of the Ministry of Food's advertisements in the successful *Kitchen Front* campaign. Indeed, wasting food was a crime punishable by substantial fines. The Ministry's inspectors made regular checks of restaurant and domestic dustbins; they also had a right to inspect domestic store cupboards, as a guard against black market activities.

The Ministry assured the nation that it was not being deprived. 'What we can get is good for us. A great deal of what

we cannot get is quite unimportant.'[7] It also tried to impress on people that it was not necessary to overeat to be well fed; quite the contrary. To do so was wasteful and unpatriotic: 'If you eat more than you need, you are wasting food as surely as if you had thrown it away. So eat what you need, no more. Buy wisely and cater strictly. For your health's sake, as well as your country's, remember that "Enough is as good as a feast." Save food! Save money! Save cargo space for munitions!' the Ministry tirelessly impressed on the public.

Nothing was to be left on the plate, as the wartime poster proclaimed: 'A clear plate means a clear conscience.' Indeed, far from eating too much, some women were going without so as to give their husbands and children extra portions. They discovered they could ward off hunger by smoking.

If you did, by any chance, have any scraps, there were pig bins placed outside restaurants and on the streets of every borough. Families routinely put any kitchen scraps into the local pig bin. Even bomb-damaged food carrying dirt, debris and broken glass was not to be discarded. The borough's chief sanitary inspector would examine it and decide whether it could be treated and made fit for human consumption or passed on for animal feed. If not, it was destroyed.

To boost the rations, small groups of people banded together to run their own clubs keeping poultry, rabbits, pigs and bees under licence from the Ministry of Food. Each member of a pig club would contribute their kitchen waste to the animal's feed for the year and the pig, having reached the statutory 100 pounds in weight, would probably be slaughtered at Christmas under the supervision of the Ministry inspector and divided among them.

Top: Old-age pensioners hoeing cabbages for the 'Dig for Victory' campaign.
Middle: The moat of the Tower of London has been put to excellent use and is proving fertile ground for all these vegetables.
Bottom: No effort was too small and no one was too young to start planting seedlings and tending vegetables.

Strict limits were placed on the number of animals that could be kept: more than 20 hens meant that some eggs had to be handed over to the Ministry. Domestic poultry keepers had to surrender their entitlement to shell eggs in order to obtain feeding stuffs for their hens. Local newspapers ran informative columns for such clubs and lectures were given on keeping hens, pigs and rabbits.

The ordinary householder was urged to 'Dig for Victory'. In domestic gardens flowers gave way to vegetables, while by 1943 there were 1,500,000 allotments nationwide. School playgrounds, bomb-sites, railway sidings, dumps, even cemeteries were pressed into service. Mr Allpress had his own allotment on a railway siding, putting in the hours digging when he wasn't at work. Betty grew carrots and runner beans in the garden at home, and the family liked to grow mustard-and-cress on flannel in a saucer placed on the kitchen windowsill as a treat for Sunday sandwiches.

Every newspaper carried its gardening column, specifically devoted to the growing of vegetables. There were classes and gardening tips were swapped in the office or at the bus stop. Publishers produced a spate of books on the subject. Amateur Gardening's *War-time Gardening for Home Needs* came with the label 'A National Food Handbook' and the reminder, 'By Helping Yourself You Help the Nation'. On the jacket flap there was a message from the Minister of Agriculture:

'To smallholders, allotment holders and those who have a reasonably sized garden – to those also who may be termed backyarders – you can help, help perhaps more than you realise, to feed yourselves and others. I ask for the fullest possible co-operation. The results of your work are of vital importance.'

There was fierce competition to obtain an allotment and any allotment holder not doing his bit was likely to be evicted.

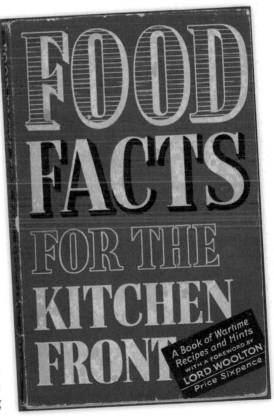

The Ministry of Food embarked on a food education programme for the nation. A small staff of dieticians and cookery specialists provided expert advice, which was passed on to the public in the form of practical demonstrations – Marguerite Patten gave demonstrations at Harrods in Knightsbridge, for example – and through a barrage of advertisements, broadcasts, 'Food Facts' in the press and *Food Flashes* at the cinema. Every morning after the BBC eight o'clock News Freddy Grisewood would introduce the *Kitchen Front* programme. Dr Charles Hill would broadcast hints and tips on food in a stirring, positive and upbeat manner. Ambrose Heath, Constance Spry and Mabel Constanduros gave recipes. Anyone who had something interesting to contribute was invited on to the programme. The avuncular Lord Woolton would appear with the popular characters 'Gert and Daisy' – Elsie and Doris Waters – in *Feed the Brute*, the content of their comic dialogue being easily

Above: *Food Facts for the Kitchen Front* was an invaluable handbook in the Ministry of Food's campaign to educate the public on healthy eating.

absorbed by listeners. Food slogans would be interspersed with encouragement, such as 'Carry on Fighters on the Kitchen Front! You are doing a great job.'

Most wartime cookery books, especially *Food Facts for the Kitchen Front*, laid heavy emphasis on a vegetable-based diet. Certainly in the Allpress household a stew with plenty of vegetables was a popular dish for the evening meal. Oatmeal was frequently added to minced meat, stews and stock, as a nutritious filler. 'Even if you like a meat and vegetable meal best,' the book advised, 'you can feed well on a course of vegetables alone. Or if you are near the end of your meat ration, an extra vegetable will transform it into a substantial meal.'[8] Readers were warned not to overcook vegetables and to preserve the vegetable water for soup or stock. Ideally, they could add raw grated carrot and cabbage to pies or use them to make a salad instead of lettuce.

'Potato Pete' became a popular cartoon character in the Ministry's campaign to encourage the public to consume more potatoes – 'a rich store of all-round nourishment.' 'It is an energy food and a protective food,' the public was told. 'It contains Vitamin C – the vitamin we miss when fruit is scarce.' Potatoes should be cooked in their skins to preserve the full nutritional value. There were dozens of recipes involving potatoes, including a potato omelette, which required only 'one egg (if you have it)'. Women were even advised that 'well-seasoned mashed potato and chopped spring onion and parsley make an excellent sandwich filling'.

Similarly, the Ministry's 'Doctor Carrot' cartoon character, carrying a doctor's bag marked 'Vitamin A', advised people to 'Call me often and you'll keep well'. Carrots and potatoes were the two main ingredients of the famous wartime dish, Woolton pie, a vegetable dish thickened with oatmeal and topped with either potato or pastry made from national wholemeal flour. Carrots, like beetroot, were used as sweeteners in cakes and to make marmalade. Children munched on carrots rather than sweets, which were rationed to 2 ounces per person per week.

Thanks to the Ministry's educational drive and their own ingenuity, British women like Mrs Allpress were doing a grand job devising healthy meals for their families from the limited ingredients, although it must have been very wearing, year after year, given all the time it took to do the shopping and constantly keeping abreast of changes in the rations and points systems.

The Allpresses were fortunate in that Nellie worked in the catering trade. She was able to offer her mother valuable assistance by spending her half-day off on Wednesday making pies which kept the family going for three days. Flour was not rationed, but if Nellie was short of butter or margarine, she could follow the recipe for 'economical pastry', which required only 1 ounce of cooking fat mixed with 4 tablespoons of milk to make enough pastry for four people. She could dispense with fat altogether by mixing 8 ounces of flour, 1 level teaspoon of baking powder and a pinch of salt with a quarter of a pint of milk and water, or

Top left: The Ministry used the cartoon character 'Potato Pete' to impress on the public the value of the potato as a rich source of all-round nourishment.

Left: With sweets rationed and ice-cream unavailable, wartime children make do with carrots on sticks. They seem to be enjoying them.

she could take a tip from *Food Facts for the Kitchen Front* and add the invaluable potato to the mix: 'It can save us flour and fat when we use it in making cakes, scones, puddings and pastries.'[9]

Nellie had a meal at work, which helped stretch the family rations, while John, a schoolboy until 1943, would have benefited from one of the government's new welfare schemes which provided children with a hot meal at school five days a week.

As if trying to produce meals from the limited and monotonous repertoire was not challenging enough there were fuel shortages. Housewives were told to leave inessential cooking until after 10 o'clock in the morning. The needs of the war industry came first. Towards the end of the war the fuel shortage was so severe that people were being advised not to have toast for breakfast. As an extreme fuel-saving measure the Ministry of Food's pamphlet *Food without Fuel* was anxious to demonstrate how a meal could be cooked in a hay box. A meat stew that would take 30 minutes to cook on the stove would take three and a half hours in the hay box. Not surprisingly, the hay box method did not really take off.

Below: Ration books did not have to be produced to eat in a restaurant, but customers were limited to one protein course only.

For those who could afford to there was always the option to eat out at a restaurant. In theory, since coupons did not have to be surrendered for restaurant meals, there was nothing to stop people procuring as many meals as they could afford in a day. The government, however, realized that some restrictions must be applied to eating out, not only to guard scarce supplies, but also to avoid exacerbating social tensions.

In July 1940 it became illegal to serve more than one main course containing protein per person in a restaurant, the restricted dishes being marked on the menu by one or two stars. The supper menu at branches of the popular Lyons Corner House, for instance, offered three courses, of which only one might be a two-starred dish. The following dishes merited two stars: Spam salad, pilchard salad, cheese and pickled cucumber salad, chopped meat and white bean salad, ham omelette, creamed fish with mashed potatoes, stewed lamb with vegetables and potatoes – all served with an additional nutritious baked jacket potato.

From June 1942 a maximum charge of 5s was imposed on all restaurant meals, although grand establishments such as London's Savoy could demand an extra cover charge, for the flowers on the table and so on. Wine was extremely expensive and spirits were in short supply, because only so much precious grain could be diverted into making them. The 5s maximum charge generally meant that previously exclusive restaurants became more accessible: it was a democratizing process, just as much as rationing was.

In spite of the adequacy of the wartime diet, a Wartime Social Survey[10] in 1942 found that men working in heavy industry felt hungry. As war workers in the factories put in long hours, they had little or no time to queue for food and no energy to cook it when they got home. Rather than fiddling with the ration for this specific group of people, the Ministry of Food decided to provide workers with canteens, where they could buy extra meals – they were, after all, receiving good wages. From 1943 it was compulsory for firms employing more than 250 people to have a canteen. They served double the meat allowance permitted in ordinary restaurants and all for less than a shilling.

In the interests of social justice and to offer flexibility, the Ministry of Food also encouraged local authorities to open 'British Restaurants', affording everyone the opportunity to eat 'off the ration' at affordable prices. To save costs, these restaurants operated on a self-service basis. Eating out at a British Restaurant occasionally would have been an option for the Allpresses, but it seems that Mrs Allpress was doing such a sterling job feeding her family at home that they had little need to eat out. The restaurants provided respite for harassed housewives and were a godsend to those working long hours, unable to afford the time to queue at the shops, or who lacked the facilities to cook, and to working mothers.

Pooling food supplies and scarce fuel resources to feed a crowd – or, indeed, a large family such as the Allpresses – was much more economical than it was for a single person or couple producing a meal themselves. With six members of the family living at home – Mr and Mrs Allpress, Nellie, Eva and Betty and John – the family could combine rations for six people, stretching them that little bit further than a single person or a couple could. Indeed, the rations were such that Mrs Allpress might have more of one foodstuff, bacon, for example, than she would normally have bought in peacetime. Nellie recalls that they sometimes swapped foodstuffs with neighbours.

◆

The biggest disappointment of 1945 was that the food situation did not improve with the peace: it grew worse. In the previous two years the government had built up food stocks of 6,500,000 tons – importing about 2,000,000 tons more than was consumed in 1943 – but decided to conserve these stocks rather than increase the rations. They knew that a world food crisis was looming and that once the war was over Britain would be obliged to send food to the starving people of Europe.

At the shops, scarcities and queues were worse than ever. As early as 23 May 1945, barely two weeks after VE Day, Colonel Llewellin, who had succeeded Lord Woolton as Minister of Food in November 1943, announced cuts in the rations. The meat ration of 1s 2d a week was to be maintained, but one seventh of it was to be taken in the form of tinned corned beef over the next five months: fortunately, corned beef hash had become a popular dish. The cooking fat ration was to be reduced from 2 to 1 ounce a week; bacon or ham from 4 to 3 ounces a week; the sugar ration, already reduced to 8 ounces, was to be maintained, although there was to be no extra allowance for Christmas, as there had been in 1944. One egg per person per fortnight might be managed and 2½ pints of liquid milk per person a week. The points allowance was to be reduced from 24 to 20 per four-week period. By the summer of 1945, it took 12 points to buy a tin of salmon, 17 for a small tin of Spam and 54 for a large one, 4 points for a tin of baked beans and 2 for a tin of sardines, so that the 20-point allowance did not go far.

There was no hope of the situation improving in the foreseeable future, not least because shortly after VJ Day on 2 September 1945 the USA abruptly terminated the Lend-Lease agreement. From now on Britain, left virtually bankrupt by the war, would have to pay for her food imports, as well as repaying her wartime debt to the USA. There would be less for everyone for years to come.

Housewives like Mrs Allpress would no doubt have been incredulous had they been told when rationing began in 1940 that it would continue for 14 long years – eight years more than the war itself. They had won the war on the kitchen front. Now, as they entered the era of austerity, they had to win the peace.

Right: Food rationing became even more stringent after the war. By 1946 these housewives had had enough.

NO MORE RATION CUTS
WOMEN OF BAYSWATER
AND PADDINGTON!
COME AND SIGN THE
OTEST TO THE MINISTER OF FOOD
ST FURTHER CUTS IN
UR RATIONS.

8
War-winning Fashion

'It made you very economical with things ...
If you'd spent your coupons, that was it.' [1]
Betty Allpress

The Allpress sisters liked to make the best of themselves. They did not have much money to spend on clothes, but they were clever and inventive with what they had. Eva had a smart black dress, for instance, which she wore with different accessories to ring the changes. Mrs Allpress was 'good with her needle',[2] both making and constantly altering clothing for each of the children when they were small. All her daughters could sew and knit, and indeed, were to pass some of the hours spent in the Anderson shelter during the war knitting. They were used to making many of their own clothes and were already all too familiar with making do and mending – readapting clothes, rescuing buttons, turning sheets sides to middle, darning stockings and socks. All this meant that they would be able to adapt easily to wartime restrictions, when it was good for morale to look one's best, yet unpatriotic to be a fashion queen or a clothes glut.

Clothes rationing was introduced on 1 June 1941, freeing up factory space and 450,000 workers for the munitions industry. As with food products, clothing manufacturers were encouraged to produce a more limited range.

Left: Rationing meant that you had to take care of your clothes and mend and adapt them as required. New clothes were in short supply.

The British generally welcomed clothes rationing, since it meant fair shares for all. For the sake of the war effort, it was permissible for men to look shabby. 'We must learn as civilians to be seen in clothes that

A.R.P.
BoilerSuit
in Navy
or Brown
drill. For
ambul'nce
driving
and Voluntary
A.R.P. work.
Sizes 36 and 38.
39/6

Left
Zipper Shelter Suit,
in shepherd's plaid
wool. Tailored and
warm, elastic cuffs
and ankles. Navy,
Burgundy **69/6**

ANTI-CONCUSSION BANDEAU
B.102. Designed by a nerve specialist to ward off the harmful effects of concussion from bombs and to protect the ear-drums. The aerated rubber lining with millions of air cells smothers the "shatter" element of concussion. Suitable for children and adults. In Black, Brown, Navy, Saxe, Wine, Beige and other colours. Sizes 6⅞, 7, and 7⅛.
PRICE
Post 6d. extra **5/11**

gloves, a
d several
e comfort
that might

Above: Winston Churchill was a great advertisement for the boiler suit. These fashion pages advertise a shelter suit, an anti-concussion bandeau and a boiler suit for ARP work.

are not so smart, because we are bearing … yet another share in the war,' Oliver Lyttelton, the President of the Board of Trade, told the nation. 'When you feel tired of your old clothes remember that by making them do you are contributing some part of an aeroplane, a gun or a tank.'[3]

Women should look smart, but it was regarded as unpatriotic and shameful to flaunt new clothes. Posters and advertisements depicting the swastika-infested Squander Bug, who jumped up and down gleefully every time a woman spent money unnecessarily, was there to remind them that they were only playing into Hitler's hands.

Clothes had become much more expensive, anyway. By the time rationing was introduced, they cost 69 percent more than they had in 1939, partly owing to the introduction of purchase tax in October 1940. Most garments and footwear carried a 16 percent tax, but silk and gloves – the materials having been imported – veils, hairnets, belts, suspenders, shoe laces, corset laces and hair pins carried 33 percent tax, a rather disproportionate amount of this extra tax being carried by women, who wore these items.

Of course wages had also increased and there were plenty of good causes to which people could redirect their spare cash. They could lend the money to the government by buying saving stamps, or they might contribute to 'Warships Week' or 'Wings for Victory Week'. There were also 'Spitfire Funds', where people from a particular town clubbed together to raise enough money to buy a fighter plane.

By 1942 when American servicemen started to arrive, the booklet *Over There* warned them: 'If British civilians look dowdy and badly dressed, it is not because they do not like good clothes or know how to wear them. All clothing is rationed and the British know that they help war production by wearing an old suit or dress until it cannot be patched any longer. Old clothes are "good form".'[4]

For the first 12 months from 1 June 1941 everyone in the country was to receive 66 coupons in the ration book. Clothing coupons could be used in any shop, unlike the food coupons, which had to be used in the shop where the holder was registered.

Every item of clothing was given a points value, according to how much labour and material were needed to produce it. Initially, a man's overcoat or lined raincoat required 16 coupons, plus the cash, a woman's dress 11, a cardigan five, a pair of pants three, a bra, two, and a handkerchief, one. By the end of the war, however, the cost of a woman's winter coat advertised at Clapham Junction's Arding and Hobbs cost 18 coupons and £14 7s 6d, a considerable sum when the average weekly wage was £4 to £5. Items of children's clothing were given a lower points value, to take account of the fact that they were constantly outgrowing their clothes and needing new ones.

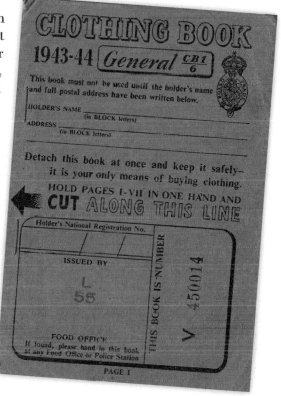

By 1943 a detachable clothing coupons section was issued with the main ration book, so that each member of the family could look after their own, as opposed to the food ration books, which were usually kept by 'Mum', who did the food shopping for the whole family. When a new set of clothing coupons was issued, unused coupons from the previous one remained valid; they could be carried over. In theory, it was illegal to offer loose coupons and retailers were not supposed to accept them, but in fact this was widely practised, especially as parents often sacrificed their own coupons for clothes-conscious daughters, or people gave their coupons to a friend who had an urgent need for them – getting married, perhaps.

A little bit of 'fiddling' among family and friends eased the pressure and did not result in clothes shortages for others. Of course, the same did not apply to retailers, who could sell clothes only in exchange for the correct number of coupons. Eva Allpress, who worked in a draper's shop, recalls that customers were always asking them to break the rules, but they couldn't.

Above: Clothes rationing began on 1 June 1941. Everyone received 66 coupons for the first year. After that the number of coupons per person was steadily reduced.

Manual workers and miners were given extra coupons to buy working clothes, but nurses had to surrender 10 coupons a year for their uniform and the few still in domestic service were required to hand over coupons for the uniform their employers expected them to wear. Parents of children at private schools were similarly disadvantaged, since schools made no concessions to the situation and expected pupils to be supplied with school uniforms in their entirety – meaning that the rest of the family often had to pool their coupons to provide it.

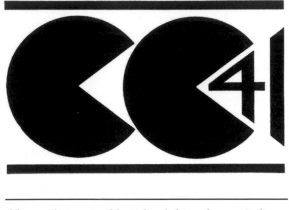

Above: The insignia of the Utility clothing scheme – Civilian Clothing, 1941 – was synonymous with good design and value for money.

The rich were less hard hit by rationing than everyone else. When it came to food, they could afford to eat in restaurants. As to clothing, they had large wardrobes of quality clothes to see out the war. Young women who reached adulthood during the war might borrow their mothers' pre-war evening dresses; alternatively, they could follow Scarlett O'Hara's example in the film *Gone with the Wind* and run up a gown from an old curtain.

Middle-class diaries record a steady dwindling of clothing as the war progressed. Whereas before the war a man might buy two new suits a year, now he had to decide between a new suit, an overcoat or a raincoat; where he might have bought three shirts at once, now he would buy only one, if he was lucky. Meanwhile, as double cuffs were no longer provided, his wife would have to cut off the tail of his shirt in order to make new cuffs for it.

The working class were at a disadvantage from the start. The scant clothing they possessed generally consisted of cheap, insubstantial items made of poor-quality material with mean seams, often bought at market stalls. Cheap clothing was not really cheap, because it had a short life. Shoes and boots, often bought 'on tick' (paid off weekly over many weeks) were badly made and needed frequent repair.

Even with coupons, cash was also required. The poor were often unable to afford clothing and were tempted to sell their coupons. They found ready buyers among black marketeers and the well-to-do. The 'black market' cost of coupons rose from about 2s 6d for a whole book in 1941 to £5 by 1944, while the rate for individual coupons rose from 3d to as much as 3s.

Genuine second-hand clothing was exempt from coupons and still available at market stalls. Second-hand clothes dealers were doing well out of the war. Women whose husbands had been killed or were POWs or missing were glad of the money they could obtain by selling his clothes to dealers.

When someone died, his or her unused clothing coupons were supposed to be returned to the Registrar of Births and Deaths. It is perhaps not surprising how many people seemed to have one last shopping bonanza before they died, because few of these coupons were actually returned.

Mothers often went without in order to clothe their families and it was usually out of their coupon ration that scarce household items, such as linen and towels, were acquired. The Board of Trade's *Make Do and Mend* booklet remonstrated: 'It isn't fair to expect the housewife to be the only one who gives up her coupons. Everyone in the household

must contribute coupons when new towels are needed.'[5] People were advised to take their towel with them if they had to go away and they must bring their own towel to the hairdresser's.

In February 1942 Hugh Dalton, a Labour politician, became President of the Board of Trade. A month later he announced a further crackdown on the amount of labour and cloth expended on clothing. Utility fashion was launched. It was men who took the brunt of the cuts and proved most resistant to the changes. All jackets must be single-breasted with only three buttons on the front and none on the cuffs. Only three pockets were permitted on a jacket and two on a waistcoat. Trouser legs were to be only 19 inches wide and elastic waistbands were forbidden. Socks were reduced from knee to ankle length.

Dalton's ban on trouser turn-ups caused uproar. Even Members of the House of Commons begged him to reconsider. He refused to bow to pressure. The annihilation of trouser turn-ups would save millions of square feet of cloth a year, he claimed. It was a small price to pay for the war effort. 'Some must lose lives and limbs,' he said, 'others only the turn-ups on their trousers.'[6] Tailors who made trousers too long 'by mistake' so that they might be turned up were prosecuted. As a final blow to male pride the age level at which boys went into long trousers was raised to 12; happily for John Allpress, he had already achieved that rite of passage.

Top: Trouser turn-ups were banned in order to save material.
Above: Utility clothing was introduced in 1941 to save on labour and materials. The simplified designs, produced by Britain's leading fashion designers, were applauded.

Utility had a more beneficial effect on women's clothing. Hallmarked on the garment by two abstract-looking 'C' shapes dovetailed with 41, denoting Civilian Clothing, 1941, it became synonymous with good, unfussy design and value for money. In order to make Utility appealing to women, the government asked the Incorporated Society of London Fashion Designers, which included such luminaries as Captain Molyneux, Hardy Amies, Norman Hartnell, and Worth, to produce designs for the key staples of the female wardrobe: a top coat, a suit, an afternoon dress and a cotton overall dress. Evening dresses, which upper- and middle-class women had routinely worn before the war for dinner, the theatre and the opera, were not included, since such fripperies were now frowned upon.

The designs were submitted for the Board of Trade's approval and a selection of them was then mass-produced.

In Utility, women of all classes had access to well-designed clothing at affordable prices, for a ceiling was placed on the prices retailers could charge. The average price of a suit was 92s 10d, a coat 83s 7d, a cotton dress 17s 10d, a blouse 21s 5d. Utility clothing did not carry purchase tax. It was essentially democratic, the society woman sharing the same designer as the factory girl.

As with men's clothing, the emphasis was on simplicity. There were to be no fancy trimmings, unnecessary buttons or pockets, extra stitching, tucks and pleats; a maximum width was stipulated for belts, collars, sleeves. The result, best personified in the classic suit or costume, was severe but elegant – a jacket which was padded at the shoulders and nipped in at the waist and a straight skirt whose hemline rose as high as 19 inches from the ground. The

Left: Women in factories started wearing turbans to keep their long hair out of the machinery, but they became popular among women generally.
Above: When Betty Allpress married Cyril McCann in 1946 she hired a traditional white wedding dress.

fashion pundit Colin McDowell believed it was the nearest thing to a civilian uniform for women in the history of dress. Similarly, the pretty frocks women and girls wore were short and straight, with cute short sleeves and a waistline to show off that svelte wartime figure.

Before the war it had been considered 'fast' for women to wear trousers, but now these were widely adopted. Women like the Allpress sisters were queuing for food, buses and trains, travelling to work long, unsociable hours, often trudging through bomb-damaged, unlit streets, or spending long, cold nights out in the Anderson shelter. Women worked in the factories and on the land, drove buses and trains, patrolled the streets on ARP duty. Trousers were warm and practical, especially as stockings were so hard to obtain. For the duration of the war they were tolerated, but the inevitable backlash came in 1945: 'It's time that women, off duty, stopped wearing men's clothes,' thundered the *Sunday Graphic*.[7]

Above: When Bill Allpress married May in 1941 the bride wore a smart suit, which would do good service for many years.

Hats had been universally worn by both sexes and all classes before the war. Perhaps because they were not rationed, they became scarce and expensive. Young women were delighted to throw off the convention. The Princesses Elizabeth and Margaret Rose made the wearing of headscarves acceptable, while turbans – worn by women in factories to keep their long hair out of the machinery – became popular among all women, as did the snood – a sort of bag of elasticated netting which would hold the hair bunched together at the back of the neck. With opportunities for hair washing or going to the hairdresser much curtailed, it was a relief to be able to bunch up the hair out of sight.

Before the war, Alice and Jessie Allpress had had lovely white weddings, even though a white wedding remained beyond the reach of most working-class people until the 1950s. In wartime a new white wedding dress was considered bad form for people of any class. Some might borrow a wedding dress and, indeed, some dresses went up the aisle many times, while others might resort to making a wedding dress and veil out of curtain lace, which was not rationed, or even parachute silk. Most brides, however, sensibly opted to invest their cash and coupons in a smart outfit that would do good service in the future. When Bill Allpress married May in 1941 the bride wore a suit with a little hat tilted on the side of her head, and similarly when Harry married Thelma in 1945 she wore a pale blue dress adorned with curtain lace. Since Harry possessed only his army boots his sisters generously gave him some of their clothing coupons with which to buy a pair of smart black shoes[8] for the occasion. When Betty Allpress married Cyril in 1946, she hired a wedding dress from a film company (the dress that had appeared in the film *Waterloo Road*) for a considerable sum in the region of £3 or £4. It was an ingenious idea.

Clothes rationing persisted beyond the war. It was no wonder, then, that when Princess Elizabeth married Lieutenant Philip Mountbatten in November 1947 her spectacular white wedding dress – to which family and friends had contributed their coupons – would make such an impact.

◆

'To wear clothes that have been patched and darned – perhaps many times – is to show oneself a true patriot,' Hugh Dalton announced in 1943, 'even when old clothes aren't exciting, they are a war-winning fashion to follow with which to speed the day of victory.'[9] With clothing rationed, it was imperative to extract the last ounce of wear out of the clothes one had. Women's magazines and the press were full of hints and tips about how to preserve clothes and re-adapt old for new. *Woman* advised its readers that their clothes would last that little bit longer if they kept their elbows off the table and their hands out of their pockets; they should keep their feet in their shoes, rather than taking them out and resting them on the heels, while gloves should never be kept on while powdering one's nose. A coat would last longer if a handbag was not rubbed up against it while walking or queuing.

The Board of Trade's *Make Do and Mend* booklet, price 3d, also laid heavy emphasis on how to care for clothes to make them last as long as possible. Clothes should be put away 'in the condition in which you will want to wear them when you take them out again'. They should be cleaned and mended before being carefully placed on hangers, with the wardrobe door shut tightly 'to keep out dust and moth'. War was declared against the moth. *Make Do and Mend* advised its readers to keep an eye out for eggs and grubs behind collars and in turnings and 'if there are any signs of moth, brush vigorously first, then iron with a hot iron over a damp cloth.' Clothes should be brushed and shaken at least once a month and hung outside – 'sun and air kill the grub' – while cupboards and drawers should be scrubbed regularly.[10]

Shoes were precious, as any woman who tramped up and down the length of Oxford Street looking for a pair of the right size or who queued for a ticket to allow her to join the queue at the shoe shop would verify. 'Have them repaired as

Above: The *Make Do and Mend* booklet was full of practical tips.

soon as they show signs of wear; in particular, never walk down the heels,' the booklet advised. 'Shoes should be put on trees or stuffed with paper as soon as you take them off because the leather is warm and supple then and can be coaxed into shape.'[11]

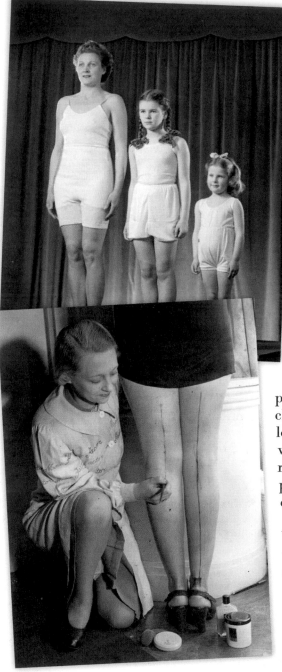

Utility shoes allowed a heel no more than 2 inches high. Wooden soles, or woodies, lasted longer than conventional soles, while wedges became popular since they provided more support than high heels, allowing the wearer to walk further or stand still in a queue that bit longer. Some resorted to wooden clogs, which never wore out, but they were desperately uncomfortable.

Mothers were at their wits' end to provide new shoes for growing children and were reluctant to force them into second-hand shoes. 'Why not exchange children's outgrown shoes?' the booklet suggested.

'In countless cupboards throughout the country, children's shoes are lying idle, not because they are outworn but because they are outgrown. What a help it would be if mothers would pass these shoes on to a friend, whose child could wear them. Or perhaps the local school, welfare clinic or some local woman's organisation may already be running a children's shoe exchange – or planning to run one. It's worth finding out, anyhow.'[12]

Women were reduced to making their own underwear. Rather than spend coupons on knickers, a woman might make up her own from blackout material or parachute silk, which were not rationed. Eva Allpress was lucky in that she was able to obtain off-cuts and throw-outs from travelling salesmen and no doubt contrived some clever purpose for them, sharing them with the rest of the family.

All women still wore corsets and these presented a constant difficulty. The three main components – rubber, steel and cotton – were all in short supply. To save on labour and inadvertently compound the problem, the Board of Trade asked the

Top: There was nothing fancy or frilly about Utility underwear, but it was warm and practical. As an example of cost, the woman's long-line knickers cost 3/11 and three coupons, while the little girl's wool vest cost 3/6 ha'ppence, plus one coupon.
Above: Stockings were precious and a woman sometimes had to do without them. Drawing a black line up the leg to look like a seam helped created the illusion that she was wearing stockings.

Corset Trade Association to have their manufacturers design a simple corset that could be made by comparatively unskilled workers, which meant only an inferior product was obtainable in wartime. The *Make Do and Mend* booklet advised:

'Now that rubber is so scarce your corset is one of your most precious possessions. Be sure first of all that it fits. In particular, don't wear one too small, as this stretches the rubber and puts too much strain on it. Bones worn in the wrong place – either too high or too low – will break. The greatest enemies of rubber are sunlight and grease. Never let your girdle get really dirty. Wash it frequently, and, if you possibly can, have at least two corsets, and wear them alternately.'[13]

Bras were another casualty of the war. As with the corset, the wearer must apply 'the golden rule of patient persuasion' when putting it on; it should never be tugged or yanked. 'A few extra minutes in adjusting it will repay you in months of longer wear,'[14] Gossard advised its customers. In extremis, a woman could make her own bra using small scraps of material from worn petticoats: 'Use an old, well-fitting brassiere for a pattern.'[15]

'Are you worried about elastic?' *Woman* asked its readers. 'Unless you're in the black market, how are you keeping your panties in the correct position, not to mention pyjama trousers now that the stuff is so scarce?'[16] Many had replaced pyjamas with nightdresses, since they took six rather than eight coupons and did not require precious elastic, while camiknickers proved practical, secured with string or buttons.

Silk stockings were the item the Allpress sisters missed most. Unless one was prepared to trade in the black market, go out with an American serviceman, or queue for hours when a rare supply came into a shop, it was virtually impossible to obtain them.

'Rinse new stockings through warm water before wearing them, and again after each wearing,' *Make Do and Mend* suggested. 'You should use your precious soap for washing them only when they are dirty. You can wash them after your bath in the same water, using soap for the soles only.'[17]

Desperate measures were applied to preserve precious stockings:

'Strengthen new stockings before wearing them by reinforcing the heels and toes with widely spaced shadow darning, and sewing two circular patches, cut from the tops of old stockings, on the tops where you clip your suspenders. Also run double rows of stitching round the tops of the stockings just above the join. When the foot is too worn to darn, a new foot can be cut from an old stocking and sewn on.'[18]

Some women went bare-legged through the summer and as far into the autumn as the cold permitted. Others drew a black line down the back of the leg to look as if they were wearing stockings, or resorted to using gravy browning or a cup of cold cocoa, applied with a sponge or cotton wool – all of which tended to run in embarrassing streaks in the rain. Leading cosmetic brands such as Cyclax and Elizabeth Arden produced stockingless cream, but this was rare and expensive.

Above: More women then than now could sew and they would habitually make their own and their children's clothes. Those who could not sew were encouraged to join 'Make Do and Mend' classes.

Fortunately, more women in the 1930s knew how to ply a needle. Girls like the Allpress sisters were taught housewifery, needlework and cookery as part of the school curriculum and they would have learned from their mother's example. They were better equipped than women today to follow the Board of Trade's 'Make Do and Mend' campaign personified by the cartoon character, 'Mrs Sew-and-Sew'.

Those who could not sew were urged to join sewing classes. The WVS and WI held 'Make Do and Mend' classes, as well as organizing groups of women to carry out repair work for others, such as the overalls of local war workers. Those who could sew were encouraged to pass on their expertise to others: 'If you are one of the clever ones who already know how to Make do and Mend, don't keep your ideas to yourself, but pass them on to your neighbours. Start a sewing party where you can pool your equipment, such as scissors, pins, piece-bags, dressmakers' dummies and sewing machines.'[19]

Newspapers worked hard to educate their readers. *The Daily Mail*'s 'Sew and Save' column provided solutions to such problems as planning a wardrobe, home dressmaking and hints to achieve smartness. Women's magazines such as *Good Housekeeping, Woman* and *Woman's Own, Woman's Weekly* and *Women and Beauty* had always shown women how to dress cheaply but smartly on a budget and were full of beauty tips and advice on how to make the best of oneself. Now they devoted their whole energies to the war effort, encouraging and admonishing their readers by turns.

Darning and patching was tedious, laborious and time-consuming, especially for women like the Allpress sisters, who already spent long hours after work on other wartime duties. 'A stitch in time now saves not only extra work in the end, but precious coupons,' *Make Do and Mend* reminded its readers. 'Always carry a needle and cotton and mending silk with you,' it urged, 'this will save many a ladder in stockings or prevent the loss of buttons; your friends will thank you, too. How many times have you heard someone say, "Has anyone got a needle and cotton?"'[20]

Washing lines revealed the full history of a family's war on the clothing front. When even darning and patching no longer served, there was still another task:

> 'When finally discarding clothes that have gone too far to renovate, be sure to cut out any good bits of material to put in your piece bag; pieces of stockinette and old corsets in particular are invaluable for patching other garments of the same type. Odd scraps of thick wool can be unravelled for darning. Be sure to have a well-stocked work basket with all the coloured cottons and mending materials you might need.'[21]

Spare scraps of material could also be pressed into service as tea cosies (to keep that precious ration of tea hot as long as possible), coverings for buttons, kettle holders and furniture polishers.

Right: A model demonstrating how old clothes can be re-worked and worn as new. She wears a black chiffon blouse made from an old dinner dress, a long black skirt made from another old dress bartered from a friend, and a white turban which can also be worn with various daytime outfits.

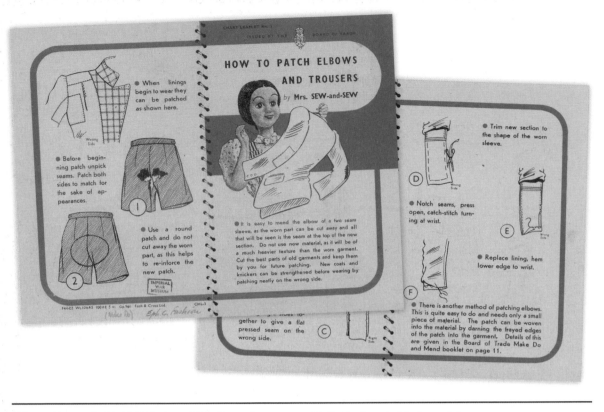

Above: The Board of Trade's 'Make Do and Mend' campaign was personified by the character Mrs Sew-and-Sew.

Opposite: Children grew out of and wore out their clothes quickly. Mothers were advised that it was more economical to exchange their clothes than to constantly re-adapt them. However, clothes could be reinforced to extend their useful life.

Knitting wool was on coupons, so that it paid to unpick and recycle old sweaters. 'New life for old woollies' ran the government slogan.

Thousands of women in the 1930s had their clothes made for them or habitually made their own and their children's clothes, using the Bestway fashion books for home dressmaking and patterns in the magazines. Now they had to take this a step further and re-adapt old clothes for new ones:

> 'Cut fabric from the backs of shirts to replace badly worn fronts, and use near-matching material for the backs. The best portions of two badly worn shirts can be used to make one good one,' was one suggestion, while 'Overcoats which are beyond renovation-repairs can be cut down into skirts or jackets for yourself, or coats, knickers and dungarees for the children.'[22]

The children were to be the recipients of a lot of these cut-downs. 'An old skirt will make one pair of knickers and a little play-skirt for a seven-year-old,' it was suggested. However, 'Since children often grow out of their clothes long before they are badly worn, mothers would probably often find it more economical to exchange clothes than to cut down an older child's clothes to fit a younger. Material is always lost in this process.'[23]

Blankets were turned into warm dressing-gowns, while worn sheets were to be given a new lease of life:

'When sheets are thin in the centre, cut them in half lengthwise, turn sides to middle, and run and fell on the wrong side. Then tack and hem the sides ... A double sheet may then be too small for a double bed, and can be used for a single one. Single sheets that are too small can be used for cot sheets or cut up for tea towels. The very finest parts of good linen sheets can be made into men's handkerchiefs or used to patch men's underwear.'[24]

Some stores offered a renovation service. It must have been very tempting to cheat and avoid the hours spent on making do and mending by letting the store take the strain. This would cost money, however, so that it was not an option for the Allpresses.

◆

To achieve the wartime look of soft curls resting on the shoulder all the Allpress sisters used to put their hair into curlers every night. Nellie recalls the night their father warned them he'd heard rattles – the signal for an impending gas attack. 'If I were you, girls, I'd take your curlers out, because I thought I heard rattles,'[25] he told them. It was impossible to get your gas mask on if you were wearing curlers.

The Allpresses' determination to look their best, despite wartime deprivations and the precariousness of their existence under enemy attack from the skies, accords perfectly with the mood of the time. Looking one's best was linked with patriotism and was good for morale.

Women were determined to keep their hair long – the film star Veronica Lake's look being much admired – even though short hair would have been more practical. With shampoo and hot water in short supply and nights spent in the air raid shelter, it was impossible to wash hair regularly. A quick steaming over a basin of hot water was supposed to put new life into hair.

With fuel shortages and the need to conserve fuel for the war industry 'a hot bath is not always possible, but a quick sponge all over with lukewarm water, to which a dash of eau-de-cologne is added, gives a fresh glow.'[26] The Allpresses washed every day, of course, but like many families – even the small proportion who owned an inside bathroom – they had a bath only once a week. On bath night they lifted the tin bath from the back wall of the Priory Grove house and brought it in to the scullery, where it was filled with hot water from the copper.

After the fall of France in 1940 the chances of finding or acquiring perfume was almost non-existent. Even something as essential as soap was rationed. From February 1942 every person was allotted four coupons for every four-week period. Soap could be bought from any retailer, and one coupon could be exchanged for 4 ounces of hard soap, 3 ounces of toilet soap, 3 ounces of soap flakes or 6 ounces of soap powder. Women had to make a choice and there was seldom enough to cover all needs, but families could pool their rations.

Two criticisms American servicemen had about British women were that their teeth were bad and they smelt. They were warned in *Over There*: 'One of the things the English always had enough of in the past was soap. Now it is so scarce that girls working in factories often cannot get the grease off their hands or out of their hair.'[27] Toothbrushes were very hard to come by. Deodorant was not universally used pre-war – talcum powder was applied to the under-arm area instead – but wartime advertisements promoted its use. 'Girls in Air Force Blue Need Odo-Ro-No' spelt one advertisement, depicting a young woman managing a barrage balloon.

Above: It was advisable to use cosmetics from a recognized brand name, and to take the container back to the shop for refills.

Cosmetics and other beauty products were limited because ingredients such as glycerin, castor oil, talc, fats, petroleum and alcohol were either in short supply or needed for the war effort, while cosmetic manufacturers' priorities switched to producing sun barriers for the military rather than creams to improve the female complexion. Before the war respectable women wore only a minimum amount of make-up. Paradoxically, during the war they started wearing more than ever before, an emphatic red lipstick such as 'Auxiliary Red' being promoted as 'a red badge of courage'.

Women got into the habit of taking their lipstick and powder cases for refills, rather than wasting money and resources on new packaging. They became adept at improvising. Soot, charcoal and shoe polish were pressed into service as eye shadow, while lard, although rationed, could be used as a cleanser when proper cleansing cream disappeared from the shops.

◆

With the end of the war people could be forgiven for thinking that new clothes and cosmetics were just around the corner. How wrong they were. Rationing continued and what quality clothing was produced was for export only, to boost the post-war economy.

In the grey, dismal era of post-war austerity the British remained shabby and threadbare, their wardrobes even more depleted. Clothes rationing became a little less stringent in 1948, but it was not until March of the following year that it finally ended, allowing women to put away their sewing kits and the nation to indulge in some new clothes.

IT IS ILLEGAL
to offer or accept
LOOSE COUPONS
of a kind comprised in a ration document
except for orders by post or in other
circumstances expressly authorised
by the Board of Trade

OFFENDERS ARE LIABLE TO PROSECUTION

9
Under the Counter and Off the Back of a Lorry

'People used to beg of you to let them have stuff, and you couldn't.'[1]

Eva Allpress

Crime flourished in wartime. The war presented the criminal with new opportunities. Bomb-damaged premises and the fact that many houses were left empty made breaking and entering a cinch. Looting of bomb-sites, sometimes while the dead and injured lay trapped, was not uncommon. Pilfering from employers was rife. Robberies from warehouses and hijacking of lorries fed the black market, which thrived as wartime scarcities bit harder and Britain entered a new era of austerity at the end of the war. Even respectable men and women were increasingly drawn into a dalliance with crime, whether it was receiving something extra from 'under the counter' or a little luxury 'off the back of a lorry'.

From the outbreak of war the government assumed complete control over the lives of the people. British life would now be ruled by Defence Regulations rather than Acts of Parliament. The government issued thousands of new regulations concerning all aspects of life, great and small. This rash of wartime legislation meant that there were simply more laws to break, even inadvertently.

The Ministry of Labour and National Service had total power to direct all able-bodied men and women of

Left: It was illegal to offer or accept loose clothing coupons – that is, those not contained in a section of the ration book with the person's name on it – but some shopkeepers turned a blind eye.

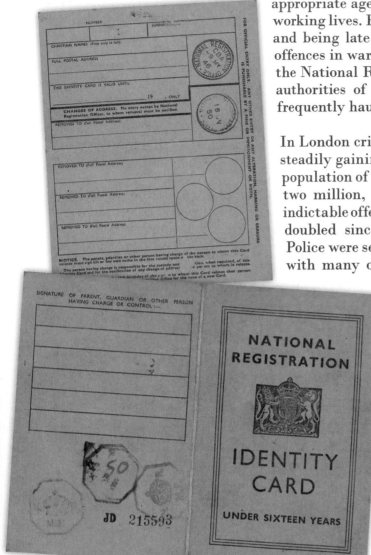

appropriate age into work and largely controlled their working lives. Failure to obey the Ministry's directives and being late or absent from work were indictable offences in wartime. British subjects registered under the National Registration Act 1939 had to notify the authorities of a change of address. Offenders were frequently hauled before the courts and fined.

In London crime was rampant and the criminal was steadily gaining the upper hand. During the war the population of Greater London had dropped by nearly two million, to 6,908,000, and yet the number of indictable offences per 1,000 of population had almost doubled since 1938. Of course, the Metropolitan Police were seriously under strength during the war, with many of its best young men in the services. In 1945 John Gosling, head of Scotland Yard's new Ghost Squad, with a special brief to infiltrate the criminal underworld and combat crime, had no illusions about the challenge facing the police:

'Against the depleted ranks of the police was ranged a new type of criminal, cunning, ruthless and well-informed. Many had served in the Armed Forces – some with distinction – and many more were deserters. They were younger, fitter, harder, more resourceful and more energetic than the pre-war criminal.'[2]

Above: Everyone had to carry an identity card bearing their name and address, even youngsters. Identity cards had to be produced on demand by the police. Deserters often carried stolen or forged identity cards.

Rationing and shortages meant rich pickings for the criminal ready to exploit the situation, according to Gosling:

'Lorry-loads of tea, sugar, butter, clothes, cigarettes and whisky disappeared from the streets or were stolen from warehouses. Jewellery and cash vanished from private houses into the pockets of thieves who worked like phantoms. Furs and rings, clothing and petrol coupons, carpets, lipsticks, typewriters, razor blades, shoes – anything with a ready cash value was loot for the army of the underworld. The figures of stolen property rose to astronomical proportions: millions of cigarettes, hundreds of thousands of forged or stolen coupons, thousands of bottles of liquor, thousands of pounds worth of jewels.'[3]

During the war most people obeyed the rules on rationing out of patriotism, but there were always some greedy consumers determined to beat the system, or who snatched at opportunities, often on impulse. As the war drew to a close sacrifice no longer seemed to be necessary, however. Impatient with the never-ending shortages, more and more previously law-abiding citizens were complicit in breaking the law.

Even so, the black market in Britain bore no relation to the black market in, say, Paris after the liberation, where in the absence of rationing to ensure fair shares for all, it raged out of control. A little black market activity could be seen as a useful safety valve, relieving the build-up of social and economic pressures, just as illegal gaming and betting offered another kind or outlet – whatever the Treasury might say about the need to direct surplus cash into war savings. The black market needed to be kept in check, however, and officials managed this by being ever vigilant and imposing fines and prison sentences on those caught breaking the law.

Nellie Allpress admits that they were short of 'little luxuries' but denies that any of the family ever participated in black market activities – even if they had wanted to, the goods were anyway too expensive for them. Others, who had the cash and were prepared to pay the inflated prices demanded for scarce or rationed items, were not so scrupulous. A Hoxton woman readily confessed: 'We didn't go without. There was a big black market operating, especially in tinned goods and American nylons which we all wanted because they never wore out. We never went short.'[4]

People were tired of hardship and longed for those little extras that made life brighter and more comfortable. The black market was there to provide them and thrived, especially as wartime restrictions were succeeded by post-war austerity.

'No one thought they was doing anything wrong buying this stuff,'[5] a Walthamstow woman claimed. But it was wrong. It was against the law – even treasonable, since it undermined the war effort.

The *Daily Mail* reminded readers that goods bought 'off the ration' were stolen goods. Just as culpable as the black marketeer was the housewife who bought produce from her friendly grocer 'under the counter' or paid for that 'little bit extra' without coupons. Uniformed police had powers to stop and search anyone carrying what looked like a suspicious package.

Stealing or fabricating ration books and clothing coupons offered an obvious opportunity for the criminal. As they were less sophisticated in design than bank notes, they were easy to forge. Illicit printing presses were busy churning them out, although it was hardly necessary, since they were so easy to obtain. Officially produced coupons could be appropriated at the printers or in the post. On at least one occasion an armed robbery was carried out on a food office – Tulse Hill on 18 May 1943 – the prize being 2,000 of the new issue of 1943–1944 ration books. As the Food Office only carried out spot checks on the number of coupons returned to them there was every chance to cheat either by putting less than the stated number of coupons, usually 500 a time, into the envelope or merely stuffing the whole envelope with newspaper cuttings.

Food Office officials were not above selling coupons themselves. An assistant at the Food Office in Hackney, formerly a councillor in the borough, extracted coupons from the office and passed them to a businessman who passed them to a restauranteur, who sold them to customers at a massive profit, of which a proportion went to the official. He received a five-year prison sentence. If the bureaucrats themselves were allowed to join the scam and get away with it, the whole rationing system would collapse.

There was a brisk trade in stolen coupons, as they were passed along a network of buyers and sellers, and offloaded on susceptible members of the public.

Arthur Harding, who had been in the East End rag trade and helped the Ghost Squad, recalled:

> 'The Ghost Squad were interested in anything that was detrimental to the war – possessing coupons, or black market business. There were people who were making fortunes for themselves out of rationing. Vast quantities of forged coupons were put on the market. In one case they were selling coupons at a shilling a time and when people who bought them came to undo them, all they found were bits of paper. The crooks in the West End were raiding the town halls to find out where the coupons were stored, and pinching the whole lot. They would sell the coupons at 4d or 6d each according to the value of the coupon. The forging was done in the West End – all around Shaftesbury Avenue, but they were sold in the East End. I knew some of the bleeding villains that was at it.'[6]

It was a criminal offence to buy rationed goods without handing over coupons. As Eva Allpress found in the draper's shop where she worked, people would beg the retailer to slip them something 'off the ration', but a law-abiding retailer simply would not or could not do it. It was best to be honest. Undercover men and women from the Board of Trade would enter shops, sometimes provoking a shopkeeper to break the law by spinning some hard-luck story to procure goods without coupons. Inspectors from the Ministry of Food would do the same in restaurants, posing as customers to ensure that the restaurant was not charging more than the statutory 5s for a meal or serving more than one protein course.

Some shopkeepers were on the fiddle, however, selling rationed goods without coupons or above the permitted price, or not returning the correct number of coupons to the Food Office. These retailers were obviously obtaining their goods illicitly, knowing that they could make a decent profit out of the transactions. An East End woman says: 'I remember taking my ration book to the butcher in Hoxton. If we gave him some extra money he would give us extra meat. There was a Welsh dairy down Cremer Street. The lady there would offer me butter and tins of salmon and other things that were difficult to get.'[7]

Given the national obsession with food after years of rationing, there was every incentive for sellers to flout the regulations, as there was always a ready market. Markets towns on the outer perimeter of London, particularly those easily accessed from the East End, did a roaring trade in illicit foodstuffs: hens officially marked for breeding were sold for human consumption; horseflesh was sold as stewing steak, and so on.

Markets were a free for all, in which coupons for food, clothes and other commodities rarely changed hands. No coupons were required for second-hand clothes, of course, making it easy to conceal or disguise the sale of brand new garments that did demand coupons. If caught selling new clothes as second-hand, stall-holders were quick to claim they were shop soiled.

Soho's Berwick Street Market, just a few streets away from Rainbow Corner, the club for American servicemen in Piccadilly, meant that it was a good place to pick up nylon stockings and razor blades, supplied by the Americans and sold under the counter and off the ration. In the East End, markets such as Brick Lane and Petticoat Lane were also doing a brisk trade, as one visitor noted:

Above: It was illegal to break the official price controls on food or to sell food without a specific licence, but markets were a bit of a free for all.

'The wife ... stopped at one of the stalls, which was being served by a woman who was wrapped in several layers of mufflers, great coats and snow boots and wore a knitted pirate's cap. She had just lifted the corner of a piece of sacking, part of the stall, and had withdrawn from under it a pair of silk stockings for a customer (her ostensible trade was in vegetables). Later, we saw her drive off in a taxi, after her day's work.'[8]

Cosmetics were expensive and in short supply, increasing the temptation to produce them illegally and sell them in markets. These cosmetics could seriously damage your health, as the Ministry of Information's documentary, *Black Market Beauties*, was at pains to point out.

Stall-holders who were selling goods without taking coupons – which they would need if they were to replenish their stock through the proper legal channels – were obviously selling stock which had been obtained through theft or other nefarious means in the first place. With the profits they were making, they could of course procure stolen coupons to buy stock, but why bother, when they were doing such a roaring under-the-counter trade? The police tended to leave the patrol of markets to the Board of Trade inspectors, who were usually pretty conspicuous. Traders relied on tic-tac men employing the hand signals they had previously used at the bookies (before the wartime restriction on horse racing put paid

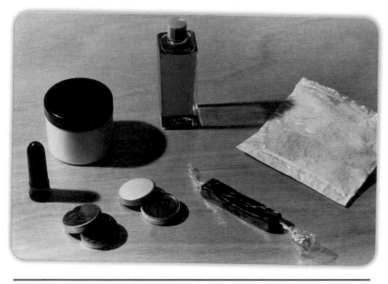

Above: Illegally manufactured cosmetics sold on the black market could be dangerous.

to that career) to warn them of the approach of undercover inspectors. If an inspector did, by chance, manage to infiltrate the market without detection he or, more usually, she would easily be led to the culprits by the size of the crowd around the stall.

◆

It was easy for black marketeers to draw others into their network. With the labour shortage, warehouses were sparsely guarded. Night watchmen often turned a blind eye, or were bribed to leave factory or warehouse gates open so that lorries could be driven directly into the yards and make a swift getaway. They worked on the understanding that if they were arrested and sent to prison, their families would be looked after while they were inside. A watchman who 'talked' when in police custody was likely to suffer 'a regrettable accident' when he was released.

One ruse was to sell stolen goods to a shopkeeper, then to rob the shop, since the shopkeeper was hardly in a position to 'squeal' to the police.

Burglaries fed the black market. By the end of the war fur coats – which were scarce, since none had been produced during the war – were the most prized loot. There was a rash of burglaries in the wealthy districts of Hampstead, St. John's Wood and Knightsbridge, as women wearing a fur coat were followed home and the house watched until she was rash enough to leave not wearing the coat, when the thieves would break in to snatch it.

There was a surge in criminal activity among women, as reported in the *Star* at the beginning of 1945.

> 'There is a slight upward grade in thefts by women pickpockets, who have been operating in the West End, and cases of highway robbery by women have been reported to the police. Thefts of bags and coats left on chairs or tables in dance halls are frequent and have been mainly traced to women. But women burglars are the problem, and Scotland Yard intends to solve it.'[9]

In an era of shortages it was all too tempting to steal from one's employer. Pilfering had always been endemic, but in wartime it took on a new urgency, as thieves either stole for themselves or to sell on. There was no problem off-loading stolen goods, because the black market was so eager to buy – acting as a stimulant to crime. 'There was a lot of thieving going on, lots of goods for sale,' an East Ender recalls. 'People would come knocking at our doors asking whether we wanted to buy things.'[10]

All levels of staff were involved in illegal activity, from management to the clerk and shop floor worker. There was an increase in white collar crime and council officials were not immune. Shortage of staff meant that supervision was slack. In Croydon an official employed by the War Damage Chattels Department investigating claims by householders for furniture damaged in the bombing was taking bogus fees. He was rumbled when he concluded an interview with the casual: 'If it is convenient to you, Mr Harrison, there is a fee of £2 2s to be paid.'[11] The claimant happened to be a war reserve police constable, who knew very well that there was no official charge for the war damage assessment service.

In wartime companies and factories were subject to myriad regulations and controls. They had to account to the various ministries for the use of the raw materials they were allotted and for the goods they were bound to supply. Even so, some businessmen exceeded their quota for production, selling the surplus on the black market, or claimed government money for employees they did not have.

By the same token, the job of honest employers was made harder still by the number of employees who were ready to steal from them. In spite of paying good wages, Ford's of Dagenham suffered theft on a grand scale. It was amazing what thieves were prepared to smuggle out secreted about their person – on at least one occasion tools were recovered that were considered so essential to production they could not be spared from the works to be shown later in court as evidence.

In the railways, wages were not good and morale was poor. Railway pay had been perennially low since before the war (a grievance that was to lead to a great deal of strike action at the war's end), and so railway employees were easily seduced by the black market. Conscription also meant that the railways had lost a lot of good men and had had to take what recruits were available, sometimes planted by the criminal fraternity.

It was impossible to guard railway depots thoroughly, so that in wartime the chances of a parcel arriving at its destination intact, or at all, were slim. Millions of pounds worth of goods in transit were stolen. 'I just took it because it is so hard to get',[12] a railway porter told the court, when she pleaded guilty with two colleagues to stealing six tablets of soap, value 2s 3d, from a van they were unloading at St. Pancras station.

'Everybody is facing the same difficulties, but we have to observe self-control,'[13] the magistrate reprimanded her, imposing a 20s fine.

As well as the railways, the docks provided ample opportunity for theft. Crates would be 'accidentally' dropped and their contents ransacked. Lifeboats would be stripped of their emergency rations. Towards the end of the war, shiploads of cigarettes were being transported to the troops in Europe, where they had become unofficial currency, and these became the thieves' prime target.

Looting of bomb-damaged houses or businesses in wartime was considered so dastardly a crime that it merited the death penalty, although the sentence was never imposed. It was not confined to the criminal fraternity; there were cases of ARP personnel, auxiliary firemen, even policemen, being charged. In Portsmouth in 1940 policemen caught looting were sentenced to 10 years' imprisonment, while in London an auxiliary fireman was given five years' penal servitude for carrying two buckets of food from a bombed grocer's shop, although the sentence was quashed on appeal. Even a group of rescue workers sharing a bottle of liquor found on a bomb-site during a long night shift was regarded as an indictable offence.

In one of many shocking cases, residents who had been evacuated from Dover during the worst of the bombing found their homes completely stripped when they eventually returned home in 1942. In south London during the V-weapon period, when whole streets of houses were damaged and left unattended, criminals had the gall to draw up in furniture vans and remove the entire contents.

There were hundreds of cases of people who would consider themselves to be law-abiding citizens taking advantage of the situation created by bombing to help themselves to other people's property. One of them had a lucky escape when she encountered a policeman as she was about to help herself to a nursery fireguard on a bomb-site. Visions of the firing squad instantly rose before her, as the policeman shook his head in disappointment.

'You can shoot me,' she blurted out.

'It's not that, Miss, I've had my eye on it to take home after dark for my own toddler.'

'Take it,' she urged.

'No, Miss,' he said sadly, 'You got it first.'[14] And he continued on his beat.

Children vandalized bomb-damaged houses and sometimes even stripped them of their valuables, as one admits:

'On one trip to Beckenham there were four of us. I don't know how, but we knew lead or metal was worth money, so we went up on the roof of a bombed-out house. We got a big box out of the shed and we filled it with lead – square bits of flat lead. We carried it home and as we got into the turning Peter's brother Bobby come out and said, "What you got there?" He went "Lead", and his brother belted him and said, "You get in, you'll get nicked, you'll get put away." So he disappeared and then Reggie, David's big brother, heard and gave him a whack and made him go in. So that left me and Charlie. We were panicking a bit. When we got to Charlie's house he didn't want to know, he was worried. So I dragged it down to my house, I took it in and my mum said, "What you got there?"

"I got some lead, Mum."

"You little bugger, where'd you get that?"

"Off a roof."

'We put it on a pushchair, rags on top, and took it to Wilson's, the scrap metal dealer down at Lower Sydenham. We got four pounds, which was a lot of money. Wilson never asked no questions. I went to Charlie and I said, "We got two pounds." So I gave him a pound and me and mum had three. That must have lasted us for ever, three pounds! We never went back for more, though. We were scared after that.'[15]

Demolition men were sometimes on the fiddle, as ARP warden Barbara Nixon observed in Finsbury:

'We did not have a great respect for the demolition workers. The "top men" were skilled, and risked their necks on the perilously insecure roof tops to collect lead in the interests of national economy. But even their efforts were nullified. One evening just after "knocking-off" time a five-ton lorry drove up, loaded the six-feet

Above: In the chaos of a bomb-site, criminals could easily mingle with the rescue workers in order to gain access to houses.

high pile of lead from the road, and drove off. Some of the lead, and some of the furniture from our square, was found by the police five months later at an auction sale in Norfolk, along with a great deal of other stolen property.'[16]

Air raids gave thieves the opportunity to either rob those in the shelters, or rob the houses of those in the shelters. Breaking into gas meters for the coins was a common pursuit of the small-time criminal.

In Walworth, Reverend Markham noted that some looters went in the guise of fire-fighters. During a raid, they would patrol in pairs down the Walworth Road. The first pair would throw a brick through a shop window and run round the corner. The following pair would empty the shop window and disappear with their loot.

Markham refused to enrol one man as an ARP warden when he discovered that he was a burglar with a van full of tools. When a business premises was hit, he would drive right into the ruins to find the safe.

Markham was so conscious of criminals snatching at any opportunity, he would have one of his men guard the dead bodies following an incident, knowing that otherwise 'their clothes would be rifled, there in the midst of the darkness and the dust, and falling bombs'.[17]

Some sites were looted even while injured people lay trapped beneath the wreckage. A man engaged in clearance work at one incident actually exercised violence on his victim, robbing a woman who had just sustained a V-weapon injury of cash and jewellery while she lay there in the rubble. He told the court he had acted on impulse. It was his first offence and he was sorry. 'Sorry!' boomed the magistrate. 'Robbing a woman who is [now] lying in hospital helpless and you say you are sorry!'[18] He was sent to prison for three months.

Looting was unpatriotic, as magistrates were at pains to point out. One described such a crime as 'mean and un-British'.

◆

Enticed by the prospect of the money to be made at home while the country was at war, many criminals were eager to avail themselves of a medical exemption certificate to which they had no right in order to avoid the call-up. An East End man, Jack Brack, had received a genuine exemption certificate from the Medical Board for a heart condition. He seized the opportunity to impersonate other men at the medical board, winning them exemptions, too. He made £200 a time. Doctors who sold medical exemption certificates were struck off. Of course, the forces did not want to recruit known criminals, any more

Above: Police swoop on and round up deserters.

than it wanted to recruit prostitutes, so that any woman who wrote 'Prostitute' under occupation was unlikely to be recruited.

For those who failed to avoid conscription, the next option was to abscond. Paradoxically, desertions increased at times when there was a lull in the fighting, suggesting that it was boredom rather than cowardice that motivated them. War took a terrible toll on family life and more often than not it was family troubles that compelled men to desert.

One poignant case involves a Shepherd's Bush couple. He applied for compassionate leave when his wife and child were bombed-out. It was granted, but he failed to return to his regiment when his leave was up. It was the wife, however, who was sent to prison, convicted of harbouring her husband as a deserter. In going to prison she had to leave her 8-month-old daughter in the charge of the Fulham Relieving Officer. Her local MP and the Soldiers', Sailors' and Airmen's Families Association (SAAFA) both wrote to the Home Secretary, Herbert Morrison, pleading for clemency. 'No normal woman can seriously be expected to betray her husband and the father of her child to the police,' the MP wrote. 'It seems to offend against every human consideration.'[19]

The woman was released on Morrison's instructions after serving only a few days of her sentence. It was too late, however, to save the life of her baby daughter, who died in the nursing home to which she had been sent. The woman blamed herself bitterly, believing that if she had not been sent to prison for sheltering her husband her baby might not have died.

British, American and Canadian military police, RAF Special Police and Naval Pickets were engaged on a perennial quest to track down deserters. A Hoxton woman remembers: 'Sometimes you would see deserters from the forces in the pubs. They would be followed by the police. Everyone could recognise the police. The deserters would go into the ladies' toilets and escape through the windows.'[20]

On 10 December 1945 military police launched a major round-up of deserters in the capital. They swooped on pubs, dance halls, pin-table saloons, restaurants, cafés and clubs, demanding identity papers. Billy Hill, one of London's most notorious criminals, scoffed at their efforts:

> 'They questioned every living soul … they checked thousands upon thousands of service passes and identification cards. From eight o'clock at night they worked until the early hours. I think they might have tumbled about half a dozen deserters…. Identity cards? They were as pieces of paper we could get any day we liked. Army passes? We could print them if you wanted them … which all goes to show how organised we were, and handicapped were the law in trying to fix us.'[21]

In what could be considered the most reprehensible of crimes, racketeers began hanging around London's railway terminals as demobilization gathered momentum. They would engage disoriented ex POWs with offers of a friendly drink, and later when inebriated rob them of their money and papers. Left with no proof of identity, it was highly likely these men would be picked up as deserters.

10
Doodlebugs and Rockets

'I remember doing the washing up and there was a terrific explosion ... this was the first rocket that we heard.' [1]
Nellie Allpress

In the early hours of 13 June 1944 the first V1 or pilotless plane crashed down at Grove Road, Bethnal Green in East London, leaving a large crater. Six people were killed and 266 rendered homeless and considerable damage was done to housing in the vicinity by the force of the blast. More of these weapons, heralded by a chug-chug sound before the engine cut out followed by silence and then the explosion, continued to arrive in salvos over the following days. On 16 June Herbert Morrison made a statement to the House of Commons announcing that London was under attack from a new weapon. Although the public had had their suspicions, it was now confirmed that these planes were pilotless – in effect flying bombs.

The government had been well aware from intelligence sources that the Nazis were preparing sinister new weapons, the first this pilotless missile, the second a supersonic rocket. The German leadership referred to these as *Vergeltungswaffe*, literally, Vengeance Weapon – Hitler's retaliation for the sustained heavy bombing of German cities by the British and Americans.

Left: A warden takes charge of a traumatized child after a V1, or pilotless plane, has crashed on a house in southern England, 23 June 1944.

It made life precarious again. After the Blitz ended in May 1941 there had been a brief lull. In 1942, in what was known as the 'Baedeker Raids', the Luftwaffe had targeted towns of historical and cultural

Below: The government was at first reluctant to announce that Britain was under attack from a new weapon, the V1, but on 16 June 1944 Herbert Morrison was forced to admit it.

This is the Gin
Gordon's
Stands Supreme

WORLD'S LARGEST EVENING NETSALE

The Evening News

NO. 19,464   LONDON, FRIDAY, JUNE 16, 1944   ONE PENNY

LATE EXTRA

PILOTLESS WARPLANES RAIDED BRITAIN

Morrison On Secret Weapon—and Counter Moves

ATTACKS MAY CONTINUE

LAST night's raid on Southern England was made by pilotless German aircraft, and more raids are expected, announced Mr. Morrison in the House of Commons to-day.

While awaiting full reports of their effect, he warned us not to stay in the streets out of curiosity if our future attacks need not be exaggerated.

Counter measures are being applied with full vigour, and the usual siren warning will continue.

Mr. Morrison's statement:

It has been known for some time that the enemy was making preparations to use this much-vaunted new weapon. A number of these weapons was used in the raids on Tuesday and their fall was scattered over a wide area. A larger number was used last night and this morning.

How to Spot Ghost Planes

1. Great Speed
2. Bright Light
3. Smoke Trail

DESCRIPTIONS of the German pilotless planes vary slightly in detail. But they agree on these points—terrific speed, bright lights, flames from exhaust, very straight course.

One correspondent telephoned this picture of them to-day:

"The planes have a distinctive rhythmic note, giving the effect of a pulsating low throb. They are much smaller than a Spitfire, but have an appearance much the same.

"They are really midget planes. At night they show a yellow glow at the rear, and in the light of searchlights streaming thick smoke can be seen being emitted from them.

OUR SCIENTISTS WILL DEFEAT IT

WHY WE BOMBED PAS DE CALAIS AREA

"Evening News" Reporter

IT should not be long before our war statisticians and the R.A.F. take the full measure of the German pilotless rocket bomber.

COOL IN STRAITS

Low Cloud and Mist

THE weather in the Straits of Dover early to-day was dull, with a low ceiling of cloud and mist.

MR. BEVIN IN BOX

Attitude to Tyne Strikers

Mr. Ernest Bevin, Minister of Labour...

FIVE-TONNERS HIT BOULOGNE E-BOAT PENS

R.A.F. DAY RAID

Air photographs taken after the great R.A.F. raid on Havre show no trace of E-boats or torpedo boats previously there. Reconnaissance pictures before the attack revealed ten E-boats and three torpedo boats.

THREE hundred R.A.F. heavies, escorted by Spitfires, attacked E-boat pens at Boulogne with 5,000-pounders before dark last night.

CHERBOURG: THREAT INCREASING SUBSTANTIALLY

Six Miles to Cut the Escape Routes: Navy Shell Havre

The Navy have been shelling military targets and harbour installations at Havre, it was revealed at Supreme H.Q. to-day.

WITH our striking power growing steadily the Allied threat to the Cherbourg Peninsula is substantially increasing, it was stated to-day at Supreme H.Q.

American troops, writes the Evening News War Reporter at Supreme H.Q., have now reached a point only six miles from Le Haye du Puits, through which runs the only remaining road and railway connecting Cherbourg with the rest of France.

Allied Striking Power Grows Steadily

EIGHTH LEAP 25 MILES

ADVANCE ALL ALONG LINE IN ITALY

ALLIED Armies in Italy have again advanced all along the front, says to-day's communique from General Alexander's H.Q.

Key Traffic Centre

Bridges Hit

BRAIN WAVES

WAR OFFICE

"DON'T stop me—I've got an idea for de-hydrating the Channel as an antidote to sea-sickness."—By Gittins.

GEN. EISENHOWER
Visits British Sector

significance – Exeter, York, Bath and Norwich – all listed in the Baedeker Guide for tourists, in revenge for the RAF's destruction of Lübeck. Londoners had again come under conventional air attack early in 1944 in what was known as the Little Blitz, but now they were confronted with a completely new kind of aerial warfare.

The V1s were going to be far more hazardous than earlier, conventional bombardments, in that they fell so thick and fast at all hours of the day and night that there was hardly any warning and little time to take cover. Alerts might go on all day with only brief periods of respite, or even continue for days at a time. It was easy to lose track as to whether there was an alert on or not, so that they became a huge interruption to the working day.

Londoners couldn't afford to relax their vigil. Tense as they were, any sudden noise – a bang for instance – made them flinch. They found themselves constantly scanning the sky and listening for the approach of the V1, whose distant hum would ascend to a raucous rattle as it drew closer, prompting the terms 'buzz bombs' and 'doodlebugs'.

The V1 was unpredictable. It would be moving in one direction, then veer away again, heading your way just when you thought the danger had passed. The sudden cut-out of the engine when the fuel ran out was the moment to dive for cover. The tension of those seconds, waiting for the explosion, must have been unbearable. People found themselves praying that it would keep moving and land somewhere else, as a Streatham man who was a schoolboy at the time recalls:

'I hadn't the time to go into the front room under the Morrison shelter, so I dived under the dining room table which was of thick mahogany. I saw through the French windows and it was coming straight at us. I think it was only about ten to twenty feet over us. Once it had gone there was a huge sigh of relief when we heard the explosion on the other side of the wood. It had landed on a small cottage off Norbury Hill and it was rumoured that the man and woman who lived there were killed.'[2]

The anxiety of constantly listening out for the weapon was wearing on the nerves. 'It makes you feel that you are just waiting your turn,'[3] a Walthamstow man wrote to his daughter in America, while others feared even to use the Hoover in case the noise drowned the sound of an approaching doodlebug.

Sleepless nights became a problem again, as a West Norwood man remembers:

'Some friends of ours in Morden said "They don't drop any over our way, so come and have a quiet night". When we got there they said "We're all sleeping in the cellar". I thought "that's confidence for a quiet night" … suddenly I found myself on the bedroom floor complete with my wife surrounded by bricks and ceiling, a flying bomb had dropped on the road 100 yards away. When we got the brick dust and muck off ourselves we went down the road to see if there was anything we could do and I came upon a head in a pile of rubble and I looked at the head and the head looked

Above: There is a tense silence as the engine cuts out, then the V1 dives to the ground.

at me and the head said "Don't get me out". It was a very shattering experience. So I said "Look chum, the electricity's gone, the gas has gone any minute now it could all go up", "But I've got no trousers on," he said. "If this lot goes up that will be the least of your worries," I said. We got him out and he was so smothered with brick and plaster that nobody would have known the difference.'[4]

Death was sudden and completely random, as Stanley Rothwell, a Civil Defence worker in Lambeth, observed:

'... we could hear the oncoming doodlebug behind us chugging like a motorbike. In front of us on a rise to the left we saw two semi-detached houses. A man was digging in a garden alongside, a little boy was running up the garden path towards the house, his schoolbag slung across his shoulder. At the doorway was a woman beckoning him to hurry indoors. The engine of the flying bomb shut off, we crouched waiting for the crunch. It glided over and past us and settled on the two houses all in the space of seconds. There was a loud explosion, a mushroom cloud of dust. Everything went up; no houses, no man, no mother and no boy. We picked up three dustbins full of pieces out of the rubble. The only way to identify where they were was the dampening dust and the cloud of flies.'[5]

If death was random, so too was survival. A Streatham boy had a narrow escape:

'A very funny thing happened during the Buzz bomb time. I had a bad bout of tonsillitis and my mother said "You stay in bed; don't move!" I was in the Scouts at this time and they had a shop just next door to the library and I decided I'm going to the shops; went up to the shops for various things and a Buzz bomb came over. I heard it cut out and went out and had a look and thought to myself "Oh, that's near home"; so I got on my bicycle and went to have a look. It landed near Fayland Avenue and we were on Pendle Road. So I dashed home. First thing I saw, there was a woman lying in the middle of the road, so I started dealing with her; I dashed off to Moyser Road and got the doctor .... But at our house the funny thing was – my bed was there, the window was there – the whole casement of the window was on my bed and the bed was flat on the floor, absolutely crushed – and I was supposed to have been in it!'[6]

The V1, with its one ton of explosive power, would inflict terrible damage. Buildings within a half-mile radius of the point of impact had their roofs ripped off, their doors blown off their hinges, their windows wrenched out and glass shattered. Modern buildings with their steel structures and reinforced concrete stood up reasonably well to blast, but the flimsy Victorian back-to-backs of the working-class districts collapsed like cardboard cut-outs. Victims could be hurled through the air by the force of the explosion, their bodies being discovered streets away or on rooftops;

Top: The pilotless planes could strike at any time, catching people as they went about their daily business. Here a bus has been hit on St. John's Hill, Clapham, killing and injuring the passengers.
Above: Death was sudden and random, as was survival. This man had taken his dog for a walk when the V1 struck, killing his wife and destroying his home.

those closest to the explosion might be blown apart, or thrown back and forth by the blast, crashing against obstacles. Blast could strip them of their clothing. They could be maimed by shards of flying glass and debris, or trapped under heavy debris.

As they were being catapulted at London at all hours, the V1s caught people going about their daily business. In June 1944 between 50 and 100 V1s a day were hitting London and its suburbs. In one of the worst incidents, on 30 June, a V1 glided over the Thames and exploded on the circular roadway at the Aldwych. It was 2.07pm, when the area was

Above: Hitler's Vengeance Weapon, otherwise known as the pilotless plane or flying bomb, earned the nickname buzz bomb or doodlebug, because of the chug-chug noise it made as it approached.

crowded with office workers on their lunch hour or queuing at the post office. Adastral House, the Air Ministry, absorbed much of the explosion, and five WAAFs who had been at the window were killed when they were sucked out by the blast. When the ghastly pall of smoke cleared, it was to reveal mutilated bodies strewn everywhere, while the leaves had been stripped off the trees and replaced with human flesh.

Frightening and exhausting as the alerts were, Londoners had not lost their sense of humour. A member of the WVS, who was helping a family in Clapham, recalls that with a doodlebug approaching the father 'grabbed each of his small children almost as if they were puppies and popped them into the Anderson shelter. He then turned round to look for his wife. Things were hot. But she was upstairs. He called out to her to hurry up. She yelled: "Wait a moment, I've got to find my dentures." "Listen, you," came the reply, "they're dropping doodlebugs, not sandwiches."'[7]

Since the V1s were being launched from Northern France they were crossing the Channel and putt-putting over the south London boroughs. Their ultimate destination was central London, but they were often falling short on the boroughs south of the Thames. A Dulwich woman, whose husband worked at the Bank of England by day and as a part-time ARP warden at night, found the tension, the broken nights and lack of sleep

unbearable – so unbearable that she was among the first to leave London, taking her children to the safety of Somerset. Over a million Londoners left town, a third of them children under the government's official evacuation scheme, others privately. In August 15,734 hospital patients and staff were evacuated to the north, Scotland and Wales, while another 8,179 patients were discharged to their homes. The purpose of the evacuation was to free up beds for the expected casualties. Many hospitals were hit, including the much-battered St. Thomas', the Royal Free, the Middlesex, St. Mary Abbott's, St. Olave's and the Lewisham.

Londoners were sleeping in the Underground again, although during this period only 73,600 were sleeping in the Tube, as opposed to 177,000 at the height of the Blitz. Fortuitously, on 9 July 1944 the first of London's new deep bomb-proof shelters, 130 feet below ground, was opened at Stockwell Underground station: the Clapham North,

Top: The rest of the country sent generous gifts of furniture and household goods to Londoners whose homes had been destroyed by the Vengeance weapons.
Above: The remains of the tailend of a V2 rocket, which came down near Southend Pier in October 1944.
Opposite: A letter confirming that this householder will receive compensation from the War Damage Commission for his damaged home – the payment of which will be deferred until some unspecified time in the future.

Clapham South, Camden Town and Belsize Park deep shelters opened over the following two weeks. The government had originally intended these new underground bunkers for its own personnel, fearing that the Nazis' new weapon would be used to deliver biological and chemical attacks. When the first V1 was proved to contain only normal high explosives, those who had feared the worst breathed a huge sigh of relief.

DEFERMENT LETTER B

BOARD OF TRADE,
Insurance and Companies Department,
Jersey Road, Osterley,
Isleworth, Middlesex

WAR DAMAGE ACT, 1943 (PART II)
PRIVATE CHATTELS SCHEME

7th. November, 1945

Reference PCS/ 48C 48418)
48D 50250)

Policy (if any) No.

Claimant Charles H. Gower

for war damage at 48, Madeira Rd. S.W. 16

on the 15/23.7.44

Amount of settlement £ 75. 10. 0d. subject to the deductions mentioned below
and overleaf.

Sir/Madam,

I am directed by the Board of Trade to inform you that the amount of the settlement of the claim as above set out has been approved by the Board.

If at any time you consider that undue hardship will be caused to you by deferment of payment, you may apply to the Local Officer of H.M. Customs and Excise for an advance payment.

Any advances which have already been made, or which may be made in the future, by the Board of Trade, the Assistance Board or H.M. Customs and Excise in respect of the said damage, and any sum chargeable in lieu of premium (see table below) will be deducted from the amount of the settlement shown above.

Payment of the balance will normally be deferred to a date to be specified in Treasury Regulations and interest will be allowed on the sum then payable at the rate of $2\frac{1}{2}$ per cent. per annum from the date of the damage to the date of deferred payment.

I am, Sir/Madam,

Your obedient Servant,

C. E. SLEDMERE

If damage occurred before 1st May, 1941, a sum in lieu of premium is chargeable as follows :

Nil on the first £300
1% on the next £1,700

$1\frac{1}{2}$% on the next £1,000
2% on the next £7,000

8802 G 1666 9/45 F A Gp 744

It meant that four of the new bunkers could be allocated to the public. Local authorities operated a ticketing system. Those who habitually sheltered in their local Underground and homeless women and children were the priorities. Each shelter accommodated 8,000 bunks.

By the end of August 1944 the Allies had seized the launch sites in Northern France and the worst of the V1 onslaught seemed to be over, although they would not cease altogether until March the following year.

Of the 9,251 V1s that were unleashed in total, 2,563 reached the London Civil Defence Region, causing 2,220 incidents, in which 6,184 people were killed and 17,981 seriously injured. Eighteen thousand houses were destroyed by the V1 and 137,000 seriously damaged, causing homelessness on a vast scale. Across London there were 50,000 removals during the V1 summer.

At a secret location in the Harz Mountains in Germany, meanwhile, a second secret weapon, the V2 rocket, was being manufactured using slave labour. The rockets, 45 feet long and 6 feet wide, could be fired from mobile launch pads, or indeed, from any flat surface.

◆

In the early evening of Friday 8 September a great explosion with a prolonged rumbling resounded over a large part of London. Nellie heard it while she was doing the washing-up in Wimbledon. The peculiar double bang of the explosion – explained by the fact that the rocket travelled faster than sound, so that the explosion on impact was followed a split second later by the sonic boom as the missile re-entered the Earth's atmosphere – was clearly heard 7 miles away at Westminster. Those in the know realized that what they had expected and dreaded but then shelved following the Allied advance across France had arrived – the first space-age missile, the V2 rocket.

In Staveley Road, a street of substantial red-brick houses in leafy Chiswick, a large crater, measuring approximately 40 feet wide by 10 feet deep, had appeared in the roadway. Seven houses were demolished and five others damaged beyond repair, while other houses in the vicinity suffered major blast damage. There was a significantly narrower area of blast damage than that produced by the V1, but then the V2 travelled 10 times faster at 3,000 miles per hour and so penetrated the earth much more deeply, causing massive damage to subterranean installations.

Obviously the denser the housing the greater the damage and number of casualties, but affluent Staveley Road had only eight houses per acre. Many of the residents had not yet returned from work, so that casualties were relatively light: 3 dead, 10 seriously injured and 10 slightly injured.

Within an hour of the explosion government officials were converging on the site. They included Duncan Sandys, a minister who was also Chairman of a War Cabinet Committee for defence against flying bombs and rockets, who now must have been bitterly regretting telling the press only the previous day that 'Except possibly for a few last shots the Battle of London is over'; Herbert Morrison and his Parliamentary Secretary Ellen Wilkinson; and Admiral Sir Edward Evans, one of London's two Regional Commissioners. People from Group Control and the local Control Centre were there, as well as the NFS and Civil Defence personnel already on the site.

Government policy was to keep the arrival of the V2s secret and there was a complete news black-out on the subject. The idea was to keep the Germans guessing as to whether the rockets were landing at all. With no information on where they were landing, they would

Above: London Region's eastern boroughs – the photograph shows an area of East Ham after an incident on 28 January 1945 – suffered the full onslaught of the V2 rocket, since it was being launched from Holland and often landing short of its target of central London.

have no chance to correct their aim. An absurd rumour was circulated that the blasts were caused by exploding gas mains. Although Londoners could laugh at this, there was growing frustration at the lack of any official statement, not least because thousands who had left the capital to escape the V1s were now pouring back again. Stanley Rothwell blamed the authorities for not warning the evacuees to stay put:

> 'The silence of the authorities observing a hush-hush attitude gave them the impression it was safe to come home. This was misleading to the people in the provinces; they were unaware of the diabolical terror weapon which was beginning to rain upon us, so back my family came. They were not indoors long before a rocket exploded nearby at the old Lambeth Baths; the blast shattered my windows showering glass over the baby that had just been put to bed. The next morning I saw them back again on a train once more from Euston to Lancashire.'[8]

The Dulwich woman who had evacuated with her children to Somerset came back, too, and was shocked at what she found. 'We catch an earlier train than planned, arriving at Paddington Station at five o'clock to an ear-splitting explosion. My heart gave a sudden lurch and for a moment I stood stock still. It could not be, yet I had heard rumours of a deadly and more lethal weapon – the dreaded and scarcely believable V-2. It was. What a nerve-wracking welcome home.'[9]

On 10 November Churchill confirmed in the House of Commons that London was under attack from the V2 rocket. The pros and cons of the two V-weapons were soon being

Above: The scene of utter devastation at Smithfield Market, London, after a V2 rocket struck on 8 March 1945. The market was at its busiest with housewives doing their shopping.

openly discussed. One commentator noted that 'People dislike [the V2's] nasty and unpredictable habit of plunking out of the blue', although 'they arrive so abruptly you don't have time to get scared – you're either dead or simply startled.'[10]

George Orwell was exasperated by the debate, writing in the *Tribune*:

'People are complaining of the sudden unexpected wallop with which these things go off. "It wouldn't be so bad if you got a bit of warning," is the usual formula. There is even a tendency to talk nostalgically of the days of the V-1. "The good old doodlebug did at least give you time to get under the table," etc. Whereas, in fact, when the doodlebugs were actually dropping, the usual subject of complaint was the uncomfortable waiting period before they went off. Some people are never satisfied.'[11]

As the V2s were being launched from Holland but falling short of their target of Waterloo Bridge and its environs, the 11 boroughs of Group 7 on the eastern side of the region were particularly hard hit, receiving 199 in total. Only four V2s landed in Lambeth, the Allpresses' previous locality, the worst incident being on 4 January 1945 when a rocket hit Surrey Lodge Dwellings, opposite Lambeth Baths at the top end of Kennington Road, killing 39 and injuring 70 people.

The Allpresses must have been glad they had moved out of Priory Grove before the arrival of the V-weapons, although Wimbledon had 36 V1 incidents. South London had been particularly hard hit by the V1s, but now the boroughs of Battersea, Camberwell, Lambeth, Southwark and Wandsworth were to receive in excess of 300 rockets. The density and poor quality of the housing in these predominantly working-class districts accounted for the above average number of deaths – 245 – and nearly 500 seriously injured.

Probably the worst 'outstanding incident' occurred in the southeast borough of Deptford a month before Christmas. It was Saturday 25 November and Woolworth's in New Cross Road was packed with women and children. At lunchtime the rocket struck. Everyone was hurled up into the air along with the debris. On the busy A2 outside the store pedestrians were flung great distances, while a bus stood still, every one of its passengers killed by the force of the blast. Civil Defence personnel worked three days and nights to locate and extract all the bodies and parts of bodies, although some people were entirely obliterated. The final toll was 168 dead and 123 seriously injured, with many others suffering lesser injuries.

Ironically, in November the government had started to cut down the Civil Defence force by just over 10,000, leaving a total force of 24,000, with the result that a number of wardens' posts had been closed.

There was to be no let-up for Christmas. After the successful D-Day landings in June some even dared to hope that the war would be over by this time. Instead, there were to be six V2 incidents in Christmas week, including a major incident on the Prince of Wales public house, between Mackenzie Road and Holloway Road, Islington, where some of the locals were enjoying a Boxing Day pint. The licensee, his wife and a barmaid were on the ground floor and escaped with minor injuries, but the cellar was full of people drinking and smoking and proved a death trap. A fire started immediately and many of the dead were charred beyond recognition. Seventy-one were killed, 56 seriously injured and 202 slightly injured.

Above: An ambulance driver and a nurse pick their way through the rubble at the scene of the Smithfield Market V2 rocket attack.

February 1945 saw 31 V2 incidents, while in March there were 36. The misery was compounded by the fact

Above: At 7.21 on the morning of 27 March 1945 a V2 scored a direct hit on a block of flats in Stepney, East London, leaving a high death toll and many injured. It was the penultimate V2 incident of the war.

that the V1 attacks resumed, the weapons being launched either from piloted aircraft or from launch sites in Holland.

Deptford suffered again when on 7 March a V2 struck a block of flats, Folkestone Gardens in Trundley's Road, killing 52 – among them entire families – while 64 were seriously injured and 70 sustained lesser injuries.

The following morning a rocket struck Smithfield Market, penetrating deep beneath the surface and bringing the whole structure down into the goods yard of the London and North-Eastern Railway below.

A quarter of a mile away two men working on the roof of the Deanery of St. Paul's were almost blown off by the blast, while a young woman working by the window of a factory in Aldersgate Street found she had a 'second sense'[12] and ducked just before the terrific blast of the explosion. The window she feared would shatter bulged in and out, but did not break.

This was the worst sort of incident. The market was crowded with hundreds of housewives, the majority from outside the neighbourhood, which meant that it would be hard to identify the bodies once they have been retrieved from under the deep mounds of rubble.

It would be days rather than hours before the casualties could be counted. Those who were found and brought out alive in the first few hours were sent by ambulance to St. Bartholomew's Hospital nearby. By one o'clock Barts had received 256 cases and had to close its doors. Surgeons operated around the clock with only short breaks. Further casualties were sent to other London hospitals.

At 7.21 on the morning of 27 March the hard-hit borough of Stepney suffered one final, terrible 'outstanding incident' when a V2 scored a direct hit on a block of flats which were home to 89 families. Hughes Mansions consisted of three parallel blocks of mansion flats. The missile completely demolished the middle block and practically destroyed the eastern block, while the western block suffered serious blast damage.

A Whitechapel fireman described the scene when he first arrived:

'As we stopped near what had been a large block of flats we were met by many people, some trying to find relatives or friends, others demented and just running around wildly. I remember one chap covered in blood running down the road carrying what had once been a whole, live baby, calling his wife, and some people grabbing him and leading him away.'[13]

Some people survived in empty pockets of the debris and were being brought out alive until late that night. The final death toll, however, was 134, with 49 seriously injured.

On the same afternoon a V2 fell in Orpington, killing one person. It was the last of over 1,300 rockets to be unleashed and the 517th to fall within the boundaries of the London Civil Defence Region. Hitler's V2 rockets had killed 2,500 and seriously injured 5,869 in London Region – of these over 1,700 had died and nearly 4,000 had been seriously injured in the first three months of 1945 alone. In addition 7,500 had received minor injuries between September 1944 and the end of March 1945. Two days later at 9.00am the last V1 crashed into a sewage farm near Hatfield in Hertfordshire.

On 2 May the remaining 24,000 Civil Defence workers enrolled with local authorities in London Region were disbanded 'quietly and smoothly'.

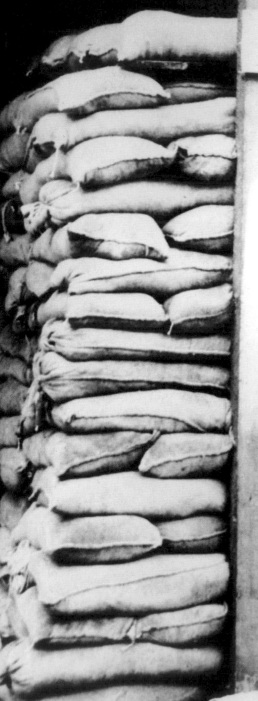

HOME SWEET HOME

11
Family Reunions

The Allpresses admit they were fortunate. None of them was killed or injured as a result of the war. Bill came home from the RAF and Harry from the Army, both having seen years of active service overseas, without a blemish. At home the family had survived the Blitz and the worst Hitler could throw at them during the V-weapons period. They had much to celebrate. Just as the war in Europe ended in May 1945 Harry came home on leave and married Thelma. Harry's friend Cyril, who had been a POW, was repatriated and married Betty the following year. Eva, in turn, married Douglas, whom she met at Betty's wedding. Douglas was a friend of Cyril's. Both of them had been in the Royal Army Medical Corps and in the same prisoner of war camp, but did not actually meet each other until they were back in London after the war. With these marriages, the war ended on a positive note for the Allpresses.

The war left no one unscathed, of course, and for many their lives were turned upside down. War had brought massive disruption to British life. Families had been broken up. Nationally, at least two and a half million women had been deprived of the presence and support of their husbands, who were serving in the forces, some not seeing them for years. Men and women had not only gone into the services, but had often worked away from home in jobs ranging from the civil service to the munitions industry, from factories to the land and the mines. Family life had been fractured by the evacuation of mothers and small children and of children on their own.

Left: The British had defiantly stood up to Hitler and the worst he could throw at them. Home, however makeshift, was more than a place – it was the loved ones who lived there.

209

Above: The war ended on a positive note for the Allpress family with a series of weddings. Here Eva is married to Douglas. To her left stand her proud parents, William and Alice Allpress.

Thousands had lost fathers, husbands, and sons to the fighting, while civilians, too, had been targeted and killed in the bombing. The mobilization of women – and the absence of many women from the home for long hours of war work – affected the family most and perhaps had the most long-lasting consequences for traditional family life. With peace and demobilization came a severe housing shortage and family reunions were often fraught with tensions.

Servicemen returning from a long period overseas were unprepared for the changes the war had wrought. Many retained a romantic picture of their wife and children, which they discovered bore no relation to the reality. They expected everything to be the same and of course it was not. In their absence, women had had to take charge of the household and assume sole care of the children. Many of them had also taken on jobs or done voluntary war work, which had given them a taste of independence and newfound confidence.

Women had written cheerful letters to their absent husbands, suppressing the more tedious details of civilian life in wartime, just as men's letters might have concealed how frightened they were or how terrible the conditions. Letters and photographs were a poor substitute for a person's presence and husbands and wives found they were virtual strangers when they were re-acquainted. Fathers had to get to know their children, and children had to learn to share their mother with the stranger who was now monopolizing her attention. There was a great deal of adjustment required as families learned to live together again.

A whole series of programmes on the BBC attempted to tell those about to be demobilized what to expect. Home was unlikely to be as they had left it. Everything looked a lot shabbier. Civilians, too, had gone through a hard war. Returning servicemen must be prepared for rationing and be appreciative of any special efforts – a cake or a roast dinner, for instance – made to greet their return. They should offer to do the shopping one morning to see for themselves just what their wives had to endure in terms of queuing and shortages.

As if women weren't tired enough, they were warned to prepare for a difficult reconciliation with their husbands; they must learn to make allowances for the stranger who had returned to them, soothing their homecoming. Newspapers and magazines carried articles on the subject of 'When Your Man Comes Home'. Men had undergone terrible experiences in the war; they were weary and possibly disillusioned. Their wives must expect a long period of readjustment and be patient, loving, and understanding.

◆

As early as 1942 Ernest Bevin, Minister of Labour and National Service, set up a committee under the Paymaster General, Sir William Jowitt, to prepare for demobilization. It was surprisingly early, since at that time the outcome of the war was by no means certain and given that the armed forces had still to reach their optimum strength of 4,243,000 men and 437,000 women the following year. The USA had already entered the war, ensuring final victory, but no one could predict exactly when this would be. Once Germany was defeated, it was reckoned that the war with Japan would drag on for another two years, meaning that demobilization could be only partial, with extra troops transferred to the Far East to fight a long, bloody island-by-island campaign, all the way

Above: At No.4 Military Dispersal Centre, Regent's Park Barracks, London, a sergeant gives an illustrated talk about the stages of the release procedure to soldiers going through the demobilization process.

Above: A selection of pamphlets relating to different careers that were made available to repatriated POWs at the RAF's No.1 Resettlement Centre, Scarborough.

to Tokyo. This would at least allow for an orderly, staggered demobilization for the rest of the forces.

The basic principle was that the oldest and those who had served the longest should be released first. They would be categorized as Class A. Special priority cases – those with rare skills, returning POWs, married women and personal hardship cases – fell into Class C. Two months' service was judged to be the equivalent of a year in age. No special privileges were allotted to married men or those who had served abroad, so that a single man who had spent the entire war in England would have the same entitlement as a married man who had spent three years fighting overseas.

Bevin was determined that there should be some correlation between demobilization and the employment needs of critical industries, particularly housing. Class B, therefore, comprised those men urgently required for construction work. Their early release came at a price. They were to be retained on the active reserve, subject to recall if they left the jobs to which they were directed, and to receive three instead of eight weeks' paid leave as a gratuity.

The plan was approved by Cabinet in February 1944. What could not have been foreseen was that the war with Japan would come to an abrupt end with the dropping of the atomic bombs on Hiroshima and Nagasaki in August 1945, just over three months after the cessation of hostilities in Europe, throwing the carefully contrived plan into disarray. The new Labour Government was under intense pressure to complete demobilization, which had started as early as October 1944 with older men, as quickly as possible. In the event, the whole process was completed by Easter 1946, but this was little comfort to the men eager to get home before all the jobs and accommodation were taken.

There was widespread grumbling at the perceived unfairness of the system and impatience with the process. Servicemen were tired of rules and regulations and resentful that the government should still be trying to direct their lives.

The transition from wartime to peacetime industry was by no means smooth, however. It was imperative that Britain begin reconstruction and the great export drive to reignite the post-war economy straightaway, but with the best will in the world factories could not be turned around quickly enough. Some employers voiced concerns that they would actually have to lay off workers during the transition period, just at a time when millions more were leaving the forces and entering the jobs market. All were hampered by bureaucracy, which of course had been ubiquitous during the war and was slow to unravel in the aftermath.

The workforce would also be unpredictable. Munitions workers and dockers had enjoyed good pay under the stress of wartime necessity and would be in for a shock at peacetime wages. Some women who had been in munitions were so indignant at the low wages on offer by the textile industry that they decided not to bother.

Returning servicemen were taken to disembarkation camps and dispersal centres, where they were given their release papers and pay, a temporary 14 days' ration card – sufficient until they could secure identity cards and civilian ration books at their nearest National Registration office – a testimonial from the CO, and the all-important single railway ticket home. The next stop was the quartermaster's stores, now known as the clothing depot, where they would be given their civilian wardrobe, consisting of a hat, a suit, a shirt with two collars, a tie, two pairs of socks, one pair of shoes, a raincoat, two studs and one pair of cufflinks. Although there was a choice of suits, ranging from town to sporting, or sports jacket and flannel trousers, they were clearly identifiable as demob clothes and were often ill-fitting. Servicewomen were spared this experience. They were given 56 clothing coupons and some cash.

Top: Demob suits came in several styles and colours, yet managed to look remarkably similar.
Above: Resettlement offices were set up all over the country to advise returning servicemen, but were limited in their scope to practical matters, rather than giving the emotional help some of the men urgently needed.

New clothes of whatever style or quality had a ready sale on the black market. Demobbed servicemen often made their first acquaintance with the cold realities of post-war life when they emerged from the demob centre to be accosted by spivs with wads of cash offering to buy their new civilian outfit.

Above: Harry married Thelma in May 1945, the morning after he returned home from Germany on leave.

Under the auspices of the Ministry of Labour, Resettlement Advice Offices were set up all over the country, to ease returning servicemen back into civilian life again. They promised to do everything in their power to help solve difficulties, but in fact their scope was very narrow and they were primarily concerned with the more practical matter of finding a job rather than resolving any emotional issues. Theirs was still the era of the stiff upper lip and very often ex-servicemen felt they had no one they could unburden themselves to. Even if they tried to tell their wives, the gap between their differing experiences of war was too great and the one simply could not comprehend what the other had been through. After the camaraderie of service life, Civvy Street could be a lonely place.

The Reinstatement in Civil Employment Act was supposed to guarantee servicemen their old jobs back, but the scheme was impractical. He might have been replaced by someone else for the duration of the war and by law the substitute had to give way, but where did that leave him? It was different, of course, if the substitute had been a retired man holding the fort or a woman who knew she was only temporary. Of course, the job might no longer exist, or he might not want it back.

For the Allpress brothers, it was no great problem. Bill was happy to go back to the upholstery business and returned to his former company in Central London. Harry, meanwhile, had no wish to go back to French polishing. His excellent service record, fitness and aptitude for sports won him a job as a caretaker with Croydon Education Committee, who were opening a camp in Caterham for young people. Best of all, the job came with a cottage – just what Harry, Thelma and their baby son Michael, born in 1946 – needed. With the severe housing shortage many people had taken to squatting in empty properties, so that Harry's employer was eager for someone to occupy the cottage. It was in a poor state of repair and it wasn't until early 1947 that the family moved in, grateful to have a home of their own at last. Given Harry's skills and his love of the outdoors, it wasn't long before he graduated from caretaker to a much more central role in the running of the camp with its sporting activities.

Three years later, when it was time for young Michael to start school, Harry found another job in a less isolated location in Essex, where four new camps were being opened. He was in charge of two of them, at Danbury and Ongar, and doubled his salary.

Like Harry, many ex-servicemen did not want to return to their old jobs, even if they still existed. Many of them had been no more than boys when they left. They had matured. War had changed them. Possibly they had been promoted and held responsibilities way beyond what they could ever have hoped to achieve in their former civilian existence. They were advised to start looking for work or take training while they were still in the forces.

The Conservatives' philosophy was to leave everything to market forces, but Bevin's last act as Minister of Labour and National Service before the wartime coalition government had been dissolved was to sign a Control of Engagement Order, requiring all jobs to be filled through the Ministry of Labour's employment exchanges. The idea was to guarantee all employers a fair share of local labour. There was still conscription into the forces for men between 18 and 30: just after his brothers had settled down at home again, in 1947 John Allpress went into the Royal Electrical and Mechanical Engineers, spending the second year's service in Singapore. In 1948 the National Service Act stipulated that all young men should do two years' military service.

Above: Just as his elder brothers were settling down in civilian life, John Allpress went into the Royal Electrical and Mechanical Engineers in 1947, serving for two years.

Men who had been brought out of retirement during the war – in the police or the teaching profession, for instance – to fill posts vacated by those who had joined up were gradually replaced by the returning servicemen. Doctors in civilian practice who had often deferred retirement until after the war were said to be suffering proportionately more illness and nervous breakdowns than their patients. In August 1945 there were still 17,000 doctors in the forces: the British Medical Association wanted 5,000 of them out before the winter to ease the load on those civilian doctors who were flagging as a result of their wartime burden.

There was a huge swell of dissatisfaction among servicemen after their experience of demobilization. Cynicism set in, a cynicism that was compounded by a series of disappointments they encountered in civilian life. It is not as if their expectations were particularly high. In the spring of 1945 the British Legion had run an essay competition, in which servicemen were invited to describe their hopes for the post-war world. The overwhelming desire was for security, plenty of jobs, adequate wages and pensions for all. 'My hopes for the post war are similar to those of Sir William Beveridge,'[2] said one. 'The things I desire from peace are things which thousands of normal people want – a home, employment, and a reasonable amount of security,'[3] another confirmed.

In order of priority, the men wanted:

1.   Employment for all at good wages.
2.   Adequate housing at controlled rents.
3.   A state health service.
4.   Improved education, including higher education and vocational training for all.
5.   Adequate pensions for widows, dependents and the disabled, and subsistence allowances for the unemployed.

Although many of the wishes expressed by the men in the British Legion essay competition were to be embodied in the welfare state, few of them were to be forthcoming in the immediate future. It was not until 1948 that the National Health Service was established; of course, that was quite an achievement within a short period after the war, but by that time disillusionment had set in. The housing situation, which apart from employment was the first problem confronting many former servicemen, was dire and remained so for many years.

Above: After all the anticipation, homecoming was sometimes a disappointment. Many returning servicemen found it hard to adjust to life in Civvy Street.

Servicemen underestimated the difficulties they would encounter. The jobs, the housing, the support services to ease them back into everyday life – none was readily available. They had been warned that civilians had had a tough war and would be too wrapped up in their own problems to take any account of theirs, but it took a while for many ex-servicemen to appreciate this. They were confused, angry and resentful, especially as even their wives did not seem to be offering the sort of sympathy and understanding they felt they deserved.

Where once servicemen had been fêted, now that the war was over they were regarded as anachronism. Civilians were often resentful, believing that those in the forces had had the better deal, while after six grim years of war on the home front, all they had to look forward to was continuing austerity. There was sympathy for POWs, of course, some of whom were ill, mentally and physically. The Allpresses' friend and Betty's future husband Cyril McCann, for instance, had contracted tuberculosis in

his prisoner of war camp in Germany and had to have an operation and months of treatment after his return.

In fact, servicemen had received no great benefit for laying their lives on the line. At the outbreak of war the average wage was £3 to £4 a week: with his many years' service on Southern Railway William Allpress was on £3 10s a week. When Harry was first called up he claimed he was earning 10s a week,[4] half of which was kept back for his leave periods. By 1945 a private was earning 3s a day. If he was a married man, a proportion of his pay would be stopped to go to his wife, leaving him with 1s a week. On leaving the Army, a major with five years' service, three of them abroad, would receive release pay, allowances and gratuities amounting to £324 12s 8d, while a private with three years' service would receive £78 16s 2d. Cyril McCann's gratuity came to £78 11s.[5] Each would receive a civilian outfit worth £12. It might be some time before they found work.

Some young men coming out of the forces had no qualifications with which to get a job. The military life was all they had known. To add to their problems, some of them had married during the war and they now had small children. Wives had often stayed with their parents or moved in with their in-laws, but now the pressure would be on them to find a home of their own. As one such ex-soldier ruefully noted: 'No job, no home, no trade, and a wife and baby …. Demobilisation is not going to solve my difficulties. It puts me right into the thick of them – and there are thousands like me.'[6]

Those returning from overseas were no doubt shocked at the sight of Britain's bomb-damaged cities and were unprepared for the grim post-war austerity. In the forces they had been looked after; they had been well fed and provided with accommodation; their days had been organized and they had the company and support of comrades. Now they had to get to grips with the hardships of civilian life; they had to find employment and somewhere to live. Staying with their in-laws or sharing sub-standard accommodation, even squatting, was not the most auspicious homecoming.

◆

After years of living apart, it was very hard for husbands and wives to adjust to living together again, especially as they had endured very different wartime experiences. This was particularly so for those who had been prisoners of the Japanese, since they had not been able to communicate with their families for the three years of their imprisonment. Those who had been in regular contact through the forces postal service had less catching up to do. Even so, it was hard.

One woman living in London's bomb-devastated Isle of Dogs recalls:

> 'When he came out it was very, very difficult to get to know him again. I think it was a time when we could have easily split up. He came home and no way did I feel I could settle down with him. You had to go all through a sort of courtship again. Four years is a very long time to be apart, but gradually we got together, though things were very, very difficult because we had nothing. Our money from the army was very little and we had just the necessary things like a bed and a chair – no carpets or things like that. My home was bombed during the war. We finally found an old flat. It had an outside toilet, no bathroom. Times were very hard.'[7]

It was unrealistic to expect ex-servicemen just to slip back easily into family life. Very few could have been left unchanged by their experience of the hostilities, and there was bound to be a reaction when they came home. They were tired, often depressed and angry, and these feelings could spill over into ill-health and antisocial behavior. It was especially hard for ex POWs, who suffered psychologically and physically, as the daughter of one of them recalls:

> 'The euphoria of having him home soon wore off as our father was to suffer further bouts of malaria, added to which his nerves were very bad. He did not like any noise and we had to try and keep very quiet. He seemed to be anti-social and did not like any visitors to the house, even close family. My mother told me that he had nightmares and would suddenly wake up during the night and run towards the wardrobe thinking Japanese snipers were firing at him. Being small children we slept soundly and knew nothing of the traumas of the night. It was terrible for our mother to see him like this, not the happy homecoming she must have envisaged.'[8]

Those who had been prisoners of the Japanese often suffered from survivor's guilt and chronic illnesses: not surprisingly, the suicide rate among them was higher than in any other group of returning men.

Above: Home to a pre-fab, but a happy family reunion.

If some men who had been POWs returned home skeletally thin, their health permanently damaged, men, too, were shocked at how much their wives had changed. Many retained a romantic picture of a young, pretty wife and now found that she had aged and grown hard. 'Our wives were exhausted, some neurotic and ill through war work, lack of essential food and queuing for hours,' ex-servicemen complained.[9] Not only had the war imposed a huge extra burden on women, but for those like the Allpresses, working in London throughout the bombing, there had been many nights of interrupted sleep and always the strain of knowing that they or their loved ones might be killed at any time. Nellie admits they were worried about Bill and Harry and prayed for them constantly.

Most disconcerting of all was how much women's personalities seemed to have changed. During the war they had taken on all sorts of new responsibilities. They had experienced independence, and held a job and earned their own money or done voluntary work, and had generally become more assertive. They had made new friends, perhaps mixing with foreign servicemen and people from other social strata, which had broadened their horizons. Many husbands simply did not know how to cope with this different woman and some were jealous and resentful.

The war had seen an increase in promiscuous behaviour and infidelity. Indeed, the Germans had used propaganda to undermine morale by suggesting to British servicemen that while they were away fighting, the Americans were seducing their women back home.

Loneliness and opportunity were often the triggers for infidelity, as the romantic novelist Barbara Cartland, who was a wartime marriage counsellor, observed:

> 'It is very easy to say what a woman should do or should not do, when she hasn't seen her husband for four years ... They were young, their husbands were not fluent letter-writers – they started by not meaning any harm, just desiring a little change from the monotony of looking after the children, queueing for food, and cleaning the house with no man to appreciate them or their cooking. Another man would come along – perhaps an American or an RAF pilot ... He is lonely, she is lonely, he smiles at her, she smiles back, and it's an introduction. It is bad luck that she is married, but he means no harm, nor does it cross her mind at first that she could ever be unfaithful to Bill overseas. When human nature takes its course and they fall in love, the home is broken up and maybe another baby is on the way, there are plenty of people ready to say it's disgusting and disgraceful. But they hadn't meant it to be like that, they hadn't really.'[10]

There was an increase in illegitimacy, the rate rising by as much as three times the pre-war figure. Some of these unfortunate children were put up for adoption, since the returning husband would not tolerate the presence of a child who could not be his, but in other instances men were kind enough to accept the illegitimate child as one of the family.

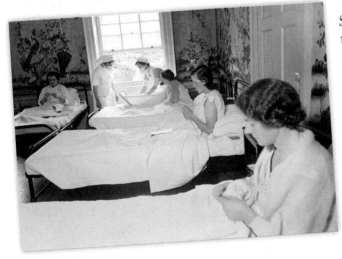

Above: Emergency maternity homes had been established in the reception areas for women to give birth away from the noise and disruption of the bombing. It was the beginning of a trend for hospital births as opposed to the more common pre-war custom of home confinements.

Some women did not trouble to hide their infidelity or were caught out by a husband's unannounced homecoming. Judges were sympathetic to gun-toting ex-servicemen who shot at wives discovered *in flagrante delicto*, but were at pains to point out that violence could not be condoned.

◆

The end of the war saw an increase in the number of marriages taking place: the rate had risen and dipped according to the fortunes of war, from the summit of 22.1 percent per 1,000 in 1940, through a slump to 14.1 per 1,000 in 1943, to 18.6 per 1,000 in 1945. There had been a wartime trend towards younger marriages. Of women marrying for the first time during the war, 30 percent were under 21.

The wartime birth rate roughly corresponded with the rise and fall of the marriage rate, although it faltered slightly in 1945 – possibly, in London at least, as a result of the disturbance and uncertainty caused by the V-weapon attacks from June 1944 to March 1945, while in 1945 itself many women were giving the housing shortage as their reason for restricting the size of their family.

Above: Husbands and wives who had spent years apart during the war had to learn to live together again.

On the positive side, the war had seen a decrease in the infant mortality and neo-natal mortality rates and in the still-birth rates. During the worst of the bombing, expectant mothers had been encouraged to give birth in the safer surroundings of the emergency maternity units that had been opened in the reception areas. The trend was set for safer births in special maternity wards, overturning the more common pre-war custom of home confinements.

Inevitably during a period of such massive social upheaval and uncertainty many ill-advised marriages took place and failed, while other established marriages broke down under the pressure of long-term separation or as a result of the difficulty of post-war adjustment. In England and Wales the number of divorce petitions filed shot up from 9,970 in 1938 to 24,857 in 1945 and jumped again to a post-war peak of 47,041 in 1947. There were also about 25,000 legal separations in 1945–1946, which represented a 150 percent increase over the pre-war level. Even without the war, there might have been some increase owing to the liberalization of the divorce laws in the Matrimonial Causes Act, 1937. Whereas previously over half the petitions had been filed by wives, in 1945 58 percent came from husbands. Adultery was the most common cause cited.

It was hard for the courts to keep pace. Divorce was still sufficiently rare for newspapers to include short notices of those granted, naming the parties concerned and outlining the reasons. In 1945 the London *Evening Standard* tended to list the numbers as a sort of score which grew ever more fantastic. On 15 January alone, Mr Justice Hodson in the Divorce Court made absolute the record total of 1,124 decrees nisi – the proceedings for which took 10 seconds.[11]

Many wartime marriages had been rushed affairs between people who hardly knew each other. Randolph Churchill, for instance, son of Winston, became engaged to Pamela Digby three days after first making her acquaintance on the telephone and they were married a month later. The marriage did not last. After long absences, those who had been quick to marry felt little or no responsibility towards each other. One such woman remembers:

'Like a lot of girls, I really married in quite a hurry in wartime. The men were in the services. We knew they were going away, going abroad, and we felt we wanted to get married. I was married on the Tuesday, and Wednesday I was saying goodbye to him. I saw him very briefly after that, and then it was three years before I saw him again. And, of course, because I had changed through the war, through the experiences, meeting all sorts of people, I'd got this sense of independence ... I thought to myself, "I can't stay with him, because I can't do what he wants, I want more out of life now". In fact, when he was sent back to his unit for demobilisation I ran off to the Channel Islands, because I knew I couldn't cope with that sort of marriage and that was the end of it. This, of course, was the effect of war.'[12]

In other cases, couples who had once loved each other found they were no longer compatible. It was hard to sustain a relationship over years of separation: a commanding officer noted that it was often all right for the first two years, but troubles and infidelities tended to occur in the third year of separation.

Above: During the war women had enjoyed a taste of independence and mixed with foreign servicemen and people from other social strata, widening their horizons.

Young women were often working away from home, so that their families could not 'police' their courtships, as they had previously done. Inevitably, where strangers were meeting outside their own neighbourhoods and where hasty marriages were taking place, there were cases of bigamy. There was a threefold increase in the number of bigamy cases during the war – enough to prompt the authorities to print a warning in every civil notice of marriage.

◆

On Wednesday 2 May 1945, 1,500 local authorities in the reception areas received a telegram: 'Operate London Return Plans'. It was the signal to put into action the meticulously planned return of the 500,000 London evacuees still in the reception areas. Of the whole country, the London children were the last to come home, since the V-weapons were mainly targeted at London, the last explosion being as late as 28 March 1945.

First, teachers had to trawl the streets of the capital, carrying out a survey on behalf of London County Council of the children's homes, noting bomb damage, serious illness in the family, imminent confinement on the part of the mother, lack of sleeping room, and other problems that might prevent the child's immediate return. Teachers were to mark their cards 'Home' or 'No Home'. 'No Home' evacuees were to stay in their billets in the reception areas until such time as their home situation was judged suitable for their return or until alternative arrangements could be made for them.

The returns reflect the dire state of housing in the capital after the bombing, but more serious still, illustrate the devastating impact of war on the family. They record fathers killed on active service; mothers who are war widows and having to work, so unable to keep the children; mothers sick or in a mental home and unable to care for the children; marriages broken up and the children being taken into care; desertions by mother or father; parents absconding altogether and not leaving a forwarding address; remarriages where the step-parent did not want to take on the children of the previous marriage; and war orphans taken into Dr Barnardo's Home.

For those children who did come home, a difficult period of adjustment lay ahead. Special care had to be taken of children under 5 who had only known life in a residential nursery and had become 'institutionalized'.

Top: Some children had formed emotional attachments to their foster mothers and would find it difficult to settle with their own mothers again.
Above: For many evacuees and their foster families, the children's return home was a wrench.

Some evacuees had spent the war in superior accommodation and were dismayed by the meanness of the homes they returned to. Where they had enjoyed clean clothes and good meals, in some cases they now had to brace themselves again for squalor. More often than not, they also had to contend with bomb-damaged school premises.

Some children had become very attached to their foster families and friends in the reception areas, felt their loss keenly and wanted to go back. Parents were advised that if the children wanted to keep in touch with their foster families, they should be allowed to do so. Children who had spent the war in the totally different environments of the USA, Canada and Australia, where they had perhaps had to make a much greater adjustment at the outset, found it very hard to adapt to their homeland again. Materially, the deprived state of post-war Britain meant that their standard of living would be sharply reversed. While most evacuees who had stayed in Britain had been able to receive visits from parents, overseas evacuees had not seen their parents for years, so would have found it all the more difficult to live with them again.

It was especially hard for children who returned to a home where siblings had been born in their absence, or who were born shortly after the war, seeming to usurp the unique place they had once held in their parents' affections. One woman recalls:

> 'Life for me changed totally. From being the cherished only child of my mother who had all her attention, I was now part of a growing family with a stranger for a father and two baby brothers who took all my mother's time. I was part of that other life "before the war".'[13]

◆

The war had spelt disruption and inconsistency in parent-child relationships. There were fewer people – fathers, mothers, grandparents, uncles, aunts, siblings – at home to spend time with children and give them the supervision and attention they needed. The adults were in uniform, or working in the war industries. Crucially, mothers spent more time away from the home, or were generally distracted by the extra demands of wartime. This great withdrawal from the home, the uprooting of homes, the ebb and flow of evacuation, the comings and goings of members of the family, the shifting of work and work places all contributed to the instability of children during the war years.

On a positive note, far more fathers came home from the Second World War than the First. With peace further adjustments had to be made in children's lives. Fathers had to get to know their children again. They were warned that the youngsters might seem rather 'out of hand' and to go easy with them. Some had been born after their father's departure, while others were too young to remember the man who had been away for two, three or four years. Even the few who had been lucky enough to

Above: Some fathers would not be coming home. Here the son of a fighter pilot takes his father's place as the man of the house.

hear their father's voice on a specially made gramophone record sent from overseas might have had a problem recognizing the man himself. He did not always look the same as the man in the photograph on the mantelpiece. One small child exclaimed when she met her father, 'But you've got legs!' The photo she had kissed every night before bed had depicted him only from the waist up. Others remembered seeing a soldier walking up the street and asking, 'Is that my daddy?' or waiting at the railway station with their mother and straining for the first glimpse of him:

> 'My mother and I stood at the barrier watching a stream of khaki-clad soldiers pouring from the train. I remember asking my mother, "Is that one Daddy?" over and over again as I had no idea what he looked like. Then suddenly one of them stopped and clasped my mother to him. My feelings were of surprise and disappointment – he was my father, but he seemed more interested in my mother – and she in him. I felt somehow I'd lost them both.'[14]

> 'The train arrived and hundreds of men in uniform alighted', another recalls. 'My father picked me up and kissed me – I didn't recognize him and hated his moustache and cried.'[15]

Many wartime children were simply not used to having a man in the house. They were shy and wary of the returning stranger.

> 'I refused to acknowledge his existence. I would not be alone with him. I ignored him totally, even when he spoke to me. I replied through my mother or anyone else present, prefacing everything with "Tell that man ..." I would not allow him to touch me. If he tried [to pick me up] I would struggle to release myself, screaming "Mummy, Mummy, tell this man to put me down." All this was very painful to him, he could never bear to talk about it.'[16]

Some fathers and children never managed to close the chasm opened by the war.

> 'I tried very hard to have a normal father/daughter relationship with my father and I'm sure he did too in his own way,' one woman recalls sadly, 'but we never achieved it. We never spoke to each other – never greeted each other on coming

home or said goodbye if we went out. Any communication was done through my mother.'[17]

With the men home it was time to re-establish the traditional family hierarchy. Father was once more the undisputed head of the household and children had to get used to his discipline. Even so, there were often quarrels over how to manage the children and much resentment on the part of the children:

'Poor Dad, his war experiences had left him in a very excitable and nervous state, so two young children soon had him worn out. As for us, we had been with Mother and Granny and we tried his patience sorely. What did we know about living with a daddy? His views on parenting emerged on a very different plane from Mother's, and there were lots of rows about who was right.'[18]

Mothers were torn between the warring factions, desperate to keep the peace, while fathers were trying to re-assert their authority. As one woman remembers:

'I was just learning how to tie my shoelaces. He tied them for me once and I promptly untied them as a game. He did them up again and I undid them again. He threatened that if I did it a third time I would get smacked. Not believing this, I undid them a third time and promptly got walloped. I ran bawling up the garden where my mother was hanging out the washing and complained, "That man hit me!" I felt he had no jurisdiction over me and was only there on sufferance. It must have been very difficult for him as he had been used to soldiers leaping to attention at his slightest command and he could not cope with a small child defying him.'[19]

Indeed, some fathers had become rather too used to barking out orders and were not prepared to make allowances for a small child. A mother who was desperately proud of the little boy she had brought up in his father's absence recalls: 'So in place of the affectionate boy I had married I found this military martinet with a large ego. He considered our boy spoilt and undisciplined and proceeded to rectify this while the baby asked me in a loud voice, "When is this man going away?"'[20]

Inevitably, children who had shared the fear and horror of the bombing with their mothers had formed an unusually close bond with them and found it difficult when a third party intruded into that relationship. One woman, who was only a few months old when her father left for war and 5 when he returned, remembers:

'No one prepared me for our meeting. I remember it so well. We were at Reading railway station on this cold December day and all of a sudden this great big man picked me up and cuddled me! I screamed the place down and nothing my mother could say or do would allow me to go near him for quite a while. It was a very difficult time. I had mostly slept with my mother and grandmother during the war, and for this man to want to sleep with my mother really made me very fed up and lost! It took years before I actually stayed in my own bed all night but I still think there was an underlying resentment.'[21]

No matter what the difficulties of adjustment for returning servicemen and their families, it was far worse for the children whose fathers did not come home. 'My pal's dad did not come home,' one man recalled. 'He had been a prisoner of war. On VE Day, the flags were up at her house but then the telegram arrived and her mother took the flags down.'[22]

Another remembers her mother's grief when she received news of her husband's death on the Western Front in April 1945. She was only 24 and never re-married. The family was sent a photograph of his grave in Germany.

> 'One day my kindergarten teacher called my mother to tell the assembled children that I didn't have a daddy. Before these days of split families, everyone else had one, and they wouldn't believe at the age of five that I did not. Anyway, I had never known him, being 14 months old when he was killed, but I did have two little dolls he bought me while marching across Europe.'[23]

◆

While the war undoubtedly caused massive upheaval in family life, what is remarkable is not the number of families who were irredeemably damaged, but the solidity of the majority of families, which saw them through these challenging times.

The Allpresses were such a family. At the height of the bombing – which they admit was absolutely terrifying – they remained calm and drew strength from each other, particularly from the father, William, who held them together. They retained a wry sense of humour about their situation. Above all, they were stoical and uncomplaining: William working long hours in dangerous conditions, often having to walk home in the dark and through the bombing after a long shift and bringing the family morning tea in the Anderson shelter; Alice, hard-working wife and mother, queuing at the shops, day after day, to feed the family while her daughters went to work; Nellie, Eva and Betty, exhausted but dutifully going to work after a sleepless night in the shelter, walking if the transport was not available, spending their evenings fire-watching and many a weekend helping in the hospital canteen; John, suffering the misery of evacuation and never quite catching up with his disrupted education. And all the while the family was anxious about the two sons serving in the Forces.

They admit they were fortunate, that the family was happily reunited at the end of the war and no one was killed or wounded. Certainly Britain was lucky to have such people in its hour of peril.

Overleaf: A returning prisoner of war is given a hero's welcome by his family and the whole village.

Notes

Chapter 1. A State of War

1. 'We knew'. Harry Allpress interview undertaken for the Imperial War Museum exhibition, 'Family in War'. Imperial War Museum Sound Archive.
2. 1,473,000 unaccompanied. Richard M. Titmuss, History of the Second World War, Problems of Social Policy, p.101.
3. 47,762,000. 'Statistical Digest of the War', prepared in the Central Statistical Office, Table 1, p.1 (1951).
4. borough was seven. LA/MBL/CD/1/74.
5. ARP committee. LA/MBL/CD/1/11.
6. anti-gas measures. LA/MBL/CD/1/18 and LA/MB/CD/1/44.
7. locating suitable. LA/MBL/CD/1/21.
8. demonstration of gas. LA/MBL/CD/1/51.
9. excess of 3,000. LA/MBL/CD/1/74.
10. six such shelters. LA/MBL/CD/1/141.
11. 83 percent. Titmuss, p.44.
12. kept in storage. LA/MBL/CD/2/81.
13. local library. IWM Sound Archives/Nellie Allpress/11893 and 32809.
14. a million death. Titmuss, p.21.
15. 2,000 canvas. LA/MBL/CD/2/294.
16. earned £3 10s. IWM Sound Archives/Harry Allpress/Ibid.
17. Lansdowne Gardens. LA/MBL/CD/2/118.
18. householders were. LA/MBL/CD/2/81.
19. Stockwell Memorial. LA/MBL/CD/2/81.
20. Fifteen thousand. LA/MBL/CD/2/116.
21. Council's minutes. LA/MBL/CD/2/281.
22. Mrs Allpress. Laura Wilson, Daily Life in Wartime, p.14.
23. Cyril. IWM Sound Archives/Cyril McCann.
24. one fireman. LA/MBL/CD/25/1156.
25. Lambeth was to. LA/MBL/CD2/281.
26. regular dances ... wedding receptions. IWM Sound Archive/Nellie Allpress/11893 and 32809.
27. families were getting smaller. See Sheila Ferguson and Hilda Fitzgerald, The History of the Second World War, United Kingdom Civil Series, Studies in the Social Services, p.2.
28. 'We were a family'. IWM Sound Archive/Eva Allpress/32811.
29. 'I am speaking'. Chamberlain quoted in Carol Harris, Blitz Diary, Life Under Fire in World War II, p.21.
30. 1,231 times. LA/MBL/CD/IV/97 Air Raid Warnings, Clapham 1939-1945.
31. 'we all took'. IWM Sound Archive/Nellie Allpress/11893 and 32809.
32. 34,750,000. Titmuss, p.413.

Chapter 2. Leave the Children Where They Are

1. 'I went to'. IWM Sound Archive, John Allpress/32808.
2. 18,000,000 ... 3,500.000 evacuees. Richard M. Titmuss, History of the Second World War, United Kingdom Civil Series, Problems of Social Policy, p.37.
3. 5,000,000 homes. Titmuss, p.37.
4. 69 percent. Titmuss, p.44.
5. John's whole school. IWM Sound Archive, John Allpress/32808.
6. 393,700 schoolchildren. Titmuss, p.103.
7. 17,000 mothers. Eds. Richard Padley and Margaret Cole, Evacuation Survey. A Report to the Fabian Society, p.220.
8. 'Suitable accommodation'. Ibid.
9. one north London. Ibid, pp.39-40.
10. John Allpress. IWM Sound Archive/John Allpress/32808.
11. 'every morning'. Titmuss, p.121.
12. repair his shoes. IWM Sound Archive/ Nellie Allpress/11893 and 32809.
13. 900,000. Titmuss, p.139, p.171.
14. 'Economic and educational'. Titmuss, p.174.
15. John Allpress. IWM Sound Archive/John Allpress/32808.
16. 200,000 children. Padley and Cole, p.200.
17. 'Back home'. Papers of John L. Sweetland, Department of Documents, IWM, 97/21/1.
18. 'from vermin'. LMA/LCC/EO/WAR/1/1.
19. billeting allowance. Titmuss, p.161.
20. contribution of 6s. Ibid, p.399.
21. Over 1,250,000. Ruth Inglis, The Children's War: Evacuation 1939–45, p.1.
22. 'Nothing, surely'.Barbara Nixon, Raiders Overhead: A Diary of the London Blitz, p.63.
23. The Chief Inspector. For his report and a description of the education of London children in wartime see LMS/LCC/EO/WAR/I/238.
24. June 1944. The numbers of children in London at various stages of the war are recorded in Greater London Record Office's We Think You Ought To Go, p.50.
25. 'The form master'. Lewis Blake, Bolts from the Blue, p.70.
26. 7,736. Inglis, p.5.

Chapter 3. Go To It!

1. 'We did'. IWM Sound Archive/Eva Allpress/32811.
2. 39 Bill was. IWM Sound Archive/Harry Allpress/Ibid.
3. Harry joined. Ibid.
4. 'there were men'. IWM Sound Archives/Nellie Allpress/11893 and 32809.
5. an old retired. Ibid.
6. no more than 20,000. Angus Calder, The Myth of the Blitz, p.27.
7. 225,000 British. Ibid
8. bombed all the way. IWM Sound Archive/Nellie Allpress/11893 and 32809.
9. 'a miracle of deliverance'. Churchill quoted in Calder, p.27.
10. 'We shall fight'. Churchill quoted in Calder, p.28.
11. 'It was the shock'. Stanley Rothwell, Lambeth at War, p.12.
12. As Nixon explains. Nixon, p.9.
13. Eva recalls. IWM Sound Archive/Eva Allpress/32811.
14. 'One or two'. Nixon, p.36.
15. 'We were given'. Ibid, p.10.
16. 'Communications alone'. Ibid, p.158.
17. 'The siren went'. Harris, p.62.
18. 'Fires were'. Nixon, p.118.
19. 'The water supply'. Harris, p.98.
20. 'Our interval'. Nixon, p.136.
21. 'He knows'. J.H. Forshaw, LMA/LCC/AR/WAR/1/29.

22. 'We cut a hole.' Papers of Reverend J.G. Markham, Department of Documents, Imperial War Museum, 91/5/1.
23. 'The other end'. Nixon, p.45.
24. 'I told you'. George F. Vale, *Bethnal Green's Ordeal*, p.8.
25. 'The next nine'. Rothwell, p.17.
26. 'It had been'. Ibid.
27. 'There was'. Ibid
28. 'We had somehow'. Frances Faviell, *A Chelsea Concerto*, pp.114–115.
29. 'The Minister'. 'Emergency Mortuary and Burial Arrangements', TNA/HLG7/762.
30. 'It was impossible'. Nixon, p.41.
31. 'When you get'. The Trustees of the Mass Observation Archive, University of Sussex, FR 2059 'Do the Factory Girls Want to Stay Put or Go Home?', March 1944.
32. 'I don't really'. IWM Sound Archive/ Betty Allpress/32810.

Chapter 4. The Blitz
1. 'War is'. IWM Sound Archive/ John Allpress/32808.
2. 'It was'. IWM Sound Archive/Nellie Allpress/11893 and 32809.
3. 'We were all'. Ibid.
4. Churchill as recorded in Hansard, House of Commons Debate 18 June 1940, volume 362, pp.60–61.
5. 'He was with'. Jon Newman and Nilu York, *What to do when the air raid siren sounds: life in Lambeth during World War Two*, p.47.
6. in Stockwell Gardens. MBL/CD/21/Civil Defence Diary.
7. 1,000 people in Lambeth. Ibid.
8. 131 patients. MBL/CD/21/259.
9. 'five nurses'. Ibid, p.45.
10. Three crew. MBL/CD/21/Civil Defence Diary; Newman and York, p.44.
11. a Clapham couple. Ibid.
12. morale in Lambeth. MBL/CD/21/263.
13. the lady. Newman and York, p.46.
14. evening of 13 October. MBL/CD/21/Civil Defence Diary.
15. One fireman. MBL/CD/25/1156.
16. On 15 October. Newman and York, p.48.
17. At the height. Ibid. Tom Harrisson, *Living through the Blitz*, p.112.
18. 'It was like'. IWM Sound Archive/Betty Allpress/32810.
19. 'signs of'. Harrisson, p.135.
20. 'In those cities'. Nixon, p.125.
21. 'the people broken'. Quoted in Tom Harrisson, p.153.
22. 'We can't'. Ibid, p.135.
23. 'Jerry has'. Newman and York, p.50.
24. She hated it. IWM Sound Archive/Nellie Allpress/11893 and 32809.
25. Thermafelt factory. MBL/CD/25/1491.
26. 'It was a gory'. Nixon, p.102.
27. In the area around Priory. MBL/CD/25/1705.
28. UXB. LA/MBL/CD/25/1806.
29. 'We've got to'. IWM Sound Archive/Nellie Allpress/11893 and 32809.
30. In Lambeth alone. MBL/CD/21/Civil Defence Diary.
31. It was nearly. Nixon, p.121.
32. 890 tons of HE bombs. Collier, *History of the Second World War United Kingdom Series. The Defence of the United Kingdom*, p.504.
33. 148,000. Calder, p.37.
34. at 1.29. MBL/CD/21/Civil Defence Diary.
35. 40,000. Titmuss, pp.559–560.

Chapter 5. After the Raid
1. 'I told Mum'. IWM Sound Archive/Nellie Allpress/11893 and 32809.
2. 'People just'. Ibid.
3. 'For many wives'. Nixon, p.138.
4. 9,000,000 square feet. Figure given in Anthony Shaw and Jon Mills, 'We Served': Wartime Wandsworth and Battersea, p.53. (Clapham Common is 220 acres, or 9,600,000 sq ft.)
5. 'The council men'. Harrisson, p.91.
6. 331,865 tons. LMA/LCC/AR/WAR/1/29.
7. 'After we looked'. The Trustees of the Mass Observation Archive, University of Sussex, FR2279 'Population and Housing in England and Wales, mid 1945', August 1945.

Chapter 6. What Are We Fighting For?
1. 'Everyone'. IWM Sound Archive/Nellie Allpress/11893 and 32809.
2. 'The sky'. IWM Sound Archive/Nellie Allpress/11893 and 32809.
3. 'The mood'. Papers of Mrs P. Bell, Department of Documents, IWM, 86/46/1.
4. 'Workers continue'. TNA/INF 1/292. Home Intelligence Weekly Reports, No.221, 29 December 1944
5. 'had seen us'. IWM Sound Archive/Nellie Allpress/ 11893/3/3.
6. 'They are perfectly'. Quoted in Peter Hennessy, *Never Again*, p.56.

Chapter 7. Food, a Munition of War
1. 'You got'. IWM Sound Archive/Betty Allpress/32810.
2. Ten acres. Lizzie Collingham, *The Taste of War. World War Two and the Battle for Food*, p.90.
3. 'If it isn't'. Anthony Heap, Diary, 29 May 1945, LMA/ACC 2243/19/1.
4. 'The first surprise'. Lola Duncan, *Home Chat*, 27 January 1945.
5. from £62 million. Collingham, p.76.
6. 'It is only possible'. Lord Woolton, *The Memoirs of the Rt Hon the Earl of Woolton*, p.209.
7. 'What we can'. *Food Facts for the Kitchen Front*, p.3.
8. 'Even if you like'. Ibid, p.12.
9. 'It can save'. Ibid, p.59.
10. Wartime Social Survey. TNA/RG23.

Chapter 8. War-Winning Fashion
1. 'It made you'. IWM Sound Archive/Betty Allpress/32810.
2. 'good with her needle'. Ibid.
3. 'We must learn'. Quoted in Colin McDowell, *Forties Fashion and the New Look*, p.82.
4. 'If British civilians'. Anon, *Over There*, p.12.
5. 'It isn't fair'. Anon, *Make Do and Mend*, p.7.
6. 'Some must lose'. Quoted in Norman Longmate, *How We Lived Then*, p.249

7 'It's time'. *Sunday Graphic*, 1 July 1945.
8. smart black shoes. IWM Sound Archive/Nellie Allpress/ 11893 and 32809.
9. 'To wear clothes'. Quoted in McDowell, p.112.
10. 'if there are'. Anon, *Make Do and Mend*, pp.3-4.
11. 'Have them repaired'. Ibid, p.4.
12. 'Why not exchange'. Ibid, p.5.
13. 'Now that rubber'. Ibid, pp.5-6.
14. 'A few extra'. Gossard advertisement in *Woman*, 10 February 1945.
15 'Use an old'. Anon, *Make Do and Mend*, p.27.
16 'Are you worried'. *Woman*, 28 April 1945.
17 'Rinse new stockings'. Anon, *Make Do and Mend*, p. 6.
18 'Strengthen'. Ibid, pp.6-7.
19 'If you are one'. Ibid, inside back cover.
20 'Always carry'. Ibid, p.8.
21 'When finally discarding'. Ibid. p.8.
22 'Cut fabric'. Ibid, p.26.
23. 'Since children'. Ibid, p.22.
24. 'When sheets'. Ibid, p.14.
25. 'If I were you'. Quoted in Laura Wilson, *Daily Life in a Wartime House*, p.19.
26. 'a hot bath'. *Woman*, 3 February 1945.
27 'One of the things'. Anon, *Over There*, p.11.

Chapter 9. Under the Counter and Off the Back of a Lorry

1. 'People used'. IWM Sound Archive/Eva Allpress/32811.
2. 'Against the depleted'. John Gosling, *The Ghost Squad*, p.18.
3. 'Lorry-loads'. Ibid.
4. 'We didn't go'. Mrs Dolly Andretti quoted in Jennifer Golden, *Hackney at War*, p.7.
5. 'No one thought'. IWM Sound Archive/Ruth and Fred Tanner/15291.
6. 'The Ghost Squad'. Raphael Samuel, *East End Underworld*, p.259.
7. 'I remember'. Mrs Dolly Andretti quoted in Golden, p,7.
8. 'The wife'. *Spectator*, 28 December 1945.
9. 'There is a slight'. *Star*, 10 January 1945.
10. 'There was a'. Mrs Dolly Andretti quoted in Golden, p.7.
11. 'If it is'. *Croydon Advertiser*, 12 January 1945.
12. 'I just'. *Islington Guardian and Hackney News*, 12 October 1945.
13. 'Everybody'. Ibid.
14. 'You can shoot me'. Verily Anderson, *Spam Tomorrow*, p.151.
15. 'On one trip'. Richie White in Jess Steele, *Working Class War*, p.107.
16. 'We did not'. Nixon, p.152.
17. 'their clothes'. Papers of Reverend J.G.Markham, Department of Documents, Imperial War Museum, 91/5/1.
18. 'Robbing'. *Hackney Gazette and North London Advertiser*, 10 January 1945.
19. No normal woman'. *Star*, 12 January 1945 and 6 February 1945; *Daily Mirror*, 3 January 1945.
20. 'Sometimes you'. Mrs Dolly Andretti quoted in Golden, p.7.
21. 'They questioned'. Billy Hill, *Boss of Britain's Underworld*, p.118.

Chapter 10. Doodlebugs and Rockets

1. 'I remember'. IWM Sound Archive/Nellie Allpress/ 32809/2.
2. 'I hadn't'. Keith Holdaway quoted in Jon Newman and Nilu York, *What to do when the air raid siren sounds: life in Lambeth during World War Two*, p.51.
3. 'It makes'. Papers of George and Helena Britton, Department of Documents, Imperial War Museum (Con Shelf).
4. 'Some friends'. Bill Wilson in Newman and York, p. 54.
5. '… we could hear'. Rothwell, p.32.
6. 'A very'. Edmund De Poitiers in Newman and York, p.53.
7. 'grabbed each'. Charles Graves, *Women in Green*, p.226.
8. 'The silence'. Rothwell, p.33.
9. 'We catch'. Papers of Mrs Irene Byers, Department of Documents, Imperial War Museum, 88/10/1.
10. 'People dislike'. Mollie Panter-Downes, *London War Notes 1939–1945*, p.357.
11. 'People are'. George Orwell, *Tribune*, vol.III, p.280. December 1944.
12. 'second sense'. IWM Sound Archive/Joyce R. Barrett/ 9563.
13. 'As we stopped'. Ibid.

Chapter 11. Family Reunions

1. 'We were lucky'. IWM Sound Archive/Eva Allpress/ 32811.
2. 'My hopes'. The Trustees of the Mass Observation Archive, University of Sussex, FR2220 'British Legion Competition Essays', 14 March 1945.
3. 'The things I desire'. Ibid.
4. Harry's earnings. Interview with J. Garnier, IWM, August 2011
5. Cyril McCann's gratuity. The POW Papers of Cyril McCann, Imperial War Museum 75/74/IT.
6. 'No job'. *News of the World*, 26 August 1945.
7 'When he came'. Kit Beasley quoted in Wicks, p.45.
8. 'The euphoria'. J. Gillett, Liverpool, quoted in Barry Turner and Tony Rennell, *When Daddy Came Home*, p.83.
9. 'Our wives'. *British Legion Journal*, February 1946.
10. 'It is very'. Barbara Cartland quoted in Barry Turner and Tony Rennell, *When Daddy Came Home*, p.114.
11. 1,124 decree. *Star*, 4 January 1945.
12. 'Like a lot'. Odette Lesley quoted in Joanna Mack and Steve Humphries, *The Making of Modern London*, p.162.
13. 'Life for me'. Monica Maher, Southport, quoted in Turner and Rennell, p.90
14. 'My mother'. Carol Freeman, Sunningdale, quoted in Ibid, p.107.
15. 'The train arrived'. Diana Bites, Cowes, quoted in Ibid, p.87.
16. 'I refused'. Margaret McCleod, Milton Keynes, quoted in Ibid, p.102.
17. 'I tried'. Margaret Maher, Southport, quoted in Ibid, p.90.
18. 'Poor Dad'. Sheila Taylor, Tayside, quoted in Ibid, p.89.
19. 'I was just'. Jane Gladstone, Edenbridge, quoted in Ibid, p.96.

20. 'So in place'. Eileen Dibben, London, quoted in Ibid, p.97.
21. 'No one prepared'. Gwen Price, Reading, quoted in Ibid, p.73.
22. 'My pals'. Thomas Lee, Ayr, quoted in Ibid, p.103.
23. 'One day'. Jane Worton, Geneva, quoted in Ibid, p.103.

Bibliography

All books published in London unless otherwise specified

Abercrombie, Sir Patrick, *Greater London Plan, 1944* (1945)

Abercrombis, Sir Patrick and Forshaw, J.H., *County of London Plan, 1943* (1943)

Addison, Paul, *Now the War Is Over: A Social History of Britain* (1985)

Anderson, Verily, *Spam Tomorrow* (1956)

Anon, *The Clothing Coupon Quiz* (1944)

Anon, *How Britain Was Fed in Wartime: Food Control 1939–45* (1946)

Anon, *Over There: Instructions for American Servicemen in Britain 1942* (Oxford, 1944)

Anon, 'A Short History of the War Damage Commission' (no date)

Anon, *ARP at Home: Hints for Housewives* (no date, but probably 1939)

Anon, *Food Facts for the Kitchen Front: A Book of Wartime Recipes and Hints with a Foreword by Lord Woolton* (no date)

Bendit, Phoebe and Bendit, Laurence J., *Living Together Again* (1946)

Blake, Lewis, *Red Alert: South East London 1939–45* (1982)

Blake, Lewis, *Bolts from the Blue: South East London and Kent under V2 Rocket Attack* (1990)

Box, Kathleen, *Wartime Shortages of Consumer Goods* (Wartime Social Survey for the Board of Trade, April 1943 – January 1945)

Braybon, Gail and Summerfield, Penny, *Out of the Cage: Women's Experiences in Two World Wars* (1987)

Briggs, Susan, *Keep Smiling Through* (1975)

British Information Service, *Fifty Facts about British Women at War* (New York, 1944)

Brittain, Vera, *Wartime Chronicle: Vera Brittain's Diary 1939–45*, edited by Alan Bishop and Y. Aleksandra Bennett (1989)

Bullock, Allan, *The Life and Times of Ernest Bevin*, vol. 2 (1967)

Calder, Angus, *The People's War: Britain 1939–45* (1969)

Calder, Angus, *The Myth of the Blitz* (1991)

Clements, Sibyl, ed., *A Short History of the War Damage Commission 1941* (1962)

Collier, Basil, *History of the Second World War, United Kingdom Military Series. The Defence of the United Kingdom* (1957), (IWM/Battery Press reprint 1995)

Collingham, Lizzie, *The Taste of War: World War Two and the Battle for Food* (2011)

Cudlipp, Hugh, *Publish and Be Damned!* (1953)

Davies, Rib and Schweitzer, Pam, eds, *Southwark at War: A Book of Memories* (1996)

Dean, Basil, *The Theatre at War* (1956)

Earnshaw, Alan, *Britain's Railways at War 1939–1945* (1989)

Faviell, Frances, *A Chelsea Concerto* (1959)

Ferguson, Sheila and Fitzgerald, Hilda, *The History of the Second World United Kingdom War Civil Series, Studies in the Social Services*, edited by Sir Keith Hancock (1953)

Firebrace, Sir Aylmer, *Fire Service Memoirs* (Melrose, 1949)

Fitzgibbon, Theodora, *With Love* (1982)

Food, Ministry of, *The Kitchen Front: 122 Wartime Recipes Broadcast by Frederick Grisewood, Mabel Constanduros and Others* (no date)

Foot, Michael, *Aneurin Bevan* (1999)

Gardiner, Juliet, *The 1940s House* (2000)

Gardiner, Juliet, *The Blitz, The British Under Attack* (2010)

Golden, Jennifer, *Hackney at War* (1995)

Gosling, John, *The Ghost Squad* (1959)

Graves, Charles, *London Transport Carried On* (1947)

Graves, Charles, *Women in Green: The Story of the WVS in Wartime* (1948)

Green, Graham, *The Ministry of Fear* (1943)

Hancock, Sir Keith and Gowing, Margaret, *The History of the Second World War, United Kingdom Civil Series, British War Economy* (1949)

Hansard, House of Commons Debate 18 June 1940, volume 362.

Harris, Carol, *Blitz Diary: Life Under Fire in World War II* (Stroud, 2010)

Harrisson, Tom, *Living Through the Blitz* (New York, 1976)

Hennessy, Peter, *Never Again: Britain 1945–51* (1992)

Henrey, Mrs Robert, *London Under Fire 1940–45* (1969)

Hibberd, Stuart, *This – Is London* (1950)

Hickman, Tom, *What Did You Do in the War, Auntie? The BBC at War 1939–45* (1995)

Hill, Billy, *Boss of Britain's Underworld* (1955)

Hodgson, Vere, *Few Eggs, No Oranges* (1976)

Hopkinson, Tom, ed., *Picture Post 1938–50* (1974)

Hornsey Historical Society, *Home Fires: A North London Suburb at War* (1992)

Howgrave, Graham, *The Metropolitan Police at War* (1947)

Information, Ministry of, *Make Do and Mend* (1943)

Information, Ministry of, 'Women in War Jobs' (1943)

Information, Ministry of, 'British Women at War' (1944)

Inglis, Ruth, *The Children's War: Evacuation 1939–45* (1989)

James, Anthony R., *Informing the People: How the Government Won Hearts and Minds to Win World War Two* (1996)

Kops, Bernard, *The World is a Wedding* (1963)

Kynaston, David, *Austerity Britain, 1945–1951* (2007)

Lees-Milne, James, *Prophesying Peace: Diaries 1944–45* (1977)

London, Corporation of, *We Think You Ought to Go* (no date)

Longmate, Norman, *How We Lived Then* (1971)

Longmate, Norman, *The Doodlebugs: The Story of the Flying Bombs* (1981)

Longmate, Norman, *Hitler's Rockets: The Story of the V2s* (1985)

Mack, Joanna and Humphries, Steve, *The Making of Modern London: London at War* (1985)

McDowell, Colin, *Forties Fashion and the New Look* (1997)

McLaine, Ian, *Ministry of Morale: Home Front Morale and the Ministry of Information in World War II* (1979)

Minns, Raynes, *Bombers and Mash: The Domestic Front 1939–45* (1980)

Moseley, Leonard, *Backs to the Wall: London under Fire 1940–45* (1971)

Newman, Jon and York, Nilu, *What to do when the air raid sire sounds; life in Lambeth during World War Two* (2005)

Nicholas, Sian, *The Echo of War: Home Front Propaganda and the Wartime BBC, 1939–45* (Manchester, 1996)

Nicholson, Mavi, ed., *What Did You Do in the War, Mummy? Women in World War II* (1995)

Nicholson, Harold, *The War Years: Diaries and Letters 1939–45*, edited by Nigel Nicolson (New York, 1967)

Nicholson, Virginia, *Millions Like Us: Women's Lives in War and Peace 1939–1949* (2001)

Nixon, Barbara, *Raiders Overhead; A Diary of the London blitz* (1980)

Novy, Priscilla, *Housework Without Tears*, foreword by Lady Beveridge (1945)

O'Brien, *The History of the Second World War, United Kingdom Civil Series, Civil Defence* (1955)

Orwell, George, *The Collected Essays, Journalism and Letters of*, edited by Ian Angus and Sonia Orwell (1968)

Padley, Edward and Cole, Margaret, eds., *Evacuation Survey*. A Report to the Fabian Society (1940)

Panter-Downes, Mollie, *London War Notes 1939–45* (1972)

Priestley, J.B., *Three Men in New Suits* (1945)

Priestley, J.B., *All England Listened: The Wartime Postscripts of J.B.Priestley* (New York, 1967)

Rooke, Dennis and D'Egville, Alan, *Call Me Mister! A Guide to Civilian Life for the Newly Demobilised* (1946)

Rothwell, Stanley, *London at War* (1981)

Samuel, Raphael, *East End Underworld: Chapters in the Life of Arthur Harding* (1981)

Samways, Richard, ed., *We Think You Ought to Go: An Account of the Evacuation of Children from London during the Second World War* (1995)

Sansom, William, *Westminster at War* (Oxford, 1990)

Shaw, Anthony and Mills, Jon, *'We Served': Wartime Wandsworth and Battersea* (1989)

Short, John R., *Housing in Britain; The Post-War Experience* (1982)

Steele, Jess, ed., *Working Class War: Tales from Two Families* (1995)

Stork, *The Stork Margarine Cook Book* (no date)

Summerfield, Penny, *Women Workers in the Second World War: Production and Patriarchy in Conflict* (1984)

Summers, Julie, *When the Children Came home: Stories of Wartime Evacuees* (2011)

Thomas, Donald, *An Underworld at War: Spivs, Deserters, Racketeers and Civilians in the Second World War* (2003)

Thomas, Geoffrey, *Women at Work: The Attitudes of Working Women Toward Post-war Employment* (Wartime Social Survey, 1944)

Titmuss, Richard M., *The History of the Second World War, United Kingdom Civil Series, Problems of Social Policy*, edited by W.K.Hancock (1950)

Turner, Barry and Rennell, Tony, *When Daddy Came Home; How Family Life Changed Forever in 1945* (1995)

Vale, George F., *Bethnal Green's Ordeal 1939–45* (1945)

Weymouth, Anthony, *Journal of the War Years and One Year Later* (Worcester, 1948)

White, Richie and Steele, Jess, *Working Class War: Tales from Two Families* (1995)

Wicks, Ben, *Welcome Home: True Stories of Soldiers Returning from World War II* (1991)

Wilson, Laura, *Daily Life in a Wartime House* (1995)

Woolton, Frederick Marquis, the Right Honourable the Earl of, *The Memoirs of the Rt. Hon. the Earl of Woolton* (1959)

Yass, Marion, *This is Your War; Home Front Propaganda in the Second World War* (1983)

Papers of the following in the Department of Documents, Imperial War Museum: Mrs P. Bell, Mr and Mrs George Britton, Mrs Irene Byers, Mrs Gwladys Cox, Miss V. Hall, Miss Vere Hodgson, John L. Sweetland, Mrs R.E. Uttin

Interviews with the following from the Imperial War Museum Sound Archive: Betty Allpress, Eva Allpress, Harry Allpress, John Allpress, Nellie Allpress, Joyce Barrett, Jack Harding, Nancie Norman, Ruth and Fred Tanner

Newspapers, periodicals and magazines
Croydon Advertiser, Daily Express, Daily Mail, Daily Mirror, Hackney Gazette and North London Advertiser, Home Chat, Islington Gazette, Islington Guardian and Hackney News, News Chronicle, News of the World, Picture Post, South London Press, Spectator, Star, Sunday Express, Sunday Graphic, The Times, Woman.

I am grateful to my editor Alison Moss for her cool head and endless patience.

Currency Chart

On 15 February 1971 Britain introduced decimal currency. This chart shows the common name and value of the old currency and the equivalent amount in decimal currency.

Old currency: pounds, shillings and pence	Decimal currency
Farthing ¼ d (d from the Latin *denarius)*	$\frac{5}{48}$ p = 0.10p
Halfpenny or ha'pence ½ d	$\frac{5}{24}$ p = 0.21p
Penny 1d	$\frac{5}{12}$ p = 0.42p
Threepence 3d	1¼ p
Sixpence 6d	2½ p
Shilling 1/-	5p
Florin 2/-	10p
Half crown 2/6	12½ p
Crown 5/-	25p
Pound 20/-	£1 or 100p
Guinea 21/-	105p

In the old currency, 4 farthings equalled one penny, 12 pennies equalled one shilling, 20 shillings equalled one pound.

In decimal currency, 100 new pence equals £1. Decimal currency consists of coins in the denomination of one pence, five pence, 10 pence, 50 pence, and one pound.

Picture Credits

Conway Archive 9, 22, 125, 128 bottom, 194, 196, 197 top.

Corbis/Hulton-Deutsch Collection 58 top, 65 top; Bettmann 80; 84; Hulton-Deutsch Collection 87, 111 centre, 131, 144, 149, 184, 190, 216, 219, 228-229.

Courtesy of the Allpress family 10 top and bottom, 11 top and bottom, 56 top and bottom, 74, 167, 168, 210, 214, 215.

Getty Images/George W. Hales/Fox Photos 13; Fox Photos 19 bottom; Keystone 23; 27; Topical Press Agency 31; A. J. O'Brien/Fox Photos 33; Three Lions 34; Fox Photos 44 bottom; Keystone 53; Topical Press Agency 60; Felix Man/Picture Post 70; Fox Photos 94 bottom; Bill Brandt/Picture Post 99; Fred Ramage/Keystone 106; Central Press 111 top; Keystone 112 top; Leonard McCombe/Picture Post 120; Felix Man/Picture Post 122 bottom, 124; David Savill/Topical Press Agency 152 centre; Ashwood/Fox Photos 154 bottom; Hulton Archive 164; A R Tanner 170 bottom; Fox Photos 178; M. McNeill/Fox Photos 183; Charles Hewitt/Picture Post 187; John Phillips/Life Magazine/Time & Life Pictures 189; Popperfoto 192; A. R. Coster/Topical Press Agency 199; Picture Post 205; Hulton Archive 208; Picture Post/Hulton Archive 217; Kurt Hutton/Picture Post 224; Picture Post 225.

Imperial War Museum All cover images, (D 778) 2, 4-5, 8, (HU 36133) 14 top, (HU 36124) 14 bottom, (HU 57448) 17, (HU 36151) 19 top, (HU 36138) 20 top, (HU 36139) 20 bottom, (HU 36130) 25, (PST 57) 28, (LN 4559C) 30, (D 984) 36 top, (D 3106) 36 bottom, (D 3064) 37, (D 252) 38, (D 255) 39, (97/27/1 DE) 40 left and right, 41 left and right, (D 3723) 42, (HU 36219) 44 top, (CH 1354) 45, (PST 2904) 46, (HU 36248) 48 top, (MH 26395) 48 bottom, (PL 4511A) 50, (D 1550) 51, (PST 3645) 54, (NYP 68075) 57, (H 5842) 58 bottom, (HU 36128) 62 top left, (D 7877) 62 top right, (HU 36129) 62 bottom left, (HU 36131) 63 top, (FEQ 418) 63 bottom, (HU 36132) 65 bottom, (HU 36175) 66 top, (HU 662) 66 bottom, (FX 255537) 69, (D 2321) 71, (D 3589) 72 top, (LDP 325) 72 bottom, (HU 36240) 76 top, (CH 8323) 76 centre, (HU 36278) 76 bottom, (D 10334) 77, (IIU 687) 78, (D 2642) 83 top, (HU 1129) 83 bottom, (HU 59004) 85 top, (HU 36261) 86, (D 1553) 88, (IIU 36144) 89, (92/2042/2) 90 top right and bottom right, (HU 44272) 92, (HU 632) 93, (HU 36188) 94 top, (H 5603) 96, (HU 36308) 97, (HU 36223) 98, (HU 36253) 103, (IIU 680) 105, (HU 36206) 108 top, (CP 10637) 108 bottom, (D 10405) 109, (D 520) 110, (D 24235) 112 bottom, (D 11121A) 117 top, (D 11051) 117 centre, (D 11053) 117 bottom, (D 24187) 118 top, (D 24190) 118 bottom, (D 6103) 122 top, (HU 36268) 123, (B 7658) 126, (D 24429) 127 top, (HU 36265) 127 bottom, (P 552) 128 top, (D 2973) 129, (D 1076A) 130, (ART LD 1353) 132, (ART LD 1550) 135, (D 1709) 137, 138, (D 18844) 140, (V 110) 142, (K 74591) 145 top, (D 7966) 145 bottom, (D 17518) 146 top, (D 24984) 146 bottom, (HU 63735) 147, (EPH 3417) 148, (D 14252) 150, (PST 17009) 151, (D 9238) 152 top, (D 9346) 152 bottom, (K 98/1952) 153, (PST 20603) 154 top, (D 6573) 156, (HU 36280) 159, (PST 14954) 160, (K/74591/1) 163, (D 11587) 165 top, (D 14846) 165 bottom, (D 3586) 166, (K98/188) 169 top and bottom, (D 13088) 170 top, (D 12895) 172, (D 14798) 173, (K 87/312) 174, (PST 8294) 175, (EPH 9727) 177, (K 90/786) 180 top and bottom, (D 21215) 197 bottom, (HU 638) 198 top, (HU 36303) 198 bottom, (CH 15111) 203, (HU 36185) 204, (HU 88803) 206, (D 26328) 211, (D 26170) 212, (D 26311) 213 top, (D 24382) 213 bottom, (D 9033) 220, (D 26322) 221, (D 14124) 222, (HU 36234) 223 top, (ZZZ 4395G) 223 bottom.

London Borough of Lambeth Archive Department 15, 16, 21, 62 bottom right, 85 bottom, 111 bottom, 116, 162, 188, 200, 201.

© TfL from the London Transport Museum Collection 90.